Teaching Online

Teaching Online: A Practical Guide is a practical, concise guide for educators teaching online. The newly updated third edition has been fully revamped and reflects important changes that have occurred since the second edition's publication. A leader in the online field, this best-selling resource maintains its reader friendly tone and offers exceptional practical advice.

Second edition enthusiasts will find the updates to the third edition will help readers choose and fully integrate the latest technology tools and valuable online educational resources. *Teaching Online* builds on the original strengths of the prior editions, and offers a plethora of new teaching examples, faculty interviews, samples of course materials, and an updated resource section.

New to this edition:

- New chapter on how faculty and instructional designers can work collaboratively
- Expanded chapter on Open Educational Resources, copyright, and intellectual property
- More international relevance, with global examples and interviews with faculty in a wide variety of regions
- New interactive companion website that invites readers to post questions to the author, offers real-life case studies submitted by users, and includes an updated, online version of the resource section.

Focusing on the "how" and "why" of implementation rather than theory, this text is a must-have resource for anyone teaching online or for instructors supplementing a traditional classroom with online elements. It is also appropriate for students enrolled in Distance Learning and Educational Technology masters programs and librarians working within the context of online education.

Get updates and keep in touch with Susan Ko at:
www.routledge.com/professional/teachingonline3ed

Susan Ko, Executive Director of the Center for Teaching and Learning at University of Maryland University College.

Steve Rossen, Instructional Technologist and Electronic Librarian, formerly Manager of the Faculty New Media Center at the University of California at Los Angeles.

Teaching Online
A Practical Guide

Third Edition

Susan Ko
University of Maryland University College

Steve Rossen
Retired, University of California at Los Angeles

Routledge
Taylor & Francis Group

NEW YORK AND LONDON

First published 2004
by Houghton Mifflin Company

Second edition published 2008
by Houghton Mifflin Company

This edition published 2010
by Routledge
711 Third Avenue, New York, NY 10017

Simultaneously published in the UK
by Routledge
2 Park Square, Milton Park, Abingdon, Oxon OX14 4RN

Routledge is an imprint of the Taylor & Francis Group, an informa business

© 2004, 2008 Houghton Mifflin Company
© 2010 Taylor & Francis

Typeset in Utopia by Wearset Ltd, Boldon, Tyne and Wear
Printed and bound in the United States of America on acid-free paper by
Edwards Brothers, Inc.

Library of Congress Cataloging-in-Publication Data
Ko, Susan Schor.
Teaching online : a practical guide / Susan Ko, Steve Rossen. – 3rd ed.
p. cm.
Includes index.
1. Education, Higher–Computer-assisted instruction. 2. World Wide Web–Study
and teaching (Higher) 3. Internet in education. 4. Distance education. 5. College
teaching–Aids and devices. I. Rossen, Steve. II. Title.

LB2395.7.K67 2010
378.1'7344678–dc22

2009038899

ISBN 10: 0-415-99733-X (hbk)
ISBN 10: 0-415-99726-7 (pbk)
ISBN 10: 0-203-85520-5 (ebk)

ISBN 13: 978-0-415-99733-1 (hbk)
ISBN 13: 978-0-415-99726-3 (pbk)
ISBN 13: 978-0-203-85520-1 (ebk)

Dedicated to

Steve Rossen, June 14, 1939–April 17, 2007

My inspiration, my partner in all things,
and my constant companion.

Brief Contents ● ● ● ● ●

Contents ● ● ● ● ●

Preface   ● ● ● ● ●

In 1993, there was no World Wide Web. Today, it is something we take for granted to do our banking, search for information, order and pay for nearly every type of merchandise, post our vacation photos, chat with friends from around the world, seek advice about what ails us, listen to music, watch video, and share our thoughts, creations, and mutual interests. And we access it now not only from our desktop and laptop computers but also from a rapidly expanding array of mobile devices, from smart phones to e-readers. The World Wide Web has become a worldwide phenomenon and it truly seems to be an inseparable part of our lives.

In 1993, if you had written a book about teaching, you would not have needed to describe the basic tools of the trade—the classroom, the rows of seats, the blackboard, the chalk. These were taken for granted; they never changed.

Today, you must describe how the virtual and real worlds intertwine in a process known as teaching online. You must talk about discussion boards, streaming media, asynchronous environments, real-time chat, instant messaging, as well as social networking, and the many collaborative and interactive tools collectively known as Web 2.0.

When the first edition of this book emerged in 2000, teaching online was still a new phenomenon that made many instructors both anxious and apprehensive. They had basic questions such as: What is the difference between teaching "on the ground" and teaching online? What are the fundamental techniques? Where can you learn them? What kind of equipment or software do you use? How do you assess how effective you are?

While many instructors have long since taken the plunge, some are still asking those basic questions, and we find that many others worldwide continue to regard the prospect of teaching online with trepidation and anxiety. Even those who have acquired quite a bit of experience may still find themselves challenged by the unique demands of teaching online. And both neophytes and experienced online instructors are some-times charmed and bewildered by the astonishing array of new tools that have appeared in the years since our second edition.

This book is written for the rapidly rising population of instructors who want to teach online, who have been told to teach online (sometimes in conjunction with on-the-ground classes), who are currently teaching online (but want to improve), or who are training or encouraging others to teach online. It is also for the administrator or support staff who assist instructors in their endeavor to teach online. In other words, it is intended for lecturers, professors, tutors, teaching assistants, department chairs, academic deans, program planners, instructional design-ers and technologists, and information technology support per-sonnel at both the administrative and departmental levels.

The book is as much for the tenured professor as for the adjunct, part-time instructor or teaching assistant. Those in the K–12 education field may also find that much of the advice given here is relevant for their teaching circumstances. It is also aimed at the growing number of students enrolled in programs in educational technology, computers in education, or similarly organized courses on technology in education. It is for the college administrator who is trying to convince a skeptical and unwilling faculty member to adopt this mode of instruction, as well as for the part-time instructor who drives seventy miles a day to teach four courses at four different institutions. It is for the trainer whose students range from those to whom life on the Web is second nature to those who struggle to keep up with the constantly evolving technologies.

The book is written from the unique perspective of two authors who have taught online themselves and have trained thousands of other faculty to teach online. It is more concerned with the "whys" and "hows" of implementation than with theory, not because we do not value pedagogical theory but because it is discussed and critiqued more effectively elsewhere. Unlike other books you may have read on the subject, this is not a collection of essays, not a general overview, not a focused look at one particular aspect of online teaching and learning, not a treatment of the subject based primarily on one institutional model, nor is it—strictly speaking—a technical handbook. Rather, it is intended as a practical and concise guide both for instructors teaching completely online and for those supplementing or fully integrating a traditional classroom with online elements. It will help reinforce what you may learn at your institution if you are lucky enough to have such instructor-development resources, but it will also serve as a survival manual for those who are operating largely on their own.

Our goal is to immerse instructors in this new environment as quickly as we can, using plain language and illustrating our points with case studies from colleagues or students that we have worked with or known, representing a wide variety of different disciplines and institutions. We hope to get you up and running as quickly as possible.

● ● ● ● ●

Organization of This Book

The book is divided into three parts.

In Part I, "Getting Started," we define and describe the world of online teaching and learning and introduce the skills, training, and support you will need to become part of it. These two chapters are aimed especially at those new to online teaching, but those with experience may find it helps provide a context of online teaching as it exists today and lays out the parameters for the book to follow.

Part II, "Putting the Course Together," covers the process of converting or developing course content for the online environment while discovering new possibilities for your course. We help you take inventory of your existing course and suggest areas for innovation, while guiding you through the development process and the creation of an online syllabus. We provide advice on using different types of software environments and offer a detailed look at opportunities for incorporating diverse activities and web resources. We shed light on the often-confusing issue of making effective use of multimedia, explore some of the new tools of the Web 2.0 world, and explore matters of copyright and intellectual property as they relate to the online classroom.

Although we strive to make the topics in Part II easy enough for beginners to grasp, we believe there is much here to offer even experienced online instructors. Carefully chosen examples from real-life instructors help illustrate the approaches and solutions outlined.

In Part III, "Teaching in the Online Classroom," we focus on some of the techniques you will need to become an effective instructor, whether you teach totally online or a true blended course, or are enriching classroom instruction with exercises on the Web. We discuss how to make sure your students are prepared for online classes, provide suggestions on the much-overlooked topic of online classroom management, and describe ways to integrate online activities into the face-to-face classroom. Finally, we discuss how online teaching can revitalize your career and how to keep current with the pace of change.

As a handy reference, resources are collected together and augmented in the Guide to Resources at the end of the book. We have included a section concerning online education research and theory for those who would like to pursue such topics. Because web addresses change so frequently, we urge you to consult the publisher's web site for updates, corrections, and new references.

Terminology is often a barrier for those unfamiliar with the Internet or computer software. Thus, there are numerous short definitions and boxed sidebars throughout the text to help you understand the narrative. A Glossary at the back of the book includes those terms and offers additional assistance. When a term is introduced and appears in bold font, that indicates you can find it in the Glossary even if there is no sidebar definition given.

●●●●●

What's New in This Edition

While we have maintained the original approach, outlines, and topics of this book, you will find that some chapter numbers and many chapter dimensions have changed. New technologies and the pedagogy needed to exploit it have resulted in many updates and revisions to this edition. Additionally, in recognition of the expanding field of online and blended education and its global reach, we have included new examples and a consideration of how the issues play out in different parts of the world.

Outdated illustrations of course management software and processes have been eliminated due to the greater familiarity of current readers with basic web technologies and the wide availability of such examples on the Web.

End-of-chapter resource sections are now subsumed into a more convenient and accessible location at the end of the book in an expanded resource section. This resource section is also available online at the book's companion website.

This edition features a new interactive companion website that invites you to keep in touch with Susan Ko. Located at www.routledge.com/professional/teachingonline3ed, this useful resource offers:

- an interactive blog that allows users to post questions and view author responses;
- real-life case studies submitted by readers, for examples of how the book is being used in the field;
- an online version of the resource section, where readers can find updated sources and removal of dead links.

● ● ● ● ●

Acknowledgments

We would like to acknowledge the special assistance of our editors for this edition, Heather Jarrow and Sarah Burrows of Routledge. We would also like to thank Suzanne Thibodeau and Peter Glassgold for encouraging us to find a new home for the third edition. We are deeply grateful to all the reviewers who gave feedback on how to improve the second edition. Thanks is also due to my father, Louis Schor, who passed away on July 22, 2009 and whose support many years ago enabled me to complete my doctoral studies and embark on a career in education. Finally, we would like to thank the many accomplished instructors—our colleagues in online education—who generously shared their experiences and whose many contributions have enriched this book.

Susan Ko

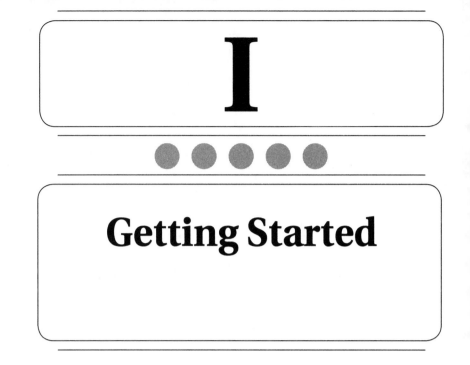

I

Getting Started

1

● ● ● ● ●

Teaching Online:
An Overview

Because teaching online is relatively new, many people don't know what it is, or how it's done, or even what some of the terms used to describe it mean. Others may have a notion of what's involved, but they don't know how to get started, or they feel some trepidation about handling the issues they may encounter. And there are now many who have taught online, but feel that they are have barely scratched the surface in terms of learning how best to adapt their teaching to the new environment. Perhaps this range of feelings is because the online environment is so different from what most instructors have encountered before.

Teaching online means conducting a course partially or entirely through the Internet. You may also see references to online education as **eLearning** (electronic learning). It's a form of **distance education**, a process that traditionally included courses taught through the mail, by DVD, or via telephone or TV—any form of learning that doesn't involve the traditional classroom setting in which students and instructor must be in the same place at the same time.

What makes teaching online unique is that it uses the Internet, especially the World Wide Web, as the primary means of communication. Thus, when you teach online, you don't have to *be* someplace to teach. You don't have to lug your briefcase full of papers or your laptop to a classroom, stand at a lectern, scribble on a chalkboard (or even use your high-tech, interactive classroom "smart" whiteboard), or grade papers in a stuffy room while your students take a test. You don't even have to sit in your office waiting for students to show up for conferences. You can hold "office hours" on weekends or at night after dinner. You can do all this while living in a small town in Wyoming or a big city like Bangkok, even if you're working for a college whose administrative offices are located in Florida or Dubai. You can attend an important conference in Hawaii on the same day that you teach your class in New Jersey, logging on from your laptop via the local café's wireless hot spot or your hotel room's high-speed network. Or you may simply pull out your smart phone to quickly check on the latest postings, email, or text messages from students.

Online learning offers more freedom for students as well. They can search for courses using the Web, scouring their institution or even the world for programs, classes, and instructors that fit their needs. Having found an appropriate course, they can enroll and register, shop for their books, read articles, listen to lectures, submit their homework assignments, confer with their instructors, and receive their final grades—all online.

> **virtual classroom** (also known as online classroom or virtual learning environment)   Any online environment in which instructors and students "meet" and interact for course activities. This term applies to environments in which communication may be either **asynchronous** (people do not have to be online at the same time to communicate) or **synchronous** (in real-time) or a combination of both.

They can assemble in **virtual classrooms**, joining other students from diverse geographical locales, forging bonds and friendships not possible in conventional classrooms, which are usually limited to students from a specific geographical area.

The convenience of learning online applies equally well to adult learners, students from educationally underserved areas, those pursuing specialized or advanced degrees, those who want to advance in their degree work through credentialed courses, and any students who simply want to augment the curricular offerings from their local institutions. No longer must they drive to school or remote classroom, find a parking space, sit in a lecture hall at a specific time, wait outside their instructors' offices for conferences, and take their final exams at the campus. They can hold a job, have a family, take care of parents or pets, and even travel. As long as they can get to a computer or other device connected to the Internet, students can, in most cases, keep up with their work even if they're busy during the day. School is always in session because school is always there.

So dynamic is the Web that new technologies and techniques are emerging all the time. What's commonplace one year becomes old hat the next. The only thing that seems to remain constant is people's desire to transmit and receive information efficiently and to communicate with others, no matter what the means. That's what drives people to shop, invest, and converse online, and it is this same force that is propelling them to learn online as well.

Online education is no longer a novelty. In the United States alone, nearly 20 percent of all higher education students in fall of 2007 were taking at least one online course (see the 2008 Sloan Consortium survey, Staying the Course—Online Education in the United States, 2008, http://sloan-c.org/ publications/survey/staying_course). In places like South Korea, where Internet usage is ubiquitous, according to a 2008 report, over 55 percent of South Korean Internet users reportedly used the Internet for the purpose of accessing education and learning, both informally and as part of structured programs (see 2008 Informatization White Paper at www.ipc.go.kr/ ipceng/index.jsp).

Worldwide, online learning is taking place in a variety of environments and combinations. There are students using mobile devices to communicate and collaborate with instructors and classmates, others gathering in local computer labs to connect with central university resources to bring previously unavailable classes to far-flung portions of a nation, and there are degree programs offered fully online for which students need never set foot on a physical campus.

But all this freedom and innovation can sometimes be perplexing. If the conventional tools of teaching are removed, how do you teach? If school's open twenty-four hours a day, seven days a week, when is school out? What is the role of the instructor if you don't see your students face to face? Do you simply deliver lectures and grade papers, or are you more like a facilitator, moderator, or colleague?

And what if you're among the many instructors who teach face to face but maintain a **web site** as well? Does making your course notes available online mean that coming to class will become obsolete? How do you balance the real and virtual worlds so that they work together? And if information can be presented readily online, what should class time be devoted to: Discussions? Student presentations? Structured debates? Even more challenging, if your course is conducted and class activities occur both online and in face-to-face sessions, how do you create a learning experience for your students that is integrated and coherent?

There is no prototypical experience of teaching online. Some instructors use the Web to complement what they teach in class. Others teach entirely on the Web. Some institutions have sophisticated hardware and software that they make available; others offer little more than the bare bones to instructors.

You will get a sense of these differences in the chapters that follow. For the time being, take a look at two hypothetical instructors working online.

● ● ● ● ●

The Range of Online Experiences: Two Hypothetical Cases

The first of our hypothetical instructors, Jim Hegelmarks, teaches philosophy entirely online. The second, Miriam Sharpe, teaches a first-year physics course in a conventional classroom but uses a web site to help her students review material and get answers to their questions.

Western Philosophy, a Course Taught Entirely Online

Jim Hegelmarks's course in Western philosophy is now in its third week, and the assignment for his class is to read a short commentary he has written on John Stuart Mill's *Principles of Political Economy*, portions of which the class has studied. He has asked the students to read his commentary and then respond in some detail to a question he has posted on the online discussion board for his course.

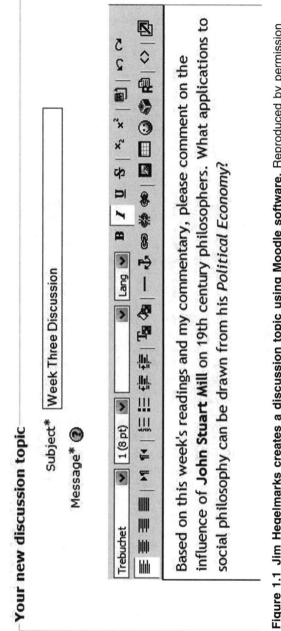

Figure 1.1 Jim Hegelmarks creates a discussion topic using Moodle software. Reproduced by permission from Moodle.

Connecting to the Web from his home, or sitting in a local coffee shop with his laptop and wireless connection, Hegelmarks types the **URL** of his class web site into the location bar of his Firefox browser and is promptly greeted with a log-in screen. He types in his user name (jhegelmarks) and his password (hmarks420); this process admits him to the class.

Hegelmarks's course is conducted using a **course management system** (or **virtual learning environment**) which his university has adopted for all online courses.

course management system or software (CMS), also known as virtual learning environment (VLE), learning management system (LMS), learning platform, online delivery system   A software program that contains a number of integrated instructional functions. Instructors can **post** lectures or graphics, moderate discussions, invoke chat sessions, and give quizzes, all within the confines of the same software system. Not only can instructors and students "manage" the flow of information and communications, but the instructor can both assess and keep track of the performance of the students, monitoring their progress and assigning grades. Typical examples of a CMS are those produced by Blackboard and eCollege, or adopted from "open source" products such as Moodle or Sakai. Your institution may have yet another proprietary system of its own, and there are many others in use or being developed all over the world. To keep track of some of these systems and to compare their various features, you might want to visit the EduTools site (www.edutools.info/course). These systems, as well as many of the tools which are continually being added to these systems, are discussed in more detail in Chapter 6.

The main page of Hegelmarks's course contains a number of navigational "buttons" he can use to manage the course. His commentary is posted in a section that is set up to display text or audio lectures, but the area he's interested in today is the discussion board, so that's where he goes first. With his mouse, he clicks on the navigational button that leads to the discussion board and reviews the messages that have been posted there. Several of the students have posted their responses to the assignment. He reads through the responses on-screen thoughtfully, printing out the longer ones so that he can consider them at his leisure. Each posting is about fifty words in length.

After evaluating the responses, Hegelmarks gives each student a grade for this assignment and enters the grade in the online gradebook, which can be reached by clicking another navigational button on the course's main page. Each type of graded assignment, including participation, has a section reserved for it in the online gradebook. He knows that when students log on to the class web site to check their grades, each student will be able to see only his or her own grades—no one else's grade will be visible. Hegelmarks also knows that those who have failed to complete this assignment will be able to monitor their progress, or lack of it, by looking at the gradebook online.

What concerns Hegelmarks now is that only five of his fifteen students have responded so far. Because it's already Friday, and there's a new assignment they must do for the next week, he decides to take a look at some of the statistical information that the course management system offers for tracking student progress. What he finds is that of the ten students who haven't responded to the question, eight have at least clicked on (and one hopes, actually read) the commentary for that lesson, some spending more than sixty minutes at a time in that area. Two haven't looked at it at all.

Hegelmarks's first concern is with the two students who haven't even looked at the assigned commentary. It isn't the first time they've failed to complete an assignment on time. Hegelmarks sends both of them a low-key but concerned email asking whether they're having any special problems he should know about, gently reminding them that they've fallen behind.

The lengthy time the other students have been taking to read his commentary concerns him as well. From experience, he knows that students often struggle with some of the concepts in Mill's *Political Economy*. He had written the commentary and created the homework assignment in an attempt to clarify the subject, but taking a second look, he now realizes that the commentary was written far too densely. He makes a note to rewrite it the next time he teaches the class.

While Hegelmarks is still online, a student instant messages him, using that feature of this course management software, and Hegelmarks takes a few minutes to answer a question about the upcoming assignment. The question had been addressed in the classroom Q&A area, and in fact, the student seems to know the answer already, but he is grateful to receive Hegelmarks's further affirmation. Hegelmarks has the ability to make himself invisible to the students via instant messaging but he usually maintains his presence because he feels that those few students who like to contact him in this manner may need this individualized attention and reassurance.

The last task Hegelmarks completes before logging off is to comment on the student responses that he has just read and graded. He doesn't comment on each one—that would take far too long—but he composes a summary message touching on the main points his students have made, and he posts this on the discussion board for all to see.

Introduction to Physics, a "Blended" Course

Our second instructor, Miriam Sharpe, teaches an introductory physics class at a large public university. Her course, a prerequisite for anyone majoring in physics, is what we call **blended**, that is, combining both online and face-to-face activities.

The class is large, with eighty students enrolled, and Sharpe has two teaching assistants (TAs) to help her. Three times a week, she lectures to her class, using PowerPoint slides projected onto a screen to elucidate her points. Because she relies on so many slides, she has decided to post them on the course web site for students to review.

Although some of her colleagues disapprove of this practice, arguing that it will dissuade students from coming to class, Sharpe contends that relieving students of the tedium of taking copious notes during her lectures makes it easier for them to comprehend and remember the material. More important, by posting her slides online, she gives students the opportunity to review the material before coming to class. As a result, she has found that the questions raised in class, and the discussions they provoke, are far more relevant and lively.

Sharpe also uses the course web site for discussion groups. Each TA leads a discussion group of thirty students, with Sharpe handling the remaining twenty herself. In these virtual discussion groups, students can post their queries and concerns and receive a response from Sharpe, a TA, or other students. Sharpe and her TAs make a point of checking the **discussion boards** at least once a day.

Sharpe has one more major use for the web site: to post sample exams. When she first started using the site, she simply posted the exams as documents that her students could read. But after her university installed a new course management system, she was able to offer the sample exams in such a way that students could take an exam online and receive both feedback and a score. This trial assessment, she has discovered, is quite popular with her students.

Blended course (also known as **hybrid**) A course which includes both face-to-face meetings and online components. Definitions of blended courses vary from one institution to another. For example, a blended course may be defined as one in which some "seat time" is replaced by online activities, or this term may be applied to those courses in which both the face-to-face and online components are required, to differentiate the course from one in which online elements are merely supplementary. The Sloan Consortium has defined a blended or hybrid course as one in which 30–79 percent of the content is delivered online.

Since first beginning to supplement her class with online materials two years ago, she has gone from a rudimentary web site which was maintained by her TAs to software that easily permits her to upload most materials on her own. The greater ease of using today's software has actually encouraged Sharpe to more readily conceive of activities that can be implemented online. Now that all her students are readily able to access the Web, she has no qualms about requiring students to perform certain activities online. This year for the first time she has begun to require students to use the university's **wiki** software to compose their group project reports rather than have them use valuable time on campus to accomplish that portion of their work. By using the wiki software rather than simply having students post projects to the discussion board, Dr. Sharpe gains another advantage— she is able to track each individual's contribution to a group project through the wiki's recording of each edit.

Wiki Software which allows for the collaborative creation and editing of content in web page format without knowledge of programming code. Various built-in controls allow for the setting of different authoring permissions and the tracking of each contribution and different versions over time. The online encyclopedia, Wikipedia, is a prominent example of the wiki format.

• • • • •

Teaching Online: The Basics

Now that you have some idea of what it's like to teach online and what some of the basic terms and concepts are, you may be thinking about how to teach your own class online. Later chapters will go into detail on many specific aspects of the task. Here we comment on some of the basic pedagogical considerations involved in teaching courses like those of our two fictional instructors, Jim Hegelmarks and Miriam Sharpe.

Teaching a Course Entirely Online

Perhaps the most daunting task is to plan a new course that will be taught entirely online, particularly if you've never taught online before. Composing the syllabus, assembling the exercises and quizzes, weighing the criteria for grades—all this presents a set of unfamiliar challenges.

Yet closer inspection reveals that the approach to solving such problems is similar to what you would use "on the ground." The same instructional strategy you've learned for a live classroom—setting the goals of the course, describing specific objectives, defining the required tasks, creating relevant assignments— applies online. Similarly, if you're converting an existing course into an online version, your basic approach need not change.

Where the online course differs is in technique and in discovering the new teaching and learning opportunities afforded by the new online environment. In a classroom, you have your physical presence—your voice, body language, intonation, expressions, gestures—to help you communicate with your students. Online, at least for the majority of the time, you don't. In a classroom, a smile can be a powerful signal of approval. Online, it's reduced to a ludicrous little **emoticon** :)—characters that look like a person grinning. In a classroom, the instructor is often the "sage on the stage." Online, the instructor is more like the "sage on the page." It is the written word, at least for now, that conveys the crux of what you want to say. Increasingly, there are opportunities to inject audio or video to relieve that burden of text.

While these opportunities existed in previous years and were discussed in earlier editions of this book, the pace of change has picked up so that the easy-to-use tools for instructors to produce audio and video are now more widespread and cheaper (if not free) than ever before. Also, many more students are able to access these audio and video communications than was previously the case. However, for most readers of this book, these non-text methods for communicating and presenting are likely still secondary to the ubiquity of text-based communications.

The fact that the majority of online teaching is still done using the written word puts an inordinate emphasis on style, attitude, and intonation as they are expressed in print. A sarcastic aside, a seemingly innocent joke, shorn of an apologetic smile or a moderating laugh, can seem cold and hostile to the student reading it on the screen. None of the conventional ways of modifying ambiguous or ironic statements—the wink, the raised eyebrow, the shrug, and the smile—is available with online text. Thus an instructor communicating with the written word must pay particular attention to nuances.

> **Emoticon** A text-based or graphic symbol used in online communications to express emotions that might otherwise be misunderstood when relying only on text. The word comes from combining emotion with icon. Text-based emoticons are formed from keyboard characters, like the smiley face :), and are usually designed to be read from left to right in Western cultures, but may be created to be read vertically (^_^) in Asian cultures.

In a physical classroom, moreover, you're always there to listen to your students or observe their interactions. Online, you're there only sporadically, at the times when you log on, whereas your students may post their comments at any time of day. These circumstances modify the instructional role you play, making you more a facilitator or moderator than the expert from whom all knowledge flows. Indeed, online courses depend heavily on the participation of students. As an instructor, you need to step back a bit from the spotlight in order to allow the students to take a more active part. Perhaps you will intervene only when the flow of conversation strays too far off the mark or when you need to summarize the conversation in order to progress to another point.

Conversely, online participation is just as important to the student as it is to you. What makes the Web such an attractive medium—the ability to communicate instantly with anyone in the world—is what drives students to the Internet rather than to a conventional classroom. If, when they log on to the course, all they can do is read the voluminous course notes you have posted there, they will soon become frustrated and drift away. And given your students' propensity to upload photos and videos, while keeping up a continuous stream of communication via text messaging, instant messaging, or other online tools, they are likely already acculturated to being active participants in the online world.

It's your responsibility to bear all this in mind when devising your course. You will fashion tasks and exercises that emphasize student collaboration and de-emphasize the traditional role of the instructor as the central figure in the pedagogical play.

This doesn't mean that an online syllabus should include only tasks that must be performed online: hunting for online material, for example, or linking to a host of other web sites. In fact, such tasks can often prove counterproductive, requiring that students stay online an inordinate amount of time. Indeed, the sort of tasks you have your students perform need not, and perhaps should not, differ from what you would have them do on the ground. They still need to go to libraries to perform the functions of sound research (unless their institution provides database and full-text resources online), and they still need to investigate, examine, and observe phenomena on their own. What's different is how they communicate what they have learned, how they talk to each other, and how you talk to them. A successful online course often includes challenging assignments that lead to publicly conducted discussions, moderated and guided by you. An online course will also find a meaningful way to incorporate the increasingly rich mix of resources available on the Web.

For instructors like Miriam Sharpe, who teach face to face but use the Web to augment the work in class, there's a somewhat different set of criteria. For these instructors, the Web may be a place to post information before class in order to inspire a meaningful in-class discussion. Or the information on the Web may help give students the proper context for a lecture, so that the lecture falls on well-informed ears rather than becoming a mere oration accompanied by the sound of pencils furiously scribbling notes (or the clicking of laptop keyboards, as the case may be).

Conversely, the web site might be used to elucidate or elaborate a point that was brought up in class. Students may begin a group project in a face-to-face session, continue it online for a number of weeks, then return to present it on campus, integrating the two modes in a series of tightly woven transitions. The Web may become a place where students can comment, critique, or analyze material in a leisurely and thoughtful way, instead of having to contend with other students in impassioned face-to-face debates. Indeed, the Web provides a safe environment for students who ordinarily might not chime in, too timid or shy to take part in discussions with those who are louder, more aggressive, or domineering. In this sense, using the Web as a means of communication can often provoke more thoughtful and reasoned discussions than might be possible in a classroom.

Later chapters will describe the options in more detail. Here, our point is straightforward:

Important! **There's no need to start from scratch to teach online. You can apply what you already know and add to it by using new tools and techniques adapted for the online environment.**

What about Support Personnel and Training?

It may have occurred to you that mastering new software and techniques is a task that ought to be handled by someone else—by computer support personnel, or instructional designers, for example, or by graduate student teaching assistants. On many campuses, however, neither the expertise nor the funds are available to provide the support each faculty member might like to have.

Most of the time, computer support personnel have to deal with problems concerning infrastructure, networks, and servers that shut down. When they respond to an individual faculty member, they're typically concerned with hardware or software problems: "I can't type the letter k on my keyboard"; "I can't download this video." Teaching assistants, for their part, won't necessarily have more advanced skills than faculty members, and are more appropriately concerned with pursuing their degrees. Instructional designers and instructional technologists are often specially hired to assist instructors, but they are seldom numerous enough to replace all of faculty's own efforts.

Many instructors who have painstakingly acquired computer skills and familiarity with the Web may even feel intimidated by the increasing ease and frequency with which their students communicate via mobile phone text messaging, socialize on social networking sites like Facebook, create and upload videos to YouTube, and, in effect, live comfortably with technology occupying a major portion of their daily life. Some instructors struggle to keep up with the ever-increasing number of technology tools available, while others worry about looking foolish to their students through a too "faddish" and superficial adoption of these tools. (Do your students even want you to "friend" them on Facebook?)

Increasingly, online programs do offer ongoing support to their instructors. But even in these comparatively proactive programs, there's a limit to how much attention and help can be offered to each faculty member, particularly as the number of online courses continues to grow. Of course, instructors who aren't based on a campus have even fewer resources to help them troubleshoot problems.

While more prevalent than in the early years of online education, still scarce is the availability of reliable and effective training for online instructors. A hodgepodge of different workshops, brown-bag lunches, and self-paced online materials may be cobbled together to ease an instructor's progress, but there are still a great number of instructors who must learn on the job. Often this means that the first course you teach is beset with errors, miscues, and miscalculations, much as may have happened when you taught your first class face to face.

Even for those who enroll in a formal training course, the results can be disappointing. Some tend to betray the idiosyncrasies of the particular person who delivers the training while others may be taught by technical staff with little teaching experience of their own. Some tend to deal with the subject as if it were a phenomenon to be researched rather than a new set of skills to be mastered and employed. To make matters worse, training is often offered in a conventional classroom or lab setting, depriving faculty members of the experience of learning online or learning online in a real-life teaching situation, i.e., alone, at their own computer.

The situation isn't entirely bleak, however. Even if your institution doesn't provide much in the way of preparation for online teaching, there are some reliable training programs offered to the public, several of which are mentioned in Chapter 14. We will also discuss with you how you might network with other online instructors for mutual support and learning. In addition, the amount of technical know-how you need before you begin is less than you may suppose. Newcomers to online teaching are likely to exaggerate the computer and overall technical expertise required. Let's address that question directly.

● ● ● ● ●

Do You Have to Be a Computer Expert?

Instructors often wonder what qualifications—especially what level of technical computer skills—they need to consider teaching online. Do you have to be an expert or an advanced computer user?

In terms of technical computer skills, an instructor needs little to start with. A very basic familiarity with computers and the Internet will more than suffice. That means knowing how to do the following:

1. Set up folders and directories on a hard drive.
2. Use word-processing software properly (for instance, cut, copy, and paste; minimize and maximize windows; save files).
3. Handle email communications, including attachments.
4. Use a **browser** such as Internet Explorer or Firefox to access the World Wide Web.
5. **Download**, that is, retrieve a file from your institution's computer network or from the Web and save it on your own computer.

If you lack some of these skills, you can pick them up on campus or in online workshops. Once you're comfortable with these basic skills, you should, with experience, be able to build on them and become more skilled. With the advent of more user-friendly and menu-driven software, it is actually getting easier for instructors to learn to teach online. For example, it is no longer necessary for most instructors to learn HTML in order to format the text they post online because the advent of **WYSIWYG ("what you see is what you get")** editors that operate very much like word-processing software are increasingly built right into the software programs instructors use to teach.

Faculty of all ranks who are enthusiastic about the possibilities offered by online teaching—and who are willing to invest some time in learning new technology and methods for the sake of personal and professional growth—are good candidates for teaching online.

This raises a question we are often asked—what kind of people make the best online instructors? Surprisingly, it is "people-oriented" people who make the best online instructors. Though these people-oriented people may initially feel the most anxiety about teaching online, their desire to reach out to their students, their empathy and interest in others, and their urge to bridge communication gaps mean that they have the aptitude and motivation to become the very best online teachers.

Important! *"Techies" don't necessarily make the best online instructors. An interest in teaching should come first, technology second.*

● ● ● ● ●

What Can Teaching Online Do for You?

Beyond the case we have made for the greater flexibility and accessibility of online teaching, the rich and diverse world of resources that becomes available, and the fact that online learning is becoming more expected and even demanded by students, is there anything else that we might say to those of you who come to this book with one arm twisted behind your back, unconvinced of the desirability of teaching online? Although teaching online presents many challenges to the instructor, there are many more benefits to be gained from the experience. Let us highlight two major benefits you may not have considered.

Heightened Awareness of Your Teaching

Among instructors who have taught online, the advantage of the process that they most commonly express is that it makes them better teachers—not only online, but also in their face-to-face classes.

Few of us in higher education have any training in teaching methods or instructional design. We learn chiefly from osmosis (being in a classroom), from mentoring by more experienced colleagues (if we're lucky), or through time spent as teaching assistants in graduate school.

Teaching online heightens our awareness of what we're actually doing in the classroom. The interactions between our students and ourselves—which often consist of fleeting occasions in the on-campus classroom—are recorded for us online, available for our review and reflection. We also have the opportunity to observe and review how our students respond to our assignments and to track the growth of understanding or incomprehension as they respond to the lessons and activities we set in motion for their learning.

This heightened awareness can be both illuminating and humbling. We find that the instructional design process becomes less implicit and more of a deliberate enterprise. Sometimes this leads us to make changes in the way we do things or to try out new approaches, not only in our online courses but in our on-campus classrooms as well.

As you reconsider your instructional methods, you may find that the rapid and flexible communication afforded by the Internet fosters some creative new approaches. Isabel Simões de Carvalho, teaching mechanical engineering at the Instituto Superior de Engenharia in Lisbon, Portugal, began to use the online classroom to support her traditional face-to-face classes and soon found herself introducing entirely new types of learning activities, taking advantage of the way that face-to-face meetings and online activities could be paired to deepen immersion in a learning activity. She was surprised by the way students seemed to rise to the occasion—"a really interesting discovery was that by asking them to do quite a bit of challenging work, one can get students to more readily engage in learning and they even enjoy it!"

When you teach online, you, too, may experience that serendipitous moment when the possibilities of the medium and your course objectives suddenly come together. Grasp that moment and shape it to enliven and enrich your students' learning!

New Connections with the Wider World

A great fear among many instructors is that all human interaction online is inevitably superficial and that such a learning environment leads to more alienation between students and instructors, and less meaningful communication among colleagues.

Communication online isn't the same as in person, but it can be both effective and satisfying. It also brings us new opportunities to communicate with, and even to get to know, people we would have no other chance to meet—either because they live at a great distance from us or because their schedules wouldn't otherwise allow them to take our classes.

At the risk of sounding heretical, we will venture the proposition that meeting online is sometimes the ideal way to get to know a student or colleague. The by-now-old joke goes, "On the Internet, nobody knows you're a dog," and by the same token, nobody knows whether you're under twenty-one or over sixty-five years old. When one of this book's authors, Susan Ko, met Gerda Lederer online, she formed a picture in her head of a woman of about thirty who had a fresh and open attitude toward life and who was bursting with creative ideas and enthusiasm for the new medium. Susan deduced from their extensive online communications that Gerda kept very current in her field of expertise, as well as up to date in her knowledge of culture and education in general. Susan and Gerda got to know each other rather well online, and eventually, when Gerda traveled to Los Angeles, they decided to meet in person. Susan was surprised to discover that Gerda was over seventy years old.

Although Susan felt that she was without any bias toward older adults, she had to admit that meeting Gerda's *ideas* before she met her in person had actually been the very best way to get to know her.

Many instructors, including the authors of this book, arrange to meet online students at conferences. Online students will also network among themselves, carry on long correspondences, and sometimes meet in person. In fact, talking extensively with another online, observing that person's interaction with others, and perhaps collaborating on a project can often form the basis of a solid friendship.

New connections with distant colleges also become possible. An instructor residing in Missouri may teach for an institution based in New York, and a professor on leave from a college in California may teach a class from a temporary post in France. In this way, instructors are often able to continue their institutional associations with their former colleges after they have moved far away from the home campus site.

With online education, cross-cultural and international collaborations become possible, without the expense and difficult logistics of travel, allowing students from different lands to exchange ideas and work in concert on projects and topics of interest to both parties.

For those who teach hybrid courses, one benefit that will be immediately obvious is the greater number of students heard from in your class—in a face-to-face class of fifty students, an instructor is lucky to get the active participation of more than a small handful of students. Many more lack the confidence to speak up in the classroom, while others may nod off or distractedly text friends on their cell phones during the in-class time. Online, especially if you establish a participation requirement, you are likely to "hear" from nearly all your students. That shy student in the back row of your classroom might end up being the most loquacious or even most eloquent contributor to your online discussion **forum**.

In the next chapter, we will begin preparing you for online teaching by showing you how to explore your institution's resources and make practical sense of what you find.

2

Scouting the Territory: Exploring Your Institution's Resources

In Chapter 1, you learned a bit about how online learning functions. Now you're ready to begin planning the online environment of your course.

But where should you start?

A good first step is to scout the territory in which you plan to operate—that is, explore the technological and administrative environment in your institution to ascertain what is possible and desirable to do. The tools an institution uses, the policies that might constrain or enable you, and the support it offers very much influence the choices you'll need to make. Before you sit down to sketch out your course, you must be certain that what you're planning can actually take place.

Colleges and other institutions, after all, don't exist in a vacuum. They have administrators, department heads, and computer support personnel, all of whom have budgets, agendas, and rivalries. Investments have been made (or are on the planning board) in computer hardware, operating systems, software platforms, computer labs, maintenance, support, and instructor training. All of these factors, in one way or another, may affect the shape of the course you plan to teach.

Of course, you can't be expected to know everything there is to know about these subjects. We aren't suggesting that you get on your hands and knees to follow the cabling from your building to the street outside or become an expert on computer software. But we are suggesting that you arm yourself in advance with a bit of practical knowledge.

This isn't as formidable a task as it may seem. If you've been working at your institution for some time, you already know much of the information. What you don't know you can usually find out by visiting the institution's web site or by scheduling a few informal interviews with your department head, chief administrator, or computer support person. Perhaps your institution has a special unit dedicated to helping faculty learn about teaching online or at the very least, a unit that offers some technical training on using whatever software tools your institution may have adopted. If you know what questions to ask and what to look for in advance, you should be able to walk away with most of the information you need.

Imagine you're a new manager visiting a modern manufacturing plant for the first time. To familiarize yourself with its operations, you do a walk-through survey. You note which equipment is in use, heeding such factors as age, reliability, and maintenance records. You also notice which procedures are in force, as well as which have been most successful. You judge whether the foreperson and the floor workers seem friendly or enthusiastic, or whether that scowl on their faces denotes some deep-seated hostility you would do well to avoid. How many of the jobs are handled in-house and how many are outsourced? Do they have the latest technology, and if so, have the workers and managers learned how to use those high-tech machines effectively? Finally, how good is the end product? Is feedback from the product users incorporated into the improvement cycle?

The rest of this chapter will help you translate that metaphorical tour into specific questions to ask and ways to interpret the results.

● ● ● ● ●

Questions to Ask About Your Institution's Resources

The following sections describe some useful questions you can ask in our equivalent of a walk-through survey.

What's Already in Place?

This question is the most important of all. In practice, you'll break it down into a number of subordinate queries, such as these:

- Does your institution already provide courses online, either as completely online or blended format?
- If so, which courses?
- Who teaches them?
- What software platform(s) or tools do they use?
- Who put the courses together?
- How long did it take to put them together?
- Is there a policy in place for those who want to teach an online or blended course?
- Are there any restrictions on how much of a course can be required to be accessed online, on whether synchronous tools can be used as well as **asynchronous**?
- Is there any training in place for those who want to teach online? If so, who offers it—faculty development, academic departments, academic technology, instructional design units?
- Is there an orientation to prepare students for online learning and technical staff to support them?

Once you find out about online courses already being taught at your institution, make an effort to contact the instructors and talk to them at length. Tell them what you plan to do and solicit their reactions. Find out what their experiences have been. Ask about potential pitfalls you ought to avoid. Talk to your administrator and any other gatekeepers to the process to find out about the applicable policies.

Information gained in this way is the most valuable you can collect. Not only will you learn first-hand what's going on, but you may, if you're lucky, forge a few strategic alliances with some of the pioneers at your institution or gain a mentor.

What Kind of Software, Hardware, and Operating System Is Available at Your Institution to Run Online Courses?

It is easiest to work with the software that your institution has already made available—that way you have probable sources of technical support, and are least likely to propose using software that your students will have difficulty accessing. Some institutions offer the choice of more than one course management system to instructors while others are amenable to supporting additional tools and programs that an instructor might wish to use.

Does your college or department support only PCs or are Macs also supported for both instructors and students? What kind of **operating system**—Windows, Mac OS X, Linux, etc.—is there? This consideration is chiefly important for those enterprising souls who may want to run software programs that that institution may not supply or support. Software is written expressly for a particular operating system. Thus the **web server** you use to run your course web site must be compatible with the operating system. Or perhaps your institution is increasingly moving to make available a variety of software completely through the browser and Internet—this so-called **cloud computing** trend may mean that you have fewer concerns about hardware.

What Kind of Network Has Your Institution Set Up and What Is the Profile of Student Users?

It doesn't matter what kind of software, hardware, or operating system your college may have if the information that's being "served" has nowhere to go. The "network"—about as vague a term as the "Syndicate"—consists of whatever hodgepodge of telephone, Ethernet, coaxial, and fiber-optic cables your institution has cobbled together, complete with the hubs and routers that connect them to the campus "backbone," culminating in the "gateway" that opens to the great outside world in which you and your students live. This collection of stuff determines how quickly and effectively you and your students can communicate with each other. Collectively, it's often referred to as the "pipeline"—another vague term that conceals more than it reveals.

In investigating this pipeline through which you'll have to operate, pay attention to specific capabilities and hindrances. The kind of course you plan and the exercises you assign must take these conditions into consideration. Imagine, for instance, that your university has an adequate network on campus, with a high-speed connection to the Internet that allows you to surf the Web and fetch useful software in a matter of seconds. But if a considerable number of your students live in rural areas where they are limited to dial-up access from off-campus, you won't want to create the type of course exercise in which they're required to go on extended searches online for material or information. Staying online can often be both costly and frustrating for a student connecting from home via a relatively slow modem. Nor will you want to schedule a lot of synchronous **chat** sessions or include video resources when you know that the connectivity is tenuous. Your student body may also include military students or other workers who are restricted by firewalls that make it difficult for them to use any programs that require downloading to their own computers. The computer support units on campus generally have information on how students are accessing the campus servers and this information is valuable for your planning.

If, on the other hand, there are adequate on-campus labs or laptop computing programs that can be accessed by students who will be on campus at regular periods to take a blended course, you may be able to use a certain amount of more sophisticated resources and software by taking advantage of and planning ahead for students to avail themselves of these campus-based computing resources.

You also need to consider where you yourself will be working most of the time. If you'll work mainly at home you will want to obtain unlimited high-speed Internet service with a local private **Internet service provider** (**ISP**). Also, if you anticipate spending part of the class time away from your normal environment, make sure that you find out about arrangements for access when traveling. Check ahead with your hotel to find out if there is **wireless** (also known as "**wi-fi**" for "wireless fidelity") or other high-speed connection service for your laptop, or if there is a business center that offers reasonably priced Internet access. Or consult an online travel guide to find out if there is an Internet café or some other facility in the city you plan to visit. Travelers increasingly discuss such accommodations on the Web, offering helpful advice about connecting in a foreign country or town. Finally, you may be able to use a **smart phone**, that is, one that allows you to access the Internet, class email, and your university web sites, to keep up with your class during a trip of relatively short duration.

What Kind of Computer Support Does Your Institution Provide?

Computer support comes in various sizes and shapes. Some colleges have computer support personnel who are strictly network maintenance types, with no time for wild-eyed academics. Still other institutions have well-meaning but somewhat inexperienced administrators in charge who aren't thoroughly familiar with what an educational web site can provide. The best have personnel who know their trade and are able to communicate what they know to faculty members.

So get to know your local computer support personnel or instructional technologist and ask the appropriate questions. Will the individual assist you in an instructional media lab or come to your office to help you with such mundane details as improving a scanned graphic in Photoshop? Will they videotape your lecture and then post it online for you? Or perhaps there are extensive online tutorials or workshops that you can avail yourself of to learn specific skills?

Will your students receive support and advice during office hours only or through a 24/7 tech help desk service? Or will you and your students be essentially on your own?

The answers to such questions will help you determine just how complex and demanding your online work can be, as well as which methods and software programs might best accomplish the task. Above all, you will want to avoid making choices that force you to be the main source of technical support for your students. While this was quite common during the early years of online teaching, it was never an ideal situation for an instructor to be spending a good deal of time doing something other than teaching.

What Kind of Instructor Training and Support is Available?

Learning how to teach online is an ongoing process that includes not only mastering new skills, but also a cycle of review, reflection, and continual revision of one's online course. By finding out what's already available at your institution in terms of training and support in the technical aspects as well as the pedagogical approaches to teaching online, you can devise a plan for sustaining your efforts. As mentioned in Chapter 1, sometimes there is a hodgepodge of different resources on campus offered to instructors, while other institutions may have well-organized paths for attaining the expertise to teach online and the support personnel in place to guide you along the way.

Support for online teaching may be found in faculty development units, or it may be lodged within a special academic technology, online teaching and learning unit, or instructional design group. It may be scattered about in several different units on campus, or there may be centralized university system-wide resources available for training instructors on multiple campuses. Finally, your institutions may make funds available to support your learning from sources outside your institution.

● ● ● ● ●

Different Resource and Readiness Levels: Three Typical Scenarios

Now that you've made your walk-through survey of your institution, you should have a fair idea of what it can offer you. Of course, there are many shades of gray to consider, but in most cases your institution will fall into one of three broadly defined categories of readiness for online teaching and learning: low, middle, or high. Our descriptions of these have necessarily morphed over the years, but keep in mind that there are instructors today in rural areas and in the developing world that may find themselves in circumstances akin to those experienced a decade ago by today's most richly provided.

The Low Readiness Scenario

A college or department in the low readiness category has little or no experience offering courses online. Its web site contains administrative information, but little else. Infrastructure is minimal; while department offices may be connected to the Internet via a high-speed line, students roll their eyes heavenward when you inquire whether there are enough computers on campus to meet their needs.

You may discover that a few intrepid faculty members have found a way to offer some of their courses online, often using an arrangement with a local ISP to host their web pages, but these pathfinders have apparently accomplished this feat on their own. No one on campus, you're told, has sufficient skill, dedication, or patience to offer solid technological support. Or if you are a little higher on this readiness scale, the university may indeed offer to host course web sites. The quality of these course web sites, however, varies widely. Some contain little more than a converted word-processed outline of the course syllabus, whereas others are replete with complex graphics and links to other sites. Speaking to some of the instructors and computer support people, you learn that the **webmasters** for the existing course sites are a mix of student interns, teaching assistants, and instructor-volunteers, mostly self-taught. Hence they have different approaches and diverse sets of skills, accounting for the great variation you see in their web sites. In many cases, the instructors have done all the web site design themselves. What's more, in order to produce their courseware, these instructors had to purchase their own computer equipment, scanners, and software. Technical support for students and instructors is available only during regular office hours. The library offers a course in Internet searching for students and computer skills tutorials are available for students.

Support on campus is informal but collegial, with those pioneering instructors eager to share ideas and tips with their fellow instructors. The staffperson in charge of faculty development is eager to help, but does not know a great deal about the pedagogy of online teaching.

The Mid-Range Readiness Scenario

At a college or department in the mid-range category, the web site probably does have pointers to individual courses offered online. Many of even the completely face-to-face courses have their own web sites while **web-enhanced** and true blended courses may also make use of course management software for running their courses. It is often impossible to tell from the course listings which courses are actual blended courses requiring online activities since the university has not yet distinguished classes with supplementary web materials from those of true blended status. Also, the university emphasizes face-to-face instruction and is somewhat conflicted about publicizing online instruction. Although there are some fully online courses being offered, most have been funneled through the continuing education arm of the institution.

The university makes available two different course management software systems because there is no consensus on campus about the best solution. It may be that these are older versions of the software, but there are computer personnel and instructors who are familiar with these software systems and that does mean there are both formal and informal support networks on campus. Or perhaps the institution has contracted with an **application service provider**, a private business set up to host the latest course management software on its own servers and provide technical support as well.

There are self-paced tutorials on the university web site and a student orientation on the Web provides an introduction to using the course management software. Technical support personnel have joined with the faculty professional development staff and instructors who volunteer to share their expertise, offering a few workshops each semester on some aspect of using the Web, the basics of course management software, creating a web site or **blog**, and other related topics. There is also a small instructional media lab where instructors can make an appointment to use equipment or receive some one-on-one support. Beyond the two available course management systems, instructors are free to adopt the use of single tools to complement their web sites rather than use the course management system. Some tools are supported by the institution, while others on the public Web are simply linked to from the web site as the instructor chooses. Several instructors are experimenting with some of the new **Web 2.0** software tools available for free on the Web, choosing tools that allow their students to more easily collaborate on their work.

Overall, there is a lot of creative experimentation but little consistency in the institution's offerings.

There are several well-equipped computer labs on campus, and instructors can easily connect to the Web from their campus "smart" classrooms. There are also wireless **hotspots** for students to connect via laptops from the student lounge and library. Communication with the world beyond the college gates has become more reliable after a major institutional effort to put registration, library databases, and other services online; students attempting to connect from home to a course web site are less likely to find that networks slow down at certain points in the day when a lot of students are trying to access at once. Many students can also connect readily from their home to third-party web sites. Ultimately, all of your students have some Internet access off-campus, increasingly high speed and reliable, but still there remain students who are on dial-up and need to use public libraries or campus resources for better connection.

> **blog** Short for "web log," it is a web site on which a person (generally one person but could be more than one) posts commentary, and can allow others to respond. The blog is usually arranged in reverse chronological order and so lends itself to a journal-like series of frequent entries. The blog does not require knowledge of HTML to create, and blogging software usually provides a variety of templates that can be used without having to design a site. Visitors can choose to subscribe to the blog so that they are notified via email when a new entry or response has been made. While many blogs are public sites, used as a way to give opinions or provide the latest news on a topic, blogs can be open or permission access restricted to students in a particular class.

> **Web 2.0** Those tools and sites which allow for easy interaction and creation of content (from text to multimedia) on the Web without special technical skills, and whose structure and features foster collaboration and sharing among users. Most of these tools are available for free use. Blogs, wikis, YouTube, and social networking sites like Facebook are among the better-known Web 2.0 tools and sites available.

The High Readiness Scenario

The high readiness institution has installed a full-scale course management system for its departments or colleges. It has purchased site licenses for course management software, such as Blackboard or open-source Moodle, and has installed this software on its own web servers. Most of the online courses therefore have a uniform user interface.

Students and faculty are both provided with 24/7 tech support, either by the university itself or in conjunction with an outside provider. Library services (including full text resources available online), tutoring, advising, and other student services are all available online.

The administration, apparently eager to promote the use of computer-mediated courses, has secured grants and alumni contributions to fund the construction of labs and wireless networks on campus. Online courses are designated as such in the online catalog, while all face-to-face courses are supported by robust course web sites or use of the course management software. Beyond the main course management system used for classes, instructors are encouraged to explore and experiment with new technology tools. Periodically, workshops are offered to both faculty and students to assist them in learning new computer skills and to introduce new software programs and tools. The faculty professional development unit has teamed up with academic technology to offer a basic training course for faculty who are interested in teaching online and a generous stipend is offered instructors as an incentive for participating. Or perhaps completion of some base-line training is actually mandated before instructors can teach online.

Instructional designers and technologists are available to assist faculty with special projects. High-enrollment courses offered in multiple sections are often designed by a team of instructional designers, technical support staff, and one or more instructors working together.

● ● ● ● ●

Adapting to Your Institution's Resource Level (and Perhaps Finding What You Need Elsewhere)

Even though it may appear that only the high readiness setting offers you a good chance to succeed as an online instructor, you can be successful in all three types of institutions if you're willing to tailor your demands to the available resources. In fact, you may find that a high readiness setting, with its integrated course management applications, amounts to a "one-size-fits-all" approach that doesn't suit your particular needs very well.

The following sections offer examples of solutions you might develop in each of the three environments.

Low Institutional Readiness Solutions

As an example of a low readiness setting, imagine you're teaching introductory biology at a small rural college with few technological resources. Because this course is required for biology majors and also fulfills the college's general education requirements, it's usually quite full, with upwards of ninety students crammed into a large, poorly air-conditioned classroom. The college has no graduate program to speak of and barely enough funds to provide TAs, so you rely on honors biology undergraduates for assistance.

You lecture, you assign homework (readings in a large, expensive, and somewhat daunting textbook), you give a midterm and a final, and you hold discussion sessions three times a week, dividing up the class into groups of about thirty. On your office computer, you've created a series of overheads that you use as you lecture (as long as the bulb in the room's overhead projector hasn't burned out), and you make available to the students a set of your private course notes, complete with graphs and diagrams, for which they pay a nominal fee. Although your discussion sessions help fill in the gaps, the atmosphere is often chaotic, with the students firing questions from all sides as if they were reporters at a presidential press conference.

Clearly, you're doing the best you can with the means available. What you'd like to do is improve student comprehension of this difficult and challenging subject while, paradoxically, lightening your own formidable teaching load. To do this, you know you must find a way to communicate more efficiently with your students. The obvious solution would be to increase your office hours. But for a class of ninety-odd students, that might not be of much help. It also might prove overwhelming for you.

Given the limited means of your institution, what can you do?

Even in this difficult situation, there are ways to use online instruction effectively. Most of your students will have access to the Internet and email, even though Internet service in this rural area is somewhat spotty. The question is, how many students have access and what kind of access?

Using whatever survey tools are available to you (information from the registrar's office, in class polls, informal interviews), find out how many students either have a computer of their own or have access to a friend's or roommate's computer, or a cell phone that is connected in some way to the Internet. To this figure add a reasonable estimate of the number of students who might gain access to the Internet via whatever on-campus resources are available to them. Then calculate how long students are likely to remain online given the computing resources available to them and the prevalent fee structure for Internet service for the home offered in your area.

Your goal is to set up an email mentoring system to supplement your regular office hours and some of your discussion sessions. You want to have your students contact you when they need help.

These authors must be crazy, you may be thinking. Students are capable of firing off fusillades of messages. *Within a week I'd have a thousand emails or text messages that I couldn't possibly answer*, you're thinking. True, we respond, email can be a dangerous thing; but if used judiciously, it can lighten your workload and deepen student comprehension of course material. The keys to success are the procedures and protocols you create and enforce.

Students are encouraged to send you questions via email or **SMS (short message service)** text messaging through cell phones and other mobile devices. But you make it absolutely clear that you aren't going to respond to each and every message. Indeed, because your entire class doesn't have equal access to the Internet, you're going to collect the inquiries, group them according to subject, and provide a single answer on each subject once a week. You can email the responses to students and print out hard copies to bring to students in class who do not have Internet access. After a time, your answers will form, in effect, a page of **frequently asked questions (FAQs)**. For future classes, you might distribute this page of FAQs in class the first day and post them on the Web for those who are able to access them.

Still, even with a clear set of student expectations and procedures in place, the first time you begin the process, it may seem like an onerous task. You'll have to read each email carefully and draft your replies. This may seem like even more work than you did before. But by the second term, your workload should decrease dramatically. You will have built an impressive database of written replies to standard queries, which you can supplement as new questions come in. Your FAQ page will become a resource students can rely on. Gradually they'll learn to look at the page first before sending you a note.

But perhaps you are somewhat better off than the biology instructor cited above. Perhaps all your students have some stable access to the Internet. This will provide you more options. Perhaps your institution would be willing to set up a course **mailing list (listserv)**. A listserv requires special software that manages your email communications, capturing all inquiries automatically and rerouting them to the entire class, but this type of software is increasingly common even at low readiness institutions. A listserv makes it comparatively easier to communicate regularly with the entire class. Your weekly replies may be sent via the mailing list to all students and you can completely eschew resorting to hard copy for disseminating your replies and FAQs.

Or perhaps your institution would be willing to support a web site for your class. However, if you discover that this is a static web site only, in that materials can only be uploaded at the beginning of the term, and no one is available to make the sort of regular weekly updates you would like to post (and you either aren't allowed to or don't know how to upload materials yourself), you might want to look into one of the free web site-hosting services available. Years ago, these required a bit of finesse to operate, but now they are increasingly easy to use, with completely menu-driven features and no coding required at all. If you simply input the words "free web sites" into your search engine, you will likely find several options available to you. Having control over your web site, being able to update and edit on your own, is likely a better solution than having a static web site or one that is too difficult for you to easily handle on your own.

Using Free Online Resources

If you find that your students have fairly good access to the Internet, you have other options beyond email to communicate and interact with your students even though your institution provides very little in the way of software. There are many free services on the Web available now for those with limited institutional resources. (Don't confuse these free software and services which host programs on their own web sites with **open source** software like Moodle or Sakai which offer a free license but require that one install and manage the software on your own or the institution's server.)

Beyond the free web sites mentioned earlier, there are programs for creating and hosting blogs, wikis, or other communication and collaborative programs readily available for free. Your decision to use these is of course contingent upon your students having access to a computer or mobile device with which they can access these programs online. Students without the latest software on their computers may be able to use free web-based document programs accessed through a browser like Google Docs (docs.google.com) for word processing, spreadsheets, presentation, and for collaborating online together as well. These types of services are known as the previously mentioned cloud computing, and they allow users to access software without that software needing to reside on their own computers. But in evaluating these services for use with your class, you will need to match up their capabilities with the computing and Internet access levels available to your own class as well as your desired teaching approaches. For example, a blog hosted on a free web site will work well for you to post

> **open source software** Software in which the underlying source code is made known, collaboration in its development is encouraged, and which is distributed with the ability for others to use and modify. Linux is an example of an open source operating system, while Moodle and Sakai are examples of open source course management software.

materials and students to ask questions or post comments or for students to post individual reflective assignments, whereas a wiki might serve better as a means for collaboration by your students, but perhaps may involve more time online than you might want to require. We will discuss more on how to teach with some of these programs and tools in subsequent chapters of this book.

One issue you may need to consider is that many free online sites feature advertising. While you may feel that advertising on these sites does not provide the most appropriate atmosphere, as long as your institution does not object, you will probably find that many of your students seem unbothered by the ubiquitous commercial features of free online services. Nevertheless, if you do want to use only non-commercial web sites, look for resources designed specifically for educators, like Nicenet (www.nicenet.org), Edublogs (www.edublogs.org), PBworks (http://pbworks.com/academic.wiki), or Wetpaint (www. wetpaint.com), which have either limited advertising or none. All of these resources allow you to create materials without having to know HTML or possess special technical skills. Using these types of resources, you may feel as if you've made the leap from the Stone Age to the Information Age in one effortless bound. Note that beyond the free services offered there are often premium subscription levels available at many of these sites for a fee that allow users more features, more control, or more storage space. Let's look at just two examples of these services and what you might be able to do with them.

Edublogs offers hosted blogging software for educators, whether K–12 teachers or university instructors. The service offers some simple how-to videos, and they also feature discussion forums where educators can post inquiries, help one another, and offer tips. Once you have set up a blog for your class, you will find that you have these capabilities, among others, depending on your service level:

- You can control who accesses your blog and who doesn't.
- You can create course materials by uploading documents or simply copying and pasting your content into the blog.
- You can allow students to post their responses in discussions

related to your content and receive emails letting you know when students have posted in the discussion, thus cutting down on the number of times you must log on to see if students are responding.

- You can allow students also to be notified when someone has posted a comment to the same piece to which they have responded.
- You can set up blogs for your students to create their own presentations.

With PBworks or Wetpaint, you can create a place for your students to collaborate on a project or research and contribute resources or simply post responses for a series of different class topics. Such resources are continually adding features, but you may find that you are able to:

- post your course materials by copying and pasting;
- use ready-made templates designed for courses;
- add discussion forums;
- control permissions for students in regard to editing and contributing;
- track the process of collaboration and see who made edits and when;
- create distinct folders for different topics;
- set up email alerts to let users know when new postings have been made.

Through using one of these free tools, you may discover that you are able to use the online environment to enrich learning for your students and, after an initial investment of time in planning and creation of material, to relieve some of the burdens of teaching as well.

Mid-Range Solutions

If you teach in an institution like the one described in our mid-range scenario, you have many more options than those in a low readiness setting.

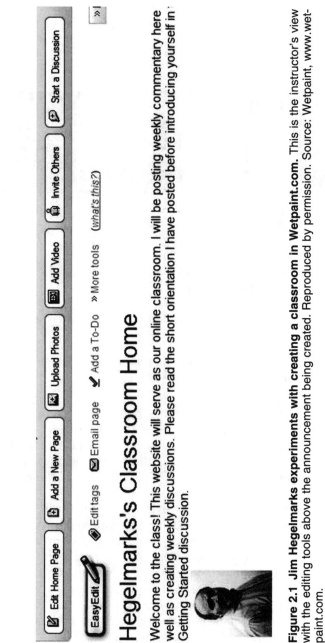

Figure 2.1 Jim Hegelmarks experiments with creating a classroom in Wetpaint.com. This is the instructor's view with the editing tools above the announcement being created. Reproduced by permission. Source: Wetpaint, www.wet-paint.com.

Philosophy 101, Jim Hegelmarks

Just another Edublogs.org weblog

Welcome to the Philosophy 101 Blog!

September 7th, 2009 by hegelmarks in Uncategorized · 1 Comment

Welcome to the **Philosophy 101** course! I am your instructor, Jim Hegelmarks, and I'll be using this blog to post my weekly lectures. However, I will ask you to post your questions and comments in our CMS classroom discussion board under the forum designated for each week's lecture rather than here.

Figure 2.2 Hegelmarks tries out blog software on Edublogs.org. Reproduced by permission from Edublogs.org.

For one thing, your students either have a computer at home, with generally good access to the Internet, or can use one of the many computers available in campus labs. Thus you can feel somewhat at ease in using the Web to help teach your class and you may have been asked to teach a blended or online course.

While you have both course management software and/or tools that you are free to use, not all are supported by your university. You are pretty much free to pick and choose what you will do to support your blended course, but despite some support from workshops and technical staff, you are largely on your own in deciding what to do. You realize that it will take quite a bit of time for you to compose your material and try out the various course management and software tools and you may find the plethora of choices daunting in itself.

Or maybe not. Beyond the help you may find at your institution through workshops and contacting those colleagues who have pioneered such efforts, you may also find help in the global village. Now is the time for you to discover one of the great benefits of teaching on the Web—the incredible creativity and generosity of a vast percentage of its citizen proprietors. For the instructor like yourself, willing to take the technological plunge but wary of sinking too deep, there are numerous resources available to buoy you up. Some of these are fellow educators who are happy to share their experience, and some of these are web resources that are free, or that cost so little that either you or your institution may decide they are affordable. The free web resources mentioned above in connection with low readiness institutions are available to you as well, and you may find that you can greatly expand upon the use of some of the tools and sites. For example, if your institution does not have blogging software installed on its server, you can use one of the free blogs as discussed above, but can also make use of some of the more sophisticated **multimedia** integration features, given that your students have fewer problems with access.

High Readiness Solutions

In the high readiness scenario, the institution has seemingly everything in place for you to teach online or hybrid courses. The course management system and additional tools are already adopted and ample training is available for you to fully prepare yourself for the task. You can rest assured that your students will be adequately oriented and supported when they encounter technical problems by the 24/7 help desk. You are also secure in knowing that students can get the help they need from library, tutoring, and advising services offered online.

You may think that in such a technological heaven, your troubles are over. However, academic institutions can be notoriously rigid. Having installed a course management system, they often begin to act like poker players nursing a good hand. They tend to stand pat, not drawing any cards and not discarding any either. When new software becomes available or new technologies come into being, they tend to dismiss these developments as too expensive, too difficult to implement, not practicable, or not necessary "at the present time." Often they would like to be more flexible, but costs and staffing as well as the need to prioritize on behalf of the greatest number of students make them slow to respond to developments. There is also the fact that as the emergence of new technologies gathers momentum, it is often hard to tell which tools have long-term promise and which are simply a passing wave. As an instructor, you are most concerned with teaching and even if you are not much of a "techie" you are paradoxically more likely to spot a new tool that will have relevance for you than are many of your technical staff or administrators.

Important! *No one knows everything, not even your computer support personnel. Even in a high-tech world, you have to do a little homework of your own to stay on top of new developments and be sure that those around you are on top of things as well.*

One other word about living in a high-tech, high readiness institutional environment: No institution will ever be able to provide the level of support to which you may think you're entitled. The fact that your university has purchased fancy equipment and software doesn't mean that you won't have to learn some skills. Sooner or later, you'll have to learn how to use the course management software, how to find and download graphics, and how to record an audio file, just as instructors once had to learn to use the overhead projector, tape recorder, or yes, how to navigate the Web.

In the following chapters you'll learn about these skills and how to master them or how to find programs that will do a great deal of the work for you. We will also tell you how to find the training and resources you need to keep up with the dizzying pace of new technology. For the time being, click open your existing syllabus document (or pull it out of that desk drawer). We're about to redesign your course for online.

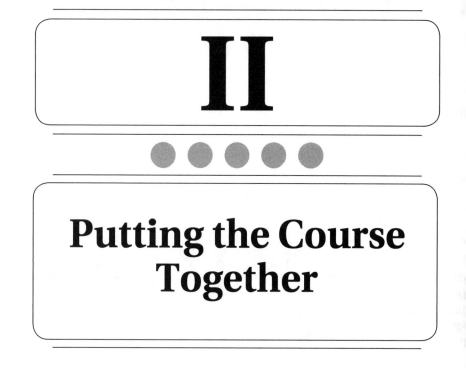

II

Putting the Course Together

3

●●●●●

Course Design and Development

A ll right. You've taken the grand tour of the campus and are now familiar with the lay of the land.

You're ready to get down to work, to convert your on-the-ground class to one online. You open your syllabus and stare at it. It reads just like it always did: It has your name, a description of the class goals and objectives, your grading policy, a schedule of your office hours, and a week-by-week listing of assignments and quizzes.

Nothing very exciting—just the same old stuff. You take your syllabus, which you wrote using a word-processing program, perhaps convert it into an HTML page (or ask instructional support staff to do so), and upload it to be displayed online. Or perhaps your institution has a handy web template (a pre-made form) or your course management system requires you to do little more than fill in the text fields with the appropriate information. You call several of your colleagues to tell them to have a look at your page. They congratulate you on your good work and tell you that it looks just fine. Your students, on the other hand, never look at it twice. Why should they, once they've printed it out?

Our point is this:

> ●⦂● *Important!* **Putting your class online doesn't mean**
> ●⦂● **copying your lectures and syllabus word for word.**
> ●●●●

Rather, converting your course to an online environment means adapting it to use some of the tools available in the new environment. If you teach a blended class (one that's both face-to-face and online), the conversion involves using the Web to complement what you do in class. If you're teaching exclusively online, it involves recasting your entire class in an online shape. And perhaps you are not converting your face-to-face class at all, but creating an entirely new course for delivery online. In either case, if you want the resulting class to be a coherent and effective learning experience, you need to think about purposeful design and development of your course.

●●●●●

Two Examples of Course Design and Development

Let's have a look at some actual instructors who have gone through this process. Here are two different situations: a speech course delivered completely online and an engineering course that's a blend of face-to-face and online components.

A Speech Course Taught Entirely Online

Mary Jane Clerkin developed a speech course for delivery as a completely online course at Berkeley College where Mary Jane not only teaches but also functions as coordinator of online faculty support. Clerkin began teaching online in 1998 but had taught Oral Communication in a face-to-face delivery format for many years before developing the online version to launch in fall of 2004. The challenge as she saw it was to promote the same type of interaction, "the same give and take" in the online course as had always been present in the on-site version. Another concern she had was to establish a sense of community in the online class. Finally, she needed to find a way to demonstrate to students that it was not necessary to have a live, face-to-face audience apart from their classmates in order to learn to speak effectively.

While learning objectives and the core syllabus remain the same as in the on-site version, the use of technology was key to transforming this course for online delivery. Beyond the Blackboard course management system used at Berkeley, there was a need for tools that could provide the essential elements of speech—voice and body language. While the course is almost entirely asynchronous, Clerkin also makes limited use of Pronto Instant Messenger to allow students to talk in real time. Wimba Voice Boards allow for both the instructor and students to speak to each other using their own voices in an asynchronous mode. Students are required to buy a simple webcam along with their textbook so that they can see themselves as they present and practice until they are ready to post their speech for peer review in the Blackboard discussion forum. Clerkin notes that "the opportunity to practice and improve their delivery skills after viewing their videos makes a difference—they practice until the background, lighting, and delivery are to their satisfaction." She structured the course to provide three types of review. First, there is the self-review involved in the student's perfecting the speech video before submitting it to the discussion forum. Second, there is the peer review in the discussion area, using a rubric created by Clerkin for this purpose. Finally, after each speech is presented, she emails the student to provide individualized instructor feedback as well.

Clerkin assigns a textbook that is accompanied by an excellent companion web site that offers many resources, including links to famous speeches. Another resource for the course is a library liaison who visits the online class to give pointers on the research process and to explain how students can use the library databases to find the materials they need for their speech topics.

Clerkin gives detailed directions for each technology tool and how it is to be used in the introductory section of her course. Several of these introductions use video as well as text to deliver instructions. Beyond these techniques used by Mary Jane Clerkin to orient her students, Berkeley College provides a network of services to prepare or offer on-demand help to her students. All students take a Road to Success in Online Learning tutorial, developed by Clerkin, before taking their first online course. A help desk is also ready to assist through phone or live online help and an instructional designer is available to help instructors prepare materials.

Although she begins her course with a video introduction that serves to personalize the course, she says that she:

prefers not to use this to model good public speaking. The companion website has many good models of excellent public speakers. However, I always use one or more of the students from a previous class to model good speaking techniques. Not feeling that they have to measure up to professional speakers, or even to the professor, makes them more comfortable. And students also explain the challenges they faced and how they overcame challenges and developed through practice.

Mary Jane Clerkin views the asynchronous elements of the course as benefiting students in many ways.

The Voice Board allows students to reflect before responding in a debate. More thoughtful and comprehensive dialog is promoted and modeled by the professor. Online students can practice diction exercises and listen to themselves and their peers as they attempt exercises that promote good enunciation.

She also feels that the lack of a "live audience" is more than outweighed by the communication and community that takes place in her online class,

Every night our television newscasters inform us of the day's events. They are excellent public speakers, and their content and delivery is no less effective because their audience of millions of viewers is not personally present. So too, our students reach all of the members of the class no matter where they are located. Overall, this asynchronous speech course permits a heterogeneous group of students from different parts of the world to come together in a learning environment that encourages and facilitates active participation.

A Blended Mechanical Engineering Course

Isabel Simões de Carvalho teaches an Energy Production and Management course at an engineering school, Instituto Superior de Engenharia, in Lisbon, Portugal. Her students are in their first year of a mechanical engineering Masters degree program.

Her institution is committed to face-to-face instruction and generally follows a traditional lecture format, but Isabel had been gradually adding web-enhanced approaches to the course, working on her own initiative. Not only did she incorporate appropriate topical resources available on the Web, but she also augmented her course, first by adding class email, and then an online discussion forum, and eventually adding elements that were provided with true course management software. Not originally having any course management software available through her institution, Isabel arranged for course management software and hosting through her family business connections.

Her class evolved into a true blended class only through trial and error. Initially, in introducing email and discussion forums, she found herself swamped by the extra work involved in responding to students outside the face-to-face class (F2F) meetings. "I remember thinking 'what did I get myself into?' Time management was really an issue what with trying to read all the messages and get back to the students. So I also started to provide some feedback at F2F. This and other 'small' issues led me to recognise the power of delivering a blended course."

The students in the classes responded enthusiastically to the addition of this online activity, but she began to realize that merely adding online elements was not sufficient, and that what was needed was a true redesign of her course to effectively blend and integrate face-to-face and online elements.

> *I began to try different structured activities. A more effective integration of the F2F with the online became an objective. I worked a lot of different assessment formulas and tried them for a couple of semesters. This was a challenge!*
>
> *I started to take some time at the beginning of the course to explain to students the objectives of such a teaching and learning methodology. This has proven to be important in ensuring their engagement and success in the course.*

Carvalho has a strong philosophical bent toward active learning approaches. Based on her past experimentation, she has evolved a set of assignments that seem to work well within this framework. Among these are an individual assignment that requires students to perform a "home energy audit," and a group assignment that requires students to collaborate online and present their final projects in the face-to-face classroom.

Carvalho uses the online discussion for a number of purposes. For example, case studies are presented in the online forum as part of the sharing of current events related to class topics. After field trips and guest speakers, students are asked to reflect on what they learned by posting in the discussion forum. For another assignment, each group is asked to post a peer review of two other groups' presentations.

She began to realize that she could encourage attendance in the face-to-face meetings and focus attention on lectures or other content delivered in that format by introducing online activities that could not easily be accomplished without experience of those face-to-face activities.

Carvalho notes that many of her students simply are not used to the types of methods she has implemented. Therefore, not only does she need to explain how the class operates, she also needs to invest quite a bit of time in the first weeks of each class, carefully facilitating online discussions and heightening awareness of the connections between face-to-face and online components of the course.

> *The first 4 to 5 weeks do require a lot of effort from my side to explain (better even, exemplify) how it works. These first weeks I use a lot of visual information and concentrate on the most "appealing" subjects that usually promote a lot of debate and student participation. Fora moderation is quite time consuming during this period. There is a need to start things moving and I need to be "present" quite often both to give them examples and to promote motivation with positive and encouraging messages. After this period, the process seems to feed itself and my work online does decrease.*

In order to guide students and clarify what is expected of them for each task, she has introduced a series of rubrics that detail what students need to do in order to fulfill the terms of each assignment. Her approach to assessment has gradually become more complex, as she has sought to make students more self-directed in their education. By providing a variety of different activities to accomplish the same learning objectives, she has created a kind of assessment matrix that allows students more choice in how they approach learning.

As new tools have become available to her, Isabel has adopted new methods to communicate with her students. For example, she now regularly sends text messages to student cell phones to provide reminders about upcoming due dates and class events.

Carvalho has found some solid formulas for success and now has some well-tested methods in her repertoire, permitting her to simply apply these structured course elements each time she teaches. However, Carvalho still views her course as a constantly evolving project as she challenges herself to find new ways to promote deeper learning. As she faces each new group of students who bring their own dynamic to the class, "I'm often trying new activities and even the face-to-face lecturing has become one of my research topics. I try to improve and adapt to the needs of each specific group of students."

● ● ● ● ●

Initial Steps in Course Design and Development

Now that you've had a look at these examples that introduce you to the process of converting or designing a new course, you're probably wondering where to begin.

Take a look at the resources you have available to you. In addition to your syllabus, you probably have some goals and objectives, a list of assignments, required readings, quizzes, papers, and grading policies. Do you also have lecture notes that you created using a word processor? PowerPoint slides, overheads, or slide transparencies that you regularly show to your class? Audio or video materials? Some web-resource sites that you consider essential for the course? All of those elements comprise the raw material you'll use to convert your course to one that you can teach online.

It would seem at first glance that the essential task to be accomplished is to convert these elements into digital files to be posted on the Web. But the fact that someone has transformed all of his or her lectures into electronic files and transferred graphics to web pages doesn't mean that a course has been converted. In fact, this isn't even the first step! It's only the mechanical aspect of the job. We'll discuss the mechanics further in Chapter 9, but here we want to focus on more basic considerations.

As our two scenarios demonstrate, a strict translation of what you normally do on the ground into the online environment isn't always desirable. Like the art of translation, course conversion should not merely strive for a word-for-word equivalency, but should allow the new language of communication to be fully exploited. Just as there are some things one can say only in Chinese or Spanish, there are new and different forms of expression that can be attempted in the online medium. Although the communication of content and the achievement of course objectives will naturally be the aim of any course conversion process, there's a great deal more to be gained than a mere transfer from one medium into another.

Important! *If you simply post your lectures and syllabus on the Web, you haven't necessarily created a viable tool for your students. The missing element here is instructional design.*

Without necessarily becoming an expert in instructional design principles, you need to become aware of what you normally do to create a course for the face-to-face classroom and then think about applying these steps to the online course. The following sections provide a simplified view of this process, along with some additional elements that apply to the online environment.

Perhaps you will be working with an instructional designer to create your course. In Chapter 4, we will provide some tips on how instructors and designers can achieve a smooth and beneficial relationship but even if you are lucky enough to have support from designers or other personnel, it makes sense for you to familiarize yourself with the whole process and to think deeply about what you are trying to achieve with the course. After all, you probably know your existing course better than anyone else, and even if it is a new course, you will still want to tap into the teaching expertise you possess to help shape the course.

Here we will look at three elements of converting to or creating an online course: analysis, course goals and learning objectives, and design.

Analysis

You'll need to have some idea of whom your course is for, what role it is to play in the curriculum, what the basic student learning outcomes are, and what resources will be available to you and your students. Here are some questions you might want to ask:

1. What is your student audience? For example, is this course for twenty or 120 students? Is the course for beginners or advanced students? For majors or primarily nonmajors?
2. What types of materials should be made available to students online? For example, will any on-campus activities or labs be available, or must all class activities be delivered online?
3. What kind of Internet access will your students have?
   a. Will students access this online classroom from campus networks or from their homes or even mobile devices?
   b. Do most students have unlimited Internet access through the university, or do they pay for their own access?
4. What support will you have available to assist you in creating online course materials?
5. Is there an integrated suite of tools or course management software available to house your course, or will you have to create everything on your own web pages or free resource sites?

If you've done the survey of your institutional resources recommended in Chapter 2, you will already have most or all the answers to the more technical questions.

Course Goals and Learning Objectives

The difference between goals and objectives is basically the difference between things that can be known but not easily measured and those that can be demonstrated! So a goal in Ancient

World History 101 may be for students to attain a good grasp of the cultures, forces, and events that helped shape the ancient world but a more precise objective would be for a student "to identify the causes of the decline of the Roman Empire." Goals, like purposes, set the parameters of what we expect to gain from the learning experience, but objectives tell us how we will be able to know, not merely intuit, whether or not a student has learned. Learning objectives are also referred to as learning *outcomes* and they are usually expressed as expected outcomes— what we can expect students to be able to do as a result of learning.

Perhaps you are asking "why do we need to write learning objectives? No one even pays attention to those."

From the point of view of the instructor engaged in the process of designing and developing a course, we would say that writing learning objectives keeps you focused on what is to be taught, what is to be learned, and helps you in planning. (At the very least, it prevents you from going off on a tangent. However clever, amazing, and interesting that reading, resource, or activity may be, if it doesn't really serve a purpose in the course, you may want to save it for another, more appropriate occasion.) From the point of view of the students, it lets them know what is expected of them and why in the world they are being asked to do X and Y.

You may have already been given the learning objectives or expected outcomes for your course from your academic department or institution. But if you have not, we suggest that you take the time to articulate how it is you will be able to recognize that students have learned what you want them to learn.

For each unit and objective of the course, jot down some corresponding readings, activities, and assessments that you are planning to use to accomplish that objective. For example, unit 2 may cover the decline of the Roman Empire. Perhaps your objective is for students "to evaluate the different theories concerning the decline of the Roman Empire." This might be achieved by having students stage a debate; individual projects based on research into each theory, then presented in the discussion forum and critiqued by students; or writing an essay on the exam asking students to compare and contrast two theories. Or you might assign a combination of these activities.

Many instructors have no difficulty expressing their goals for the class but find it very frustrating to write learning objectives, especially if asked to do so on the sub-unit or activity level. We would discourage instructors from tasking themselves to write learning objectives for every activity, and instead concentrate on the overall course objectives and how they can be applied for one or more units of the class. A particular set of learning objectives related to research skills might be satisfied by a major project, while an objective involving critical thinking and writing might apply to several assignments distributed over a number of different units or modules of the course. And while an objective should not be overly broad, it is not beneficial for it to be too picayune either ("the student will be able to name all the Roman emperors"). The words *know, learn,* and *understand* belong in the realm of goals and if you can avoid using such terms when writing objectives, you are well on your way to accomplishing the task. Another tip is to keep overall course objectives to no more than a dozen—this will keep you focused on the essentials.

One approach for coming up with learning objectives we have found that is easy to use and apply for most instructors is that based on **Bloom's Taxonomy**, a hierarchical system of classifying different levels of thinking. Bloom's Taxonomy for the cognitive domain is familiar to K–12 educators as well as instructional designers as a hierarchical classification of learning objectives and the verbs that correspond to each task level. There are many charts and graphic representations of Bloom's Taxonomy. (See the Guide to Resources for some of these.)

Table 3.1 is a simplified version of these correspondence charts, showing sample verbs for writing learning objectives, and some types of assignments that students might be expected to produce.

A more recent version of Bloom's Taxonomy relabels these levels as Remembering, Understanding, Applying, and Analyzing, and swaps the two top levels so that Creating is at the top, with Evaluating just underneath. (See the web site www.odu.edu/educ/roverbau/Bloom/blooms_taxonomy.htm for a nice graphic representation of the old and new versions.) Nevertheless, the verbs associated with these levels remain much the same.

Table 3.1 Bloom's Taxonomy

Domains	Sample Verbs for Writing Learning Objectives	Sample Assignments
Knowledge or Remembering	Recall, tell, show, match, list, label, define, cite, name, brainstorm	Test, worksheet, quiz, labeling, table
Comprehension	Compare, contrast, demonstrate, identify, report, outline, summarize, review, explain, catalog	Outline, summary, test, identifications, review, compare-and-contrast exercise
Application	Develop, organize, use, select, model, choose, construct, translate, experiment, illustrate	Report, diagram, graph, illustration, project, video, case study, journal
Analysis	Analyze, categorize, classify, distinguish, dissect, examine, differentiate, calculate, solve, arrange	Model, report, project, solution, debates, case-study solution
Synthesis	Combine, compose, solve, formulate, adapt, develop, create, validate, design	Article, report, essay, experiment, composition, essay, audio or video product, drawing, graph, design
Evaluation	Assess, evaluate, determine, measure, select, defend, score, rank, discriminate, judge, justify, conclude, recommend	Peer and self-evaluations, chart, critique

Sharon Guan, an experienced instructional designer at DePaul University, advises that faculty should not become overly concerned with writing ever more precise objectives. She notes that:

> *sometimes objectives are very subtle in the faculty's mind and if a faculty member has no designer to work with, that faculty member should just ask herself, "what do you want students to be able to do as a result of this class and how would you know that students have learned or know how to do this?"*

She also cautions that it is possible for someone to write very precise learning objectives and yet have a poorly designed course! It is necessary to provide follow-through from articulating those learning objectives to devising the actual instructional activities so that the latter align with the former, as we discuss in the next section on design.

If you are interested in the topic of learning objectives, or want to learn how to write better objectives, there are some selected web sites under the Instructional Design and Learning Strategies category in the Guide to Resources section of this book.

Important! **Don't drive yourself crazy trying to write ever more precise learning objectives—the main point is to express as clearly and plainly as possible what it is you want students to learn and how they can best demonstrate that they have learned it.**

Design

"Design" really means the shape and direction you want your course to take. It means *purposefully* planning the course, rather than simply letting it happen. In thinking about the design of your course, you need to consider your course objectives, the preferred teaching strategies and approaches to the material that you want to preserve, and any new approaches you would like to try in the online environment. Always keep in mind two design principles: make sure that your course objectives are defined in terms of the learning outcomes that you want students to be able to demonstrate and that you align all activities, assignments, and assessments with those expected learning outcomes. Even if you have never consciously planned all these aspects of a face-to-face course, as an experienced instructor, you likely have an internal guidance system that has directed you in making instructional choices over these many years. So feel confident that you can do the same thing now, but in a more explicit fashion.

Here are some of the types of questions to ask yourself.

1. If you are designing a blended course, how can you best take advantage of each format, online and face-to-face? Are there some activities that must take place face-to-face, or do you

have the option of re-envisioning how each activity will be carried out? How will you ensure that the face-to-face and online elements are complementary, reinforcing, and integrated? (See Chapter 13 for more in-depth considerations for blended courses.)

2. Is collaborative work among students and/or peer review appropriate or desirable?

3. What are the best ways to assess your students in the context of your course or discipline?

   a. Portfolios?

   b. Multiple-choice quizzes? Self-assessment exams or graded exams?

   c. Essays, journaling, or research papers?

   d. Fieldwork reports?

   e. Individual projects and presentations?

4. What will be the balance of student-centered versus instructor-led activities? Will you mainly facilitate discussion and research, or does the course have a strong component of lecturing and instructor commentary as well?

5. How central is discussion or student presentation to achieving the objectives of the course? Do you want to take advantage of the many new tools that would allow students to generate content in text, audio, or video?

6. What are your preferred methods of presenting content?

   a. Do you have graphics or slides that you want to utilize in some way?

   b. Do you use lecture notes?

   c. Do you use overheads?

   d. Is it important for you to accommodate as many different learning styles as possible?

7. How might your available resources affect the implementation of your design?

   a. Do you have online testing capabilities? If so, would these be mainly for self-assessment or do they possess the necessary security for graded tests?

b. What forms of communication are options—for example, do you have a discussion board, a chat or other synchronous software, is there blog or wiki software available, or will you have to rely on email and mailing lists?

c. Do you have easy access to a scanner or help to convert existing slides?

d. Will you be able to use audio or video in your online classroom?

Language courses, like the speech course highlighted at the beginning of this chapter, present a number of unique challenges when delivered solely online. Gretchen Jones, who heads up the Foreign Languages Department at University of Maryland University College, was new to online teaching when she first began to teach an elementary Japanese course that she had previously been involved in developing with a team. While the course development team had developed media-rich modules that allowed students to practice and drill orally to some extent on their own, she found herself:

grappling with how to get students to practice a language orally the way we do in a face-to-face class, with the rapid fire contact and repetition within a classroom to enable students to hear and speak basic patterns and use those patterns in a specific context.

Jones found an effective approach using a few tools in the Wimba suite that allowed her to enhance student interaction. The Wimba Voice Board affords the opportunity for her students to respond to her and to classmates via asynchronous audio discussion postings, and she has made use of Wimba Voice Presenter to review basic grammar while providing images that allow her to pose questions that are made lively through these images and spark the imagination. Another form of interaction resulted from assigning student pairs to work on a skit using yet another Wimba tool, Voice Direct, which allows for real-time chat with voice. The fact that each of these tools allows for archiving and playback affords additional opportunities for review and further application.

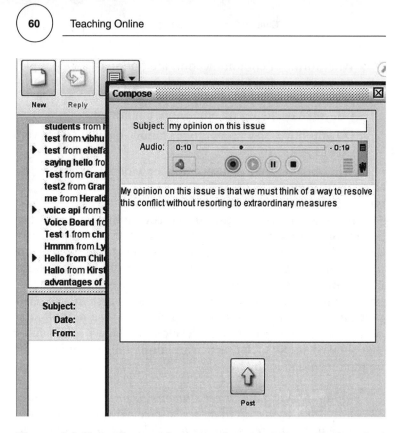

Figure 3.1 Recording and composing an accompanying text version of a message to post on Wimba's Voice Board Asynchronous Audio Discussion. Reproduced by permission. Source: Wimba Voice™, Wimba, Inc.

Beyond the transformations necessitated in approximating face-to-face activities, Jones also noted that the online environment harbors some advantages of its own. "I found that I can do more with cultural aspects of the course—I can easily create a discussion on a cultural topic and I can bring in video, audio, and images from the Web to illustrate these topics." She cautions that design and development of online activities requires real forethought and investment of time on the part of instructors.

Perhaps this is the time to consider whether a direct "translation" is either possible or desirable. Say that you have PowerPoint slides with lots of text on them. These probably won't translate very well to an online setting, although simple figures and images may be directly convertible. But look at the other side of the question as well: Do you really want to replicate the combination of lecture and slides that you've always used, or would it be possible to consider some new combination of presentation methods?

Important! *The move to an online format offers you opportunities to try out new methods and approaches. Preserving the quality of your course need not mean finding an exact translation of what you've always done in the past.*

● ● ● ● ●

Rubrics and Guidelines for Online Course Design

There are a number of systems that have been developed to guide and evaluate quality design in online courses. While some of these are intended for use only within a particular network of institutions, others have been aimed at general standards which can be adopted by any institution and then supplemented with other criteria specific to that institution. These systems can be used both to guide the design of an online course and to evaluate the quality, and if your institution does not have its own rubric or guidelines for online course design, you might find it worthwhile to consult one of the following considered here. Some rubrics include criteria that apply to the course teaching and learning stage, but all include elements related to the design phase.

The Illinois Quality Online Course Initiative rubric (www.ion. uillinois.edu/initiatives/qoci/categories.asp) comprises six main areas: instructional design; communication, interaction, and collaboration; student evaluation and assessment; learner support and resources; web design; and course evaluation. The checklist under instructional design includes such aspects as whether content is sequenced and structured, whether information is chunked, and whether course objectives are clearly presented and explicated. This rubric is available to the public at the web site noted above.

The North American Council for Online Learning (NACOL) has adopted the Quality Online Course Standards developed by the Southern Regional Education Board (www.inacol.org/research/nationalstandards/NACOL%20Standards%20Quality%20Online%20Courses%202007.pdf). Their rubric is organized into six areas: Content; Instructional Design; Student Assessment; Technology; Course Evaluation and Management; and 21st Century Skills. Under Instructional Design, the criteria for review include whether or not the course includes active learning strategies, whether multiple learning paths are provided to master the content, and whether activities address a variety of learning preferences.

California State University, Chico has its Rubric for Online Instruction (www.csuchico.edu/celt/roi) which is designed to be used as a guide for course design as well as a set of evaluation criteria. The rubric is organized into six categories: Learner Support and Resources; Online Organization and Design; Instructional Design and Delivery; Assessment and Evaluation of Student Learning; Innovative Teaching with Technology; and Faculty Use of Student Feedback.

Quality Matters™ began as a project with MarylandOnline and has grown into a widely adopted system for design and evaluation of online courses as well as a sophisticated training and peer-review program. The Quality Matters™ rubric contains forty elements categorized into eight major standards: Course Overview and Introduction; Learning Objectives; Assessment and Measurement; Resources and Materials; Learner Engagement; Course Technology; Learner Support; and Accessibility (http://qminstitute.org/home/Public%20Library/About%20QM/RubricStandards2008-2010.pdf).

Many institutions use the Quality Matters™ standards to guide their course design and others have made this rubric part of a larger system, based on their institutional needs and resources. For example, at the College of Arts and Sciences at Seton Hall University, Senior Instructional Designer Renee Cicchino explains that they have developed an online course template built upon the Quality Matters™ rubric to serve as the foundation for faculty developing online courses. She describes how this has been included in the course development process:

Before development occurs, faculty meet with the Quality Matters™ certified reviewer and their instructional designer to discuss the elements of the rubric and create a project plan and timeline for deliverables to ensure that the course is completed on time. Once development has been completed, the course is reviewed, feedback and recommendations are given to the faculty and instructional designer for review and if need be, for revision. Our online course template includes sample grading rubrics for discussion postings, sample participation requirements, as well as minimum technology requirements and tutorials. The template is populated with materials, documents and samples that are updated on a regular basis. An exemplar course is available for new faculty course developers to use as a reference. Faculty are enrolled as students so they can experience the course from the student perspective.

If your institution is neither a subscriber to Quality Matters™, nor has a course design rubric or systematized approach, you may be interested in any of several of the basic courses they offer that are available to non-subscribers through the Quality Matters™ organization (www.qualitymatters.org/Training.htm) or through the Sloan Consortium workshop program (www.sloan-c.org).

Whether you seek additional training or merely review some of the existing course design and quality standards rubrics, you may find that these resources serve to broaden your thinking about the course design process.

● ● ● ● ●

Course Development

The development stage involves the actual creation of a syllabus, class schedule, content, and exams, as well as activities the class will follow. Having assembled your materials and analyzed the needs of your class, with your course objectives and basic design considerations in mind, and an outline or table in hand, it's now time to make a few decisions about what you're going to do.

Some Help in Getting Organized

Even before you begin to create your syllabus, you should draft the course goals and objectives along with a general outline of the major units of your course and their topics. In some cases, you may want to follow the order of your main required textbook, while in others you may have more freedom to organize the units.

Some institutions supply their instructors with course planning templates, but it is easy to create one on your own. A basic table should include columns and rows to list your course objectives, each weekly unit or module of the course, major content (main readings, instructor presentations, web resources), types of interaction and activities (discussions, group work, blogging, weekly email or announcement, etc.), and any major assignments and exams that you already know about at this point. For those teaching a blended course, the template should specify what is to be accomplished online and what is to be done in the face-to-face classroom. Such a simple template as this can help supply the basic building blocks you need to create your syllabus.

Table 3.2 is an example of this type of simple planning template for a unit of a course on Cultural History of Ancient Rome.

One can add a column for a timeline of development, and for those developing a course with the assistance of others, the roles played by each person and any due dates can be indicated as well. If there are particular skill attainment objectives that need to be embedded throughout the course, one might add a column; see the Guide to Resources section of this book for links to some course design and development planning charts from a variety of institutions.

The instructional sequence of activities is something that you need to consider when planning your units. Sequencing means to arrange your assignments and activities into a logical order that will allow students to attain the learning objectives. For example, students will read the text and the instructor commentary prior to discussing all topics in an asynchronous forum prior to writing a reflective essay—all steps but the last to take place in week 2 of the course with the essay due at the end of week 3. While this sequencing is something you naturally do

Table 3.2 Example of Simple Course-Planning Template

Course Objectives and Targeted Skills as Applied to a Unit and Time Period	Instructor-Generated Content, Communications, and Feedback	Class Interaction and Activities	Readings, Web Resources	Assessments—Graded Assignments, Exams, Projects, etc.
Unit 3: Age of Augustus (Time span: four weeks)	Audio lecturette and text transcript providing commentary on historical, social, and cultural aspects of Augustan Rome—in three fifteen-minute segments	Discussion in weekly forum based on readings and resources	Textbook, pp. 12–65	Participation credit for weekly discussion according to rubric
Course Objectives that apply to this unit:		One weekly discussion involving debate on social or political issue of the period, with students assigned to argue a particular position	Electronic full-text articles on Augustan society	Short essay based on questions related to readings from either Ovid, Virgil, or Horace
1. Identify key historical events and persons of the period	Weekly announcements in the online classroom; biweekly reminder emails and text messages; weekly office hours via chat		Web resource on literature of the period focusing on primary texts: Ovid, Virgil, and Horace	Short online self-assessment quiz on key events, dates, and persons—students get credit for taking quiz
2. Analyze the social and political framework of the period	Feedback in the form of comments and follow-up questions in the weekly discussion;	Formation of study groups and initial organizational meeting; group creates outline in wiki		
3. Critique representative works of literature from this period	Automated feedback preloaded by instructor for self-assessment quiz; Individual feedback from instructor on short essay			
Targeted skills: Critical thinking, essay writing				

when planning a face-to-face course, it requires a bit more fore-thought in the case of an online or blended class.

Whether your units comprise one week or several, you will need to work out the sequence in terms of weekly units, because that is how students approach an asynchronous online class and the week remains the basic building block of an online syllabus, as explained in Chapter 5. So, if your units are each of multiple weeks, you will want to further break down your planning template by weeks, either by adding columns to the above sort of template or simply transferring that task to your creation of the syllabus schedule to nail this down.

The activities in most college classes can probably be divided into a few large categories:

■ *Instructor-generated content and presentation:* Typically this includes lectures, simulations, charts, and graphs, as well as computer-assisted presentations using tools like PowerPoint, the creation of audio or video files. Guest lecturers are also included in this category.

■ *Discussion/interaction/communications:* Small-group, guided discussion sections run by teaching assistants are a common format for discussion. So are question-and-answer sessions as adjuncts to lectures, labs, and exams. In seminars, instructor presentation and discussion are often combined. Problem-solving sessions, case studies, and other types of interactive work can also be carried out in the discussion area. Feedback loops, instructor announcements, and emails as designed and scheduled elements help build in a strong basis for effective communication and interaction during the course.

■ *Group-oriented work and student-created content:* Collaborative, cooperative, and other peer activities are included here. These might include a group project, peer-reviewed compositions, journals in the form of blogs, and an independent project presented to the entire class.

■ *Research:* Research may be conducted either by individuals or in groups. A separate category may be carved from research to encompass practical applications, experiments, fieldwork, interviews, and apprenticeships.

■ *Assessment:* Assessment activities typically involve exams, essays, and projects; all graded assignments; peer-based strategies; portfolios that combine different types of work; and evaluation and credit for participation. Rubrics can serve to guide students as they undertake an assignment as well as provide the basis for grading that assignment.

Let's look at some of the factors you need to consider in converting these various types of course activities to an online format.

●●●●●

Instructor-Generated Content and Presentation: Lectures and Commentary

Lectures and commentary are probably the most common method of presenting content in a traditional college classroom. Often they're accompanied by slides, blackboard writings, or computer-assisted PowerPoint presentations.

To translate this type of activity into an online environment, you can use several different online formats alone or in combination. Here are some notes on these possibilities, along with their advantages and disadvantages.

Text Text in the form of web pages is still a logical choice for converting lecture materials. Compared to a conventional lecture, text on a web page has the advantage that students can copy the materials and make their own notes; in addition, they have more time to reflect on what you've said.

The main pitfall here is trying to transcribe your speech without taking into consideration that the lecture will be read, not listened to. You don't want to create documents that are tediously formal or that appear as overly long blocks of text when viewed on a web page.

Also take into consideration the readability level of your lectures and commentary—make sure your text is appropriate for the student audience in regard to level of course offering, and the expected proficiency that students will bring to the subject. If you only have experience giving informal lectures to your students in the face-to-face classroom, give your written lectures a bit more scrutiny. Without your voice and body language and pauses for questions, the text must carry the full freight of what you are trying to say. Some instructors have been introduced to the idea of submitting their text through a "readability index" (these include the Gunning Fogg, SMOG, and Flesch-Kincaid systems), software for which is often available online (see our Guide to Resources for some links to these). These indicate the relative ease of reading, in some cases providing an indication of the number of years of education that a person can be expected to need in order to easily comprehend your text. Keep in mind that these provide only an estimate based on a formula, but if you find that your text aimed at freshmen is judged to be closer to graduate student level, you might want to take another look at your text with an eye to making some revisions. Taking readability into account does not mean that you must "dumb down" your content—only think about how you can communicate it more clearly online.

Tips for Writing Online Text

■ Strive for a style midway between casual speech and formal writing.

■ Chunk your writing into short paragraphs with space between them.

■ Use headings, italics, colors, and other indicators to allow the eye to quickly take in the gist of the presentation but don't overwhelm the viewer with multiple colors and a hodge-podge of styles.

■ Intersperse graphics or present them via links.

PowerPoint Slide Shows As we mentioned in earlier chapters, you can incorporate PowerPoint slide shows into a web page or upload them to most course management system classrooms. Remember, though, that in the face-to-face classroom, the students have you to observe, but online the slides themselves must carry the entire presentation. Therefore, design, images, and graphics are essential to the success of such presentations.

Keep in mind, too, that slide presentations, when they involve a large number of slides and click-throughs, can be very tedious to the viewers. If you wish to use slide-show presentations, divide up your slides and test them so that each segment takes no more than ten minutes. That will make it easier for students, not only to initially absorb, but also to find particular segments for review. Don't try to directly replicate long PowerPoint presentations that are mainly bulleted text. If your slides are primarily of this type, consider converting them into short text paragraphs with bulleted items. This web page format can replace your slides.

Narrated Slides, Audio or Videotaping, and Screen-casting
Narrated slides can be an effective way to present materials online. However, you should avoid simply narrating bulleted text. Here are some tips for using narrated slides effectively online:

■ Make sure each narration extends over a series of slides rather than stopping for five or more minutes on one slide.
■ Use a casual narration with lots of color in the voice.
■ Use graphics, arrows, video snippets, or other visual means to enliven the presentation.

A narrated slide presentation is particularly good for taking students through a series of steps—say, the steps for learning a computer software program. Audio alone or in narrated slides can also be a very effective instructional method in foreign languages, art, and music. Audio might be used to replace a short lecture or a guest lecture. Audio can also serve as a personalized introduction to the course or to the instructor. In the latter case, a short audio welcoming message might be combined with a still photo. How to create audio is discussed in more detail in Chapter 9.

Some online programs feature videotaped lectures that have been converted into streaming video files on the institution's web site. You can see many examples of these on YouTube university sites. Although this is indeed an option, it isn't a particularly good choice if students in your part of the world don't have high-speed connections or the latest computer or smart-phone equipment, or if you have little institutional support for such delivery. In addition, in some areas of the world, there's the familiar problem of "net congestion": when the Internet gets *busy*, the student will find that the video being streamed will become garbled, or the picture will blur or drop out altogether. For these reasons, even though many students do enjoy the videotaped presence of an instructor, a little video may go a long way.

For many instructors, video is increasingly attractive as YouTube and other online sites provide the resources to stream video and have eliminated the need for their institution's support for hosting these. But if you look at some of the YouTube EDU (EDU signifying YouTube's videos and channels from higher education sources) videos, you will see that there is a downside to just having staff record you in a classroom, however tempting that may be from the standpoint of saving time. What happens in the on-site classroom does not always translate very well to the computer screen, unless the institution has the appropriate equipment and knowledge about how to do this and the instructor adapts his or her techniques. It's a little like watching a video of a theater production or pirated movie filmed by someone in the audience. You might find that while you enjoy listening to the lectures, the video portion doesn't add much to your comprehension. Best are those in which the video production has sought to present the lesson with the remote viewing audience in mind (close-up shots, reproduction of what's written on the board, and questions from the classroom student audience repeated by the instructor for the benefit of the remote audience).

Effective uses of streaming video might include a demonstration of a science experiment or a presentation of vignettes for a language course. For longer or numerous videos, or if your students do not have good Internet connectivity, consider distributing the material via DVD.

But it isn't always necessary to create a streaming video. Many demonstrations can be created on your computer using **screencasting** programs, like Jing or Camtasia, that capture the entire sequence or an edited version of what you display on a computer screen. (Check to see if your computer already comes preloaded with a screen-casting software program that might serve your needs.) Or, if you have access to a collaborative synchronous program like Wimba Live Classroom, Adobe Connect, or Elluminate, you can record a presentation, and place the link in your classroom so that the presentation can be accessed asynchronously. These types of demonstrations allow instructors to be both focused and customized in their approach.

When offering audio and video, you should also take into consideration students' disabilities as well as learning preferences. Always prepare a text transcript or summary for the benefit of those who have sight or hearing disabilities. This will also serve to give all students other options for accessing the material, including those who have technical problems and those for whom the text option is a learning preference. You can best prepare your transcript or summary before making your video or slide narration. Preparing transcripts afterward is quite labor intensive. By creating the text materials ahead of time, you also generate, in effect, a script or **storyboard** from which you can more efficiently produce your audio or video. See Chapter 9 for more information on creating these types of multimedia presentations.

Instructor Presentation: Simulations and Experiments

Before you go to the trouble of creating these yourself, you may want to see if there is an online subscription service or publisher web site that already has the kinds of simulations you want.

If you already have your own computer simulations and experiments, or want to create them, it may be possible to have students access them via a web page. But you should test any simulations under the real conditions in which students will access them. If they involve long download times they may prove less effective than you wish. In that case, if your class is a blended one, you may want to continue using a computer lab for these activities.

But what if no actual lab is available, and you have a large number of computerized simulations to demonstrate? In such cases, you might consider distributing your simulations on a DVD. This will require extra preparation on your part and perhaps the enlistment of instructional media services as well but it is not a costly or overly complicated endeavor. See Chapter 7 for more discussion of simulations.

Discussion/Interaction/Communications

Earlier, we mentioned the following types of discussions that are normally held on an on-the-ground campus: those facilitated by teaching assistant as small-group guided discussions; question-and-answer sessions as adjuncts to lectures, labs, and exams; and seminar models in which instructor presentation and discussion are often combined. All of these may be successfully transported to the online environment.

In planning these activities, however, you'll need to decide which can best be carried out in an asynchronous (not-in-real time) forum and which in a real-time, synchronous mode. Here your audience and course analysis comes into play. If you're conducting a primarily face-to-face class, for example, you may want to have all real-time discussion carried out in the live classroom and utilize an asynchronous forum for follow-up discussions that allow for more reflection. Or you may want to utilize an asynchronous forum for preparatory exploration of topics before the face-to-face discussion takes place.

If your course is entirely online, a synchronous mode of discussion might seem to offer the best parallel to face-to-face interaction. Yet if students are logging in from multiple time zones or are primarily working adults, the synchronous mode will allow too little flexibility in scheduling.

Later chapters will discuss specific strategies and techniques for getting the most out of both asynchronous and synchronous discussions. The following sections look at factors you need to consider when planning your course discussions.

Asynchronous Discussion   To prepare for your use of asynchronous discussion opportunities, you should first decide on how you want to use discussion in relation to your presentation and assignment elements in the course. In other words, decide whether discussion topics will closely follow the questions you raise in your lectures and other presentations, or whether the topics will provide opportunities to introduce additional materials and further applications of ideas you've presented.

For example, one instructor we know ends each short online lecture segment with two or three questions. The discussion scheduled in coordination with this lecture starts out by repeating these questions and having students respond to them. After the discussion based on the questions, the teaching assistant may then open up the forum to additional questions.

What about a seminar type of discussion? Even though a face-to-face seminar is synchronous, you will find it possible to organize the same type of activity in an asynchronous mode. To do so, you need to create a segmented lecture or dialogue. First, you create some initial or topic questions to pose, or short minilectures followed by a series of questions. After allowing an interval of time (say, two or three days) to permit students to respond to the initial minilecture or question, you proceed to ask some open-ended questions, such as, "What other ramifications might there be to this set of circumstances?" or simply, "Are there any other aspects of the lecture that you want to comment on?" Questions may be prepared in advance and used or not used as you deem appropriate.

Asynchronous Discussion in Math and the Sciences

Some instructors we know in various sciences—including some of the social sciences, computer science, and math—have told us that discussion isn't an appropriate activity for their students. Their idea of discussion is that it's connected to the realm of the soft, fuzzy, inexact, and ambiguous fields of the humanities. We believe, however, that all instructors can utilize discussion forums in online environments.

A good example of a "hard" use of online discussion is a question-and-answer forum. From such a forum a "frequently asked questions" (FAQs) page can be created to serve as review material. In fact, posting a FAQs page can eliminate some of the chit-chat and elementary questions that, however essential, are time-consuming for the instructor to answer; thus, it can permit the instructor to broach new or more in-depth topics.

Another use of the discussion forum is to ask students to offer possible solutions to problems. Discussion then consists of ana lysis of these solutions, with the instructor contributing comments as well. Some instructors have a slightly different approach to this process: First, they receive and evaluate the solutions; then they choose the best ones to post and discuss with students online. John Beyers, who teaches Developmental Math for the University of Maryland University College, uses the discussion area to have students choose a "problem of the week." Each week all students are responsible for posting their solutions to math problems and Beyers gives feedback concerning process and answer, all right in the discussion forum so that all students get the benefit of seeing these sample problems resolved.

The discussion area may also be used to post student homework or to allow students to present projects. Questions may then be posed by other students, and the instructor may offer his or her input for the benefit of the entire class. Students in the sciences can benefit from seeing how others approach the material.

Discussions that are coordinated with assignments must be scheduled to allow enough time for reflection and response. If assignments are presented in the online classroom and students are asked to comment on them, guidelines and procedures must be set up in advance to make sure that the discussion is structured and focused. Even though this activity may be asynchronous, you will probably not want to allow unlimited time for participation, especially if one of your goals is giving students feedback that they can apply to their subsequent assignments.

You'll also have to decide who will lead discussions—you, the instructor; the teaching assistant; or a student or group of students appointed for this purpose each week? What guidelines will you use for teaching assistant or student facilitated discussions?

Synchronous Discussion   Most synchronous discussion is still text-based chat, although audio and video chat have become much more popular.

In chat, everyone participating must log on to a particular site at the same time. The entire conversation then takes place in real time, although some chat software does permit saving the chat transcript so that it can be read (or listened to) after the actual event. **Instant messaging (IM)** is a form of chat that is most often between two people, although it is increasingly possible to IM multiple users. The distinctions between chat and

IM are gradually blurring, but for the purposes of this book, you can think of chat as taking place in an online classroom site to which one or multiple users are invited or able to enter, while IM involves summoning another who is online to chat privately.

Your course management software package may already include a real-time chat tool, or you may be familiar with chat from the great number of online services like Yahoo. Whatever the special features of a specific chat tool, the basic process of participating in a text-based chat generally remains the same: As each participant types in a phrase, his or her words appear on the screen, automatically prefaced by the name of that participant. For example, if Susan and Steve have a chat, the beginning of the transcript might look like this:

SUSAN: Hi, Steve, glad you could make the chat.
STEVE: Glad to be here. Let's talk about this week's assignment.

Depending on the features of the chat software, Susan and Steve's conversation might be accompanied by photos, or even **avatars**, which are graphic representations of each person. Or Susan and Steve might have their **webcams** activated so they can view each other as they converse.

While chat is more spontaneous than asynchronous communication, adequate preparation and forethought are still essential to its success. The timing of chats, for example, is an important factor in planning.

If your students reside in different time zones, you'll need to make multiple times available for the same discussion topic: Say, topic A will be discussed on Tuesday at noon US Pacific time and the same subject repeated on Thursday at 7:00 P.M. US Pacific time. (A web site like the World Clock www.timeanddate. com/worldclock can be a helpful resource for students to ensure schedules are synchronized.)

You might indicate to students that you'll be surveying them to find the most convenient times for all. Or you may set up two or more chat times and require that each student sign up for a particular time slot so that you can control the number participating in each session. You need to decide all of this ahead of time.

Chat is fast-paced and has the potential to be a confusing format for instruction with multiple students. A specific topic and the response to it often may be separated by other questions and comments, making it difficult for an instructor and students to follow a train of thought.

Important! To get the most out of chat, we recommend that students be given adequate preparation by announcing the topic to them ahead of time and publicizing the rules for the conduct of the chat.

For example, you may have a series of questions that you want students to think about before the chat. Or you may have students view a web resource or read a particular passage before the chat. See Chapter 11 for tips on how to facilitate chat in an effective manner.

Some synchronous chat tools are accompanied by a **whiteboard** or other types of shared display spaces. The whiteboard is an online version of the traditional blackboard that allows an instructor or student to draw or write on the whiteboard in real time (and in some cases to use math and science symbols as well) while students can type in their questions using the chat function. The questions appear, chat style, in the space below the whiteboard. Other types of shared display spaces permit instructors to guide students to view an external web site or an uploaded document. The instructor can then write on the displayed web page, initiate chat discussion, and encourage student questions about the site being viewed by all.

Collaborative real-time programs such as Wimba LiveClassroom, Elluminate, and Adobe Connect provide chat space for students who may wish to ask questions during a presentation or who do not want to use audio tools. They may also allow for **application sharing**, that is the software may allow the instructor or student to give access to the computer desktop of the other party and provide assistance in real time. For example, the student may be asked to share his desktop to show the instructor how he has worked out a problem on his spreadsheet, allowing the instructor to enter corrections while discussing the errors the student has made. Or the instructor may display a document on which she has highlighted certain features and examples in order to better discuss these with the students.

If you plan to use such a tool, you must plan ahead carefully to coordinate this activity with your topics and assignments. Students will need to know the protocol to follow for such an activity. For example, you might want students to first visit on their own the URL of a site to be discussed, or you might ask students to work on some preliminary problems before using the whiteboard or application sharing to show them the correct solution.

● ● ● ● ●

Group-Oriented Work and Student Presentation

All types of group activities, from peer review to true cooperative learning exercises, are possible in the online environment. To be effective, however, group activities must be well organized and properly paced. In Chapter 7, we'll discuss how to conduct specific types of group activities and presentations. Here we'll outline the considerations related to planning and implementation.

In terms of your planning, consider how many group activities will be included in your course. Also, if you decide to reconstitute groups during the course (that is, not have students remain with the same group throughout), make sure that you allow enough time for students to get to know each other and develop working relationships.

Important! *Group organization and working procedures take longer to develop in the online environment.*

Always consider in your planning how, where, and when groups will be able to meet and work together online. Also consider how you will monitor and evaluate individual contributions if this is an element you're concerned about.

Groups will need guidelines for working together. It's a poor idea to allow groups to evolve naturally. This isn't likely to happen online in a way that will be satisfying to the entire group of students. (When we see the words "Group yourselves" on a syllabus, we tend to shudder.) If it is appropriate for the particular activity, you may allow for some choice by asking students to let you know of a preference for joining certain classmates. You may want to specify a method of group organization or particular roles to be filled; for instance, a rotating chair plus a recorder and a spokesperson.

If you are teaching a blended class, take advantage of that combined delivery format by scheduling time for students to hold their first group meeting during a face-to-face class session. While not a necessity, many have found that it can provide a boost to and lay a solid foundation for the future online group communications.

Allow student groups as many avenues for communication as possible, with an emphasis on asynchronous discussion forums, synchronous chat, whiteboards, and document-sharing areas in a course management system. If an asynchronous discussion board is available to you, that's preferable to relying only on email and listservs. Email and listservs aren't the most efficient forums for group work, because documents and comments can't be viewed in sequential order without creating unwieldy email messages. For those who do not have a full set of tools for organized group activities, it may be advantageous to use a commercial service like Ning or Voice-Thread or a wiki provider. Each of these three Web 2.0-type options offers different features, advantages, and disadvantages. We will have more to say about these tools later in this book.

For each group, try to plan an ice-breaking, getting-to-know-you activity as early as possible. This can include an initial casual get-together opportunity—in a face-to-face class, for example, or in a totally online setting. Online ice-breaking activities may involve paired chats, exchanges of private email, or participation in an online student "lounge" area (a discussion area specifically set aside for casual talk among students).

Decide how you'll determine the composition of groups. For example, will groups be chosen by you via random assignment? Will they mix male and female students? Special practical considerations may apply. For instance, if students will rely heavily on real-time communication, it would be wise to factor in time zone residence when constituting the groups. Another consideration is the task itself—there are types of projects for which you may want as great a mix of diverse backgrounds as possible, while other group assignments may call for students of the same discipline or related background to work together.

How will students be graded on group work? Some instructors give a grade for the entire group, and others for each individual. This is easier to arrange online because you may specify that all group work be done in an asynchronous area visible to you or that the transcript of all chat sessions be saved and sent to you. You may want to prepare a grading rubric for students to see, in order to clarify your criteria for grading.

What role will student presentations by groups or individual students play in your course? To which assignments, activities, or topics will the presentations be connected? What will be the structure of each presentation? Will it involve a simple presentation of text, such as posting a paper or a group summary of the week's lessons? Or will the presentation involve the display of multimedia projects, an increasingly more feasible option with the advent of Web 2.0 technologies?

There are more examples of these types of activities in Chapter 7, but here we want to emphasize that such activities must be carefully planned, and areas for their implementation must be chosen or organized.

Research

Research activities, including fieldwork, may be carried out in a number of ways in an online class.

Web Research   Web research is an obvious option. There are open-ended activities, and there are guided activities. In the former, instructors typically propose web searches in which students are told to go find information on a particular topic. But in these open-ended research opportunities, it's vitally important that you give students some guidelines for both evaluating and searching out web resources. Because of the enormous growth of the Internet, open-ended research is becoming increasingly frustrating and difficult. Web search engines typically discover only a small percentage of the sites actually available.

We suggest that you not only give students some training in Web search and evaluation, but also consider providing them with initial home-base sites from which they can fan out to find others. You could offer this guidance in the form of edited or reviewed collections of **hyperlinks**. For example, there may be an economics department at a university that maintains a site of the best links related to economics. Or a reputable and well-established association or journal might provide a selective list of relevant sites in its field. These provide reliable starting points for students to begin their searches.

Another way to approach this problem is to give students your own list of pre-evaluated sites to use for their research. This is similar to distributing a bibliography for research papers in an on-the-ground class. You might want to enlist the help of your campus librarian in assembling a list of web sites for your students. Or you might encourage students to consult with their local librarians. Librarians are increasingly engaged in the review and evaluation of web sites and electronic reference materials, and they can be a great resource for students who are doing research on the Web.

Social Bookmarking Tools like Delicious (www.delicious.com), Furl (www.furl.com), and Diigo (www.diigo.com) can be part of your design for research activities on the Web, providing ways for students to work singly or in groups to **tag** (give a searchable term or topic label to a bit of information), sort, annotate, and store their web links. While social bookmarking thrives on open sharing, depending on the particular social bookmarking tool, it is possible to keep links private or confine sharing to a particular group. Social bookmarking tools vary in features, but most permit users to view how others in their selected group or the vast number of users in that bookmarking system have bookmarked the same links, how those users have annotated and categorized links, and to see what other related links those users may have discovered. Such social bookmarking tools permit students to keep their collection of links housed on the Web so that they may access them from any web browser without being tied to a particular home or work computer, and to easily widen their circle of references and pointers to research topics. The authors of this book used Delicious as a tool to help investigate, categorize, and annotate the great number of web sites that they researched and found that it was a more efficient method than simply bookmarking in the browser or copying long lists of sites into a document. Social bookmarking sites are considered part of the Web 2.0 technology tools, in that they are easy to use and involve collaboration and sharing. To keep up with the latest social bookmarking services, we suggest that you consult one of the Web 2.0 resource sites for educators noted in the Guide to Resources.

Library Research   Library research will depend on the facilities that your library or those in your consortium make available online. If your school subscribes to an electronic full-text service, that will make library research much easier for your students. There are a few databases available online free of charge, as well as many others that charge for their services.

If full-text documents aren't available to your students, you may still be able to direct students to databases that will help them expedite their in-person research at nearby libraries. Here's another case in which it's vitally important to consult with your librarian and survey the resources that will be available to your students, as well as the costs of accessing them.

Fieldwork or Internship   Fieldwork isn't as obvious an option for an online class, because it implies experimentation or apprenticeship in a live, on-the-ground environment. However, although the fieldwork itself may be accomplished outside the online classroom, its results may be presented online, and a discussion and evaluation may also be accomplished online.

If you're using field studies or internship periods as part of your class work, it's essential that you carefully schedule the before-and-after activities that will take place online. Any prerequisites, such as a secured internship position or a prearranged fieldwork site, should be stated in your course description at registration time and in any catalogs that list your course.

If a proctor or supervisor's report is required for fieldwork, this should also be clearly indicated. You will need to create the necessary forms and make any arrangements required to allow this aspect of the course to be implemented.

Assessment Considerations

As part of your planning, you will need to make some choices about the types of assessment you'll use. Any type of assignment is a potential assessment, either "formative" (part of the instructional sequence, for the purpose of measuring progress and giving appropriate feedback, not graded) or "summative" (a graded assignment or test that takes place at the end of an instructional sequence or as a final assessment of the course). Chapter 7 of this book will provide some ideas about the multitude of different ways in which you might assess your students. What matters most is that the assessment:

- is relevant to the objectives and goals of the course;
- is appropriate for the level and scope of the course content;
- is easily enough accomplished online;
- is clearly outlined to students via logically organized instructions that include the how, when, and where of online logistics.

Next, make sure that you vary your mix of assessments so that:

- there are a variety of different types of assessments, allowing students to be assessed from a number of different perspectives, using a diverse set of skills;
- the number and pacing of the assessments are appropriate for the course length and format;
- there are some options for student choice and different levels of challenges.

● ● ● ● ●

High-Stakes, Low-Stakes Testing

If online testing is available to you, you'll have to decide which types of questions to create and whether a specific test will be used for self-assessment and review (that is, low-stakes testing), or for a grade (high-stakes). If you are using low-stakes self-assessment, determine whether it will be possible for you to see the results of the self-assessment or just to record that the student has accessed the self-assessment.

Some online testing programs allow for relative security. They may be set so that students can access them only at a specific time, after obtaining a password, and they may be timed or made to record any pause in execution. Even so, if students aren't taking such tests in a proctored environment, there's naturally some possibility of fraud and cheating. However, this is also true for many testing situations on the ground. (How many large lecture classes check student IDs before exams?) To cut down on fraud and cheating in graded online high-stakes testing, in cases in which a campus-based or proctored test is not an option, you should consider the following techniques in your planning:

1. The test should be lengthy or difficult enough that it isn't easy for students to look up information and still complete the test on time.

2. A good proportion of questions should relate directly to in-class discussions or other in-class activities, including instructor lectures or case studies. Even if students can access the transcripts of such discussions, these aren't easy to locate in time to respond to timed tests. In addition, this type of question isn't easily answered by "stand-ins" who haven't actually participated in the class.

3. Don't rely only on online testing for grading individuals. Make sure you have at least two other methods of evaluation, such as essays and discussion participation. You can even include one real-time online "debriefing" that can serve as a basis of comparison with the student's other work.

4. Find out if other security measures are available through your CMS or specialized software and learn how to use them. You may have options such as issuing a password to access a test, automatic randomization of questions, setting time limits for tests, or you may be able to arrange that a student contact you before gaining access to the test or answer personal challenge questions to authenticate identity.

In transforming a traditional engineering course, Circuit Theory, to a blended approach, Jerzy Rutkowski of the Silesian

University of Technology in Poland was working with his colleagues to restructure a course to accommodate large numbers of students each year with only a small team of instructors. As part of their blended solution, they sought to redevelop the summative final exam. They soon realized that simply converting the previously open-ended questions would not be a reasonable approach. After periods of experimentation and feedback, they developed exams that emphasize conceptual understanding over problem solving and the resulting tests are close-ended, multiple-choice questions that are randomized for online access through Moodle. A great deal of planning and design went into making the test questions sufficiently challenging. They also calculated how many minutes a student who understands the concepts involved should take on the exam, in order to set a reasonable time limit for the test. Questions involving reverse reasoning skills present additional challenges to students who have only a superficial understanding of a concept. Rutkowski's redesign experience is recounted in an article in the *Journal of Education, Informatics, and Cybernetics*, available at www.journaleic.com/article/view/3461/2499.

A more sophisticated approach to security is found in the recent introduction of a number of technology solutions to online testing that have emerged involving **biometric** (verification of physical characteristics of an individual) authentication of a student (such as login via eye scan or fingerprint) and/or monitored webcams. These are implemented on an institution- or system-wide basis, and involve considerable costs and coordination planning. If you happen to belong to such an institution, you will need to attain a clear understanding of how it works and how it will impact the way you develop your exams.

For the vast majority of instructors, such biometric or other high-security testing arrangements will not be available. Therefore, instructors need to be purposeful in devising assessments so that it is not easy for students to simply plagiarize essays and papers. The more open-ended the paper topic assigned, the easier it is for students to plagiarize and the harder it is for instructors to detect cheating. For example, asking a student to "Write a ten-page paper on Augustan Rome" simply leaves too much room to forage among web sites and fulfill the assignment. A more plagiarism-proof assignment would be:

> *Write a ten-page paper characterizing the major trends in the literature or art of the Augustan era, using at least three primary source documents or images presented in our class, as well as five additional library resources. In presenting your characterizations, incorporate at least one topic from our class discussions.*

Some institutions subscribe to services like TurnitIn.com which provide feedback to the faculty member on possible student plagiarism. Or, an instructor can use a simple method like choosing an odd or unusually eloquent turn of phrase and inserting it in Google, which will often turn up the source for a plagiarized assignment. But in some cases, it is just not possible to find the evidence of plagiarism, or to detect self-plagiarism, like students reusing their papers from another class. Beyond that, it is a terrible waste of an instructor's time to continually play policeman.

A good alternative is to make sure that in setting up your grading criteria, responsiveness to the assignment requirements is made a major determinant of the grade. "Responsiveness" means that you can often avoid having to make a difficult determination about plagiarism. For example, no matter how erudite that suspect paper is, the fact that it discusses Ovid without any of the class reference points as stipulated by the assignment directions means that the student has simply not met the full set of criteria for a good score.

Portfolio methods of assessment are yet another way in which to measure student learning, ensuring that the student is assessed over time, by a progressive series of work products. It isn't difficult to assemble a portfolio of work in the online environment. The key is planning an adequate variety of activities from which students can assemble portfolios of their work. You can create a special online area, equivalent to a folder, where student work and evaluations of student work can be stored. Find out if your institution provides some sort of electronic portfolio software.

•••••

Choosing Textbooks, Coursepacks, and Software for Your Course

Even though your course may be totally online, there's no reason to discount the idea of ordering a textbook for your students. A textbook may provide the most effective and most easily procured source material for your course. (It can usually be ordered and purchased online.) Increasingly, textbooks are available both in hard copy as well as in the form of **ebooks** (electronic books). Hard-copy textbooks may be useful for those who don't want to read book-length materials completely online, and it allows them to avoid the expense and time of printing out copious amounts of text. But it is unwise to order a textbook from which you will only require students to read a few chapters. Students increasingly refuse to buy expensive textbooks that they know they will be used only sparingly in the course. Rather than assign such a textbook, choosing a less expensive ebook option or assembling an electronic "coursepack" or anthology of different writings provide better solutions. Ebooks increasingly come in a variety of delivery modes, from access on a web site or downloadable versions for ebook readers and other mobile devices. Ebooks often provide features that allow the student user to annotate and highlight the text electronically, adding to the attractiveness of this option.

A coursepack anthology of writings from different sources can also be ordered and is essential when you wish to make use of copyrighted materials to which the library does not have full-text electronic versions. Perhaps your library provides a service by which these can then be placed directly in your online classroom. Some will still want to reproduce a coursepack in print but others will find it sufficient to secure electronic rights. A hard-copy coursepack may make sense when the instructor's own authored materials aren't easily scanned into an online format or when students are best served by having a hard-copy reference.

Depending on your subject matter, you may find that you are increasingly able to assemble the equivalent of a "coursepack" from **open educational resources** available on the Web that allow for free educational use. These open educational resources (referred to as OERs) range from courseware made available by such universities as MIT to freely shared podcasts from an individual biology instructor at a community college. We will discuss more about how to find open educational resources in Chapter 8.

Some publishers provide companion web sites to support their textbooks, and the best of these can furnish your students with valuable resources. In some cases, there is a companion DVD or CD. Again, it makes little sense to require students to purchase an expensive CD/DVD textbook bundle if you are not really going to require use of that CD/DVD. Remember that you can also create your own online resources that will help students get the most out of the text, for instance, self-assessment quizzes, guideline questions for use in discussion, and web site reference lists for further exploration of the textbook topics.

In ordering software applications for use in a particular class, the pricing and compatibility of programs are important issues, as well as the analysis of your student audience. If price and lack of consistency among students are issues for your students, using open-source documents like Google Docs or another software program freely available on the Web may be the answer. The key to finding these is a web resource or blog site in your field. For example, math software can be very expensive, but there are a number of freeware programs available that have been reviewed by those involved in math education. John Beyers, the math instructor from University of Maryland University College, mentions Geogebra, a free software used in his developmental math class:

> it's quite good and can be used to draw two-dimensional figures. Like all freeware, it has its limitations, but it allows my students to sketch a graph of a function when given an equation. The graph can then be captured, copied and pasted into our discussion forum or attached as an image file.

Look to a specialized blog or a social bookmarking site like Delicious to see what sites educators are recommending, then try out and evaluate them for your needs.

● ● ● ● ●

Redesign

As institutions become more involved with online education and try out new delivery formats, course lengths, or class sizes, faculty increasingly find themselves being asked to redesign an online course to meet the new specifications. While we discuss the issues involved with different class sizes in Chapter 11, we will take a moment to address the overall issues involved in redesign of term length here.

Whether a course is shortened from fifteen weeks to ten or is lengthened from six weeks to twelve, redesign is what is required, rather than simply truncating, chopping, or stretching to try to fit the new dimensions of the course. As part of this redesign, you must revisit the course objectives because it is those intended learning outcomes that should be the main determinant of the design changes you will make.

Start with some practical steps. If you have previously taught the course, plot out the new term length on a weekly calendar alongside the schedule of your previous class (or another's syllabus) as a reference. Where do exams, term breaks, and holidays fall in the new schedule? How much time was previously devoted to introductory activities, wrap-up, review, small-group formation, visiting speakers, or library-related activities?

Try to understand your institution or department's rationale and purpose for the new course length—is it to provide more time to cover complex material? A function of student demand for shorter courses and more variety in courses? Understanding the purpose behind the change may help you as you approach redesign.

If the length of the course is shortened, be certain to find out whether the new version of the course will be considered an "intensive" or "accelerated" course—that is, is the course now expected to cover more credit hours, the same number of credits, and what is the expected time on task required of students per week?

Redesign from Longer to Shorter

Course Content

Calculate the prior weekly reading load for students, including textbooks, online lectures, etc., and now examine how many hours per week that translates to under the new schedule. Assuming the course is not now considered an accelerated version, if you expected students to read sixty pages of a textbook each week and the readings now work out to ninety pages a week, is it possible for you to trim some of the reading without negatively affecting the attainment of learning objectives?

Consider being more selective. Perhaps there are entire topics or subtopics that have proved non-essential and could be eliminated, along with their corresponding readings? If you cannot in good conscience cut any of the topics or textbook reading, consider reducing other content such as your online lectures and commentary and additional Web resource readings. You may also choose selected chapters that you can assign to students— singly or in pairs—to read, analyze, and then present in summary to fellow students in the conference area, using a special template for this activity. Sometimes a change in pacing will do, with longer reading assignments reserved for times when students are not busy with major projects and papers. When altering reading assignments, consider all text elements of the class, including any library reserved readings, or external web site materials. Make sure any cuts you make in one element or another of the reading do not undermine support for the learning objectives, assignments, or exam questions.

While "coverage" of a subject remains an important consideration, a rushed and superficial learning experience is sometimes the result when one attempts to pack too much into a shorter period. Again, the core learning objectives should be the main factor of your redesign choices.

Discussion activities

If you have created one or more discussion fora for each week of the course, start by reducing the number of separate fora to the new reduced number of weeks. Review past discussions; are there particular topics and questions that seemed to stimulate the most productive discussion in your students? If so, those are the ones you want to make sure to preserve. Are there some topics and discussion questions that might be consolidated within another forum? Finally, are there any discussion questions or topics that are not really essential and could be eliminated in their entirety?

You may want to slightly reduce the number of responses students are required to make each week while retaining the peer–peer responses built into your design. For example, if you require students to respond each week to three or four faculty-posted discussion questions as well as to two responses from other classmates, you might reduce that requirement to two responses to faculty-posted discussion questions and one response to a classmate. If you use a rubric or other clearly stated criteria to judge the quality as well as quantity of postings, you can probably preserve the desired level of interactivity in discussion.

Assignments

What are the major graded assignments and how much time on task is required for students to accomplish each?

The three main choices you have in redesigning assignments involve reworking, consolidation, or elimination.

Reworking: It may be possible to narrow down research topics or reduce the number of words/pages required for papers. Get started early on group projects, asking students to meet for the first time earlier in the course, and make all group projects more explicit and directed so that students can quickly engage in the project without spending a lot of time organizing themselves or coming to a decision about the path to take.

Consolidation: You may be able to combine two assignments that address different learning objectives or skills so that both are fulfilled in a single assignment. For example, you may have had one assignment in which you asked students to come up with their own imaginary marketing plan and another in which you asked students to analyze a company's approach to marketing. It may be possible to combine these two assignments into one in which students are asked to devise a plan to improve the company's approach to marketing. Both analytic and planning skills will come into play in the newly consolidated assignment.

Elimination: Eliminate what is no longer current for your field or does not have a good time/benefit ratio for students. That is, if an assignment has really not proved effective in the past, consider why it was ineffective. Calculate whether it can be revised, eliminated, or even replaced by something better yet less time-consuming. Perhaps in the past you asked students to write three papers on three or more related topics. This task might be replaced with an activity in which students write one longer paper that incorporates those three topics.

In redesigning assignments, be careful to ascertain any limitations to your choices. For example, if a particular assignment has been designated a key part of a program's outcomes assessment plan, or is related to prerequisites for future courses, the consequences of making changes to that assignment may have an effect beyond your own course.

Feedback and interaction

With a shorter course, you may be concerned that you will not have sufficient turnaround time to give high-quality feedback on assignments or to engage with students in discussion. Maintaining high levels of interaction and quality feedback should remain a high priority—this is not likely to be the case if you try to maintain exactly the same assignments and numbers of discussion fora that you had in your previous longer course. The best approach is to prioritize and rank your assignments and discussion topics. By consolidating assignments whenever possible, you will have fewer but more focused opportunities to give feedback. Use detailed rubrics to speak for you and conserve your time to make those individualized comments that are necessary to help your students improve their performance. For example, it may be that you can address such elements as grammar, structure of an assignment, required parts of an assignment, etc. through a rubric, freeing up your time to write comments that address the student's specific problem, shortcoming or strengths.

Redesign from Shorter to Longer

Course Content

Avoid the temptation presented by a longer course that seems to invite the addition of more and more content and activities to a course. Determine whether adding readings and activities will enhance the course or whether they simply add up to "filler." Look for those readings and activities that will add a vital new dimension to the course.

Assignments and feedback

A longer course provides a great opportunity to diversify approaches to learning. You may find that you now have time for a major project or research paper, or to structure a group project over a number of weeks.

Depth and relevance rather than simply "more" should be the goal. For example, if you previously assigned a final project, you might now find there is sufficient time for students to not only complete the final project but for you to ask them to provide an outline, first draft, or bibliography at an early stage of the project, so that you gain an opportunity to provide feedback to students before the final version is due. Or, you might allow students to share their final projects with their classmates and participate in a spirited give-and-take discussion concerning their projects.

Being able to assess students in an early stage of an assignment, to take the temperature of the class via short surveys and to use that student feedback to inform the remainder of the course, or to simply have the leisure to guide students through a more comprehensive preparation and review for a final exam are all possible advantages that come with a longer course.

A redesign template

Table 3.3 is a simple template that might prove useful for planning the redesign of a course. The example shown is for redesign of a course that is moving from fifteen weeks to a shorter ten-week course.

Table 3.3 Example of a Redesign Template

Learning Objectives for Course	Previous Assignments to Meet Objectives/New Assignments	Previous Course Content Coverage to Meet Objectives/New Content	Previous Discussion Topics and Questions/New Topics and Questions
Describe the major cultural, political, and social elements of China from 220 BC–AD 1200	Three two-page essays on three different dynastic periods/One 5–6 page paper that compares and contrasts the major elements of three different periods	200 pages of textbook readings over a period of four weeks/An instructor lecture and three focused articles of 20–30 pages each in a period of two weeks	Discussion questions distributed over four weeks/Focused discussion questions included in two weekly discussion fora

● ● ● ● ●

Some Final Tips on Course Development

Before you begin to convert or create a new online or blended course, here are some final tips:

1. Devise some sort of simple chart for yourself to plot out the major units, their objectives, content, and assignments if your institution does not supply one. There are a lot of moving parts in an online course, and a table, chart, or other planning document can help you bring these all together in the initial planning stages, make it easier to discern what is missing, and facilitate the creation of your syllabus.

2. Even though you may ultimately create web pages written in HTML or post materials within a course management system, make sure you save all content that you create, whether it be lecture notes, quizzes, or announcements, in some electronic, word-processed format, so that you'll be able to reuse or revise it for a future course. In other words, don't simply post your materials online without saving them in clearly marked files on your own hard drive, DVD, or flash drive. Include the date of the latest revision of your documents. This warning is particularly relevant for those who may use an external hosting service for their main classroom content and services.

3. When you do create your course materials, you may place them in one of the integrated course management systems or in some combination of web pages, discussion forum software, or other online software tools. Be aware that each system and tool is different. Therefore, be sure to give yourself enough time to experiment with different ways of organizing the material. Try out all major features of the system; knowing the limitations of your software will save you time in the long run. Also be sure to try out a sample unit in your course from the students' perspective, or ask your teaching assistants or colleagues to play this role and give you feedback. Then go back and make changes in your syllabus.

4. Be sure to develop a schedule for preparation and delivery of any materials that need processing by teaching assistants, technical support staff, instructional designers, or librarians. Make sure you ascertain the turnaround time necessary for anything you'll be doing that requires some mediation by others. Draw up a time line and then work backward from your due dates to plan your own work.

5. Find out if there are any institutional or departmental policy restrictions that might affect your choices for course activities, materials, online communication tools (especially the use of external hosting services and Web 2.0 tools). Another issue is the preservation of course data and student records. Perhaps your university wants you to preserve a record of communications or work posted on third-party sites. It is essential to know these restrictions up front.

4

Working with Others to Develop a Course

Wile many instructors worldwide operate largely on their own when it comes to development of online courses, a growing number of institutions committed to online education have increasingly turned to a team approach for course development. The "team" may be as small as an instructor paired with an instructional designer, instructional technologist, or other technically oriented person providing assistance, or it may be a larger group of individuals—technologists, designers, graphic artists, and programmers, along with a project manager—joined in their efforts by an instructor who most likely serves as the content expert and perhaps plays other roles as well. There may be peer reviewers from the ranks of fellow instructors, or external subject-matter experts.

In some cases the resulting course is meant to be reproduced without many alterations as it devolves to each new instructor to teach. In other situations, the team is devoted to creating only some core materials or a skeletal syllabus that are incorporated within the larger course, taught by successive instructors who each add their own materials and craft all or some of their own assignments.

From the point of view of an institution, standardization of portions (or the entirety) of online courses may be seen as a way to ensure consistent quality and scalable coverage of required content over multiple sections of a course. From the point of view of an instructor who was not involved in the development of that course, it may be difficult to force one's own shape into the existing structure modeled by others.

If you are the instructor charged with developing and teaching a course, what are the secrets of developing a course within a team approach? If you are an instructional designer or other team member, how can you most successfully approach your work with the originating instructor? And how can an instructor most effectively develop and teach a course which is completely or largely authored by others and still experience professional satisfaction?

● ● ● ● ●

A Model of Instructor–Designer Collaboration

Sharon Guan is an instructional designer, currently Director of Instructional Technology Development at DePaul University in Chicago but previously at Indiana University, where she worked with Pete Mikolaj to develop a course for the School of Business at Indiana, Commercial Liability Risk Management and Insurance. Previously offered only face to face, the course was converted to the online format and along with changing the delivery format, it was decided to take advantage of the opportunity to alter the teaching approach. In working with Mikolaj, Guan proceeded by first choosing an appropriate learning theory and then allowing the course development flow from that imperative.

Prior to working with Guan, Mikolaj had been using group projects in most of his courses, but was not always satisfied with the quality of team participation. He had tried a number of different techniques, including peer evaluation, but was still not satisfied and was looking for "a better way for building cohesion within the team and a way to build motivation." He was also concerned about how to evaluate the teams so as to assign individual student grades.

While Mikolaj had considerable industry and teaching experience, he said that he tended to be a lecturer and considered himself a rather boring lecturer at that! He credits Guan with helping him to change to a more learner-centered approach, and showing him the value of including examples, graphics, as well as guest experts in the class. He commented,

"I was relieved to find that there were other ways to convey information so that students can actually enjoy learning!"

As Guan described it, she:

> played the role of a typical designer with Pete being the content expert. He brought to me his syllabus, lecture notes, assignments and other course materials. After going through these, I suggested major surgery of course structure from chapter-by-chapter coverage to one that centered around one group project. Pete welcomed the suggestion and we worked together to fit the content into the new structure.

Sharon Guan also helped Pete Mikolaj with his questions about motivating and evaluating team members by designing a project rubric and measures for assessing individual contributions to the team.

Guan and Mikolaj shared the work along with some student workers who were available to digitize materials and create graphics. While Guan generally utilizes a formal work-flow development chart in working with instructors to ensure that all stay on schedule, she and Mikolaj met weekly and his commitment to close cooperation meant that such aids were not needed to the same degree.

In regard to working with Guan to redesign the course, Mikolaj noted that his greatest difficulty had probably been in:

> accepting the need for a more formalized evaluation than I was accustomed to using. I was not familiar with much in the way of assessment and Sharon jumped in and helped me organize an evaluation plan that fit the particular objectives we had set out for the course.

Mikolaj even found that his collaboration with Guan produced another unexpected benefit—the experiences he had with this first course resulted in ongoing discussions and analysis as he introduced additional components of learner-centered design into his subsequent courses and sought to learn from those experiments. Guan also encouraged Mikolaj to incorporate new technologies in subsequent courses, patiently coaching him through his hesitation to try out appropriate tools.

Thus what began as a collaboration to develop a new online course turned into a professional quest for Mikolaj in becoming a more effective online instructor:

> *I am learning more about how to be an effective teacher, which I feel is the ultimate reward. In close second place is the education I am getting—it's quite exciting to be learning new concepts and feel that one is at the forefront of the educational process.*

●●●●●

Advice for Instructional Designers on Working with Instructors

Sometimes instructional design seems theoretical and abstract to instructors and they may feel that the realities of teaching don't match up with the systematized and idealized instructional design principles. This can be particularly true when what's involved is designing a student activity as opposed to instructor presentation materials. Some designers may have more experience designing for self-paced instructional activities rather than instructor-led online classes. And designers who lack experience teaching may not understand the dynamic nature of teaching and classroom interaction. As Pete Mikolaj

---

Advice to Instructional Designers on Working with Instructors on the Writing of Learning Objectives

■ Discuss the objectives with instructors in terms of what instructors want students to learn and the ways that students could demonstrate that learning in the context of class assignments, readings, etc.

■ Expose instructors to some simple examples of ways to express learning objectives but do so without pressing them to comprehend complex systems—avoid jargon!

■ Help instructors in a collaborative way to refine the learning objectives so that they would be reasonably clear to both the instructor and his or her students (there's really no value in the objectives being understood only by design professionals).

said, "I discovered that not all designers were like Sharon Guan! They don't know how to motivate students, don't have that first-hand and direct teaching experience." Sharon valued the experience she had as a teaching assistant during her graduate school days as well as her engagement as a tutor, working with students one-on-one. She commented,

> *I often hear complaints about designers from instructors. That designers are too demanding and can't put up with the fact that instructors like to be creative, that they have different working styles. It's important that designers have the experience of teaching so that they understand that perspective.*

Renee Cicchino, the instructional designer at Seton Hall University in New Jersey, echoes that sentiment:

> *I believe that the online course design process is easier for those designers with some online teaching experience. In addition to being able to draw from our own online teaching experiences, I find that instructors are often able to relate better to a fellow instructor. During the course development process I share techniques that worked for me as an instructor as well as the things I look for as a past online student.*

The writing of learning objectives is an aspect of design that can cause conflicts between designers and instructors. The fact is that instructors are rarely trained as part of their preparation for teaching to write precise learning objectives. Typically, they end up writing more general learning goals. And they may find it hard to match up those learning objectives, whether written by themselves or designers, with the actual course activities that they want to occur.

Sharon Guan emphasized that rather than pressing the instructor to write ever more precise objectives, and, in the process, sometimes humiliating the instructor, the designer needs to simply discuss with the instructor what it is that students should be able to demonstrate so that the instructor knows that the student has learned. She added, "and having someone else write the objectives for you is not really that good," as much of value can get lost as the expert tries to hone the language. For example, Guan also teaches Chinese language and said, "one of my goals is that students fall in love with the language." That sort of goal is a valid one, but not easily conveyed in a precise learning objective! Each instructor has his or her goals and the designer needs to strike a balance so that the objectives emerge with clarity without being overly pedantic about the process or producing learning objectives that really do not reflect the realities of the classroom dynamic.

There are resources that can assist instructors in improving their writing of learning objectives (see the Guide to Resources section) but bear in mind that for most faculty, a little goes a long way. As Sharon Guan has characterized it, "it's an important subject, but tends to be boring for faculty." One simple way to get the concept of different levels of learning and their expression in objectives is to help the instructor locate the level of learning taking place and appropriate verbs to express that level. Instructors can readily understand the difference between rote memorization and analytic thinking. So that if the level of learning is at the basic level of demonstrating reading comprehension and memorizing facts, the learning objective might be expressed with the verbs "to identify or name" while at a higher level of thinking, the learning objective might be expressed as "to reflect on or to analyze."

Renee Cicchino finds that instructors often write learning objectives from a conceptual perspective rather than a measurable perspective, but she hastens to add, "99% of the time the objectives are actually there—they just need to be reworded in a measurable way." At Seton Hall, instructors are often given a list of action verbs based on Bloom's Taxonomy as an aid to developing measurable learning objectives. (For some online resources that use this same approach, see the Guide to Resources in this book.)

Many instructors are particularly put off by the use of jargon and designers would be wise to avoid the use of jargon in working with instructors. Guan noted, rather than use such terms as "goal driven, assessment driven and outcomes based," sit down with instructors and ask "What do you want students to be able to do as a result of this class?" and "How would you know that your students had learned this?" Even the term "deliverable," which is handy in its application to so many different types of assignments, can seem off-putting to instructors— better, says Guan, to express this by asking "What do you want the students to present to you—something concrete—to show they understand?"

Another factor which may give rise to misunderstanding is the inherent difference that exists between interactive online classes and self-paced computer-based training (often known as CBT). Some designers have in the past focused on self-paced learning modules in which the instructional content and activities must carry the entire weight of learning, because there is no teacher mediating the experience. The content is sequenced and the directions specifically oriented toward the student's completion of a series of tasks on his or her own, with perhaps interaction occurring through built-in automatic feedback and response. An instructor-led online course is different in that the instructor is expected to facilitate learning and the interaction with classmates also contributes to the learning experience— therefore there are multiple layers of interaction—with content, with the instructor and with classmates. While sequence is still important, there must be room to breathe for the instructor to play a role and to respond to the needs of students. Sharon Guan advises, "Designers need to take on the student perspective and I would recommend that they take an interactive online class to be exposed to both synchronous and asynchronous modes."

Good teaching is dynamic and designers can benefit from having had teaching experience of their own, whether in a face-to-face or online context. Short of attaining that teaching experience on their own, the designer can perhaps best make up for that lack by carefully interviewing the instructor as to what he or she would normally do in the classroom to accomplish a particular end, then helping the instructor translate that into an appropriate online mode or introducing a new approach to accomplishing the same goals. This means that the designer must accept that good instructors are more than content experts—they are also teaching experts. The designer should seek to draw out that often latent knowledge so that it is clearly manifested in the online course as it is developed. Renee

Cicchino mentions that as the designer begins to work on online course design with an instructor, if possible, one way to better grasp the teaching methods of an instructor is to visit the instructor's face-to-face class to observe and analyze the instructor's teaching style first-hand.

Three Suggestions for Designers from Sharon Guan

- Act more as a support than a consultant.
- Always do more show than tell! Earn instructors' trust by show-casing a piece of work you have accomplished such as a course, learning object, or a simple reader-friendly digital document.
- Be flexible in your way of serving the diverse clientele of univer-sity instructors—get to know their personalities, working habits, and view of instructional design.

● ● ● ● ●

Advice for Instructors Working within a Team Approach

When teaching in the face-to-face class, instructors are accus-tomed to responding to body language, questions from students and other cues that students are in need of further clarification, explanations, or assistance about what they should be doing in the course. For an online class, a good deal of this needs to be anticipated, so that students are clear about what they need to do and when and where, and the instructor can provide addi-tional emphasis, reminders, and referrals to other resources as needed. Therefore, if you are working with an instructional designer, or within an even larger team framework, it's best to approach the experience as a way to become more aware of your teaching while at the same time taking advantage of the opportunity to try out new approaches to teaching arising from the multiple perspectives afforded to you by the team.

Juanita Pardo González teaches two blended courses in English as a Foreign Language to undergraduates at Universi-dad de Los Andes in Bogatá, Colombia. Each course involves students meeting 4.5 hours per week face-to-face, with the expectation of an additional three hours per week spent online. During the first year, having had no more than a technical training course in WebCT, González began to apply information and communication technologies to one of her courses, but:

> I would just assign students to go to the course webpage to do an activity that I formerly did in the face-to-face class. The activity was a basic drill, consisting of listening and repeating phrases or words. These online drills were not required for students but just provided an additional opportunity to practice listening and speaking the language.

Not being satisfied with that first effort, she sought help in an attempt to determine the needs for a blended course. González was fortunate to belong to an institution like Los Andes which provides extensive support for the use of technology in teaching and learning. She was soon assisted by an instructional designer in creating some observational criteria and guidelines to examine what had gone on in that first class, looking at the student behavior and underlying approaches to teaching inherent in her instruction, along with the degree of consistency between the course content and her pedagogical practice. As González put it, "the goal of the process I went through was to design a blended course where I would not have to change my essential teaching style, but to find ways to apply my style of teaching to the new environment."

With these investigatory resources, she came to realize that she needed to apply a different strategy the next time the course ran:

> First, I integrated the course content to the work online, instead of simply using the webpage—I devised a cycle in my teaching that allowed me to insert the online portion into one of the steps of the teaching cycle. In this way the online component did not seem added to the course, but a part of the course.

At the same time, she also received help from another part of the Los Andes team. Their technology services provided some additional software programs to meet the particular needs of each of the courses. For example, early on, she discovered that most of the practice exercises could be done at home by students via an online lab program and that they did not need the instructor for immediate supervision of this activity. With the help of technology, she realized that with online drill and practice exercises "the students could get a faster response from the machine than from me." This freed up her time to give better and more detailed feedback to students in other activities.

Then she realized that some of her presentation could be delivered online as well, and that through the use of video, she could "allow other voices into the classroom" than just her own, and include students as sources of information as well. González even noticed that she had no need to continue lugging audio tapes around the university and to be constantly rewinding tapes to find the right place in the recording to conduct quizzes on campus, but could move these online as well, with built-in feedback. Finally, she began to add self and peer evaluation to her course, establishing clear criteria, and after demonstrating in the face-to-face class meeting how to perform these assessments, she found that students could perform these assessments quite well given clear limits and guidelines.

Later on, the instructional designer and graphics designer suggested a further remodeling of the course to bring a fresh look to the courses. Today there are numerous sections of the original course teaching the same content. González now trains new instructors in the use of technology for the course. She has also created videos to prepare students on the proper use of the online components of the course. González has moved from trying to operate entirely on her own to becoming part of the team effort to support blended classes in her discipline.

One of the most important things she learned about designing and teaching a blended course is that:

> *you must dare to let your students teach you! You have to feel comfortable with the tools and with the structure of the class in order to be able to teach it. You need to be willing to monitor and accompany your students in paths you had never planned. You need to be willing to give your students more freedom and responsibility than you have in*

traditional face-to-face classes and you need to accept the different forms in which students will take that freedom and responsibility.

John Beyers, an instructor and academic director for math at University of Maryland University College describes how he worked with a development team to transform a pre-existing course in development math into an online course that may be offered to as many as 25 sections of students in one semester. Starting out, Beyers had the syllabus, schedule of class meetings and activities, and some model assignments. It took multiple weeks and feedback from a half-dozen veteran instructors to create the new syllabus for an online course. Beyers also chose the three main textbooks before work began on creating course modules with a larger team. This larger team consisted of instructional designers, a graphic designer, a programmer, a peer reviewer, and a project manager. John Beyers played the role of both content expert and curriculum expert. Beyers describes the collaboration,

At the initial meeting, we set up goals and a timeline. The project manager was really key to the whole endeavor. Instructional designers, graphic designers and programming created learning objects to add interactivity to the math content. I was comfortable working with the team. When there was an issue of pedagogy, the others tended to listen to me as content and curriculum expert. They suggested learning objects and I would work with them on the design. Some of the advantages of working in a team are that you tend to stay on task, there's accountability in a team, more staff resources, and multiple eyes on the project.

In the role of content expert, you must recognize how a lack of content expertise can affect the ability of other team members to provide their own expertise. For example, John Beyers found that he needed to do as much rendering as possible of graphs and equations before turning these over to the graphic artists. In math, accuracy is a major issue, and graphic artists are not usually mathematicians, so the task of helping the artists more easily adapt the design and also reviewing their work for errors fell to Beyers. In the same way, Beyers had to be attentive to changes in wording suggested by the instructional designers—in math, words like "and" and "or," "equal" and "congruent" are not interchangeable! Similarly, Gretchen Jones, playing the role of curriculum specialist as part of a team developing a course in Japanese language for University of Maryland University College found that she needed to be vigilant concerning cultural subtleties. For example, the graphics designer originally presented a lovely picture of a kimono with the right lapel folded on top of the left—a way that one dresses the dead in Japan!

John Beyers noted that instructors also need to appreciate the limitations of the development enterprise when it comes to programming difficulty and expense. "I had great ideas," he noted, "but such limitations could drive what the team could and could not do. Dynamic graphs, simulations, animations—that sort of work was really the potentially most expensive and complex part of course development."

The rewards of a team approach to create course elements that can be scaled to multiple sections can be great. Beyers noted that when the course went online, the university suddenly had 4,000 new students who wouldn't have otherwise taken the course—previously they would have had to take it at a community college and transfer the credits in. Beyond that, attrition was actually cut in half,

> *in part due to the consistency in the syllabus and course modules. Previously the attrition rate was very high, students would take different versions of the course and then as they advanced to the next course in the series, they sometimes discovered that they had missed important elements and were not well prepared. So both student retention and student success (as measured by passing and enrolling in the next course in the series) have gone up as a result of this change.*

While you may be playing the role of content expert, do not hesitate to assert your teaching expertise when you sense that something devised by the team is unlikely to be workable in the classroom situation. We advise all instructors to, at the minimum, take an online class or online teaching training before attempting to act as a content expert for the design of an online course. You are unlikely to contribute much to the course if you have neither taught online nor have experience as a student in an online class.

Renee Cicchino suggests that instructors avoid becoming fixated on an exact one-to-one transformation of face-to-face into online activities. One can avoid this problem, she says, by focusing on what you want students to achieve by the activity. Cicchino states that "when we run into a problem trying to replicate exactly what the instructor wants created, we show them an alternative that creates the same outcome." For example, in developing a science course, the instructor, never having taught online, could not see how anything could replace a face-to-face classroom activity in which she had students label and color different geologic samples. The designer presented a variety of different alternatives, until reaching a resolution by which a matching exercise was created using images of the geologic samples and the course management system quizzing software.

Lori Walters teaches history at the University of Central Florida and faced a challenge in transforming a course designed for face-to-face delivery into a completely online class. Her class teaches American history through media, and students previously viewed films, television programs, commercials, and other popular media with an eye to analyzing how the time periods were reflected in these media products. When faced with moving this course online, Walters worked with an instructional designer, Debbie Kirkley, to find a cost-effective way to deliver the class while meeting the same objectives. Walters and Kirkley created a series of modules to present the essential background information on each period represented by the various forms of media. When it came to film, they made the decision not to have all students watch the same film, but rather to provide a list of approved films and allow students to rent or purchase films. A wide range of films, both current and classic, are readily available now to rent via inexpensive DVD or from a variety of online streaming video services, most of them free. This decision by Walters and Kirkley, while initially in reaction to the need to avoid incurring expensive copyright and licensing costs, unexpectedly provided an opportunity to add some personalization of student interest to the assignments. For television programs, they discovered a burgeoning supply of sources on the Web that have made vintage television shows available in a legal and freely available streaming format. Walters notes, "it is important to consider the media that students are comfortable with and constantly work with your instructional designer to find ways to incorporate those into the classes."

The instructor should not hesitate to ask the designer to share examples of what other instructors may be doing in their online classrooms to accomplish similar objectives. Seeing how concrete examples work in the context of a real class or talking with other instructors who have implemented such elements can do much to facilitate understanding between instructor and designer.

Instructors should beware of harboring unrealistic expectations of the designer. Sometimes instructors expect designers and other team members to perform all remotely technical and even routine cut-and-paste work for them, handing over a rudimentary syllabus and even handwritten notes from past lectures and exams and expecting the team members to simply "upload" and format everything for them. Some instructors even demand designers edit their content and correct their spelling! While it's unreasonable to expect all instructors to perform all technical tasks without assistance, if an instructor at the very least does not learn how to use the class software fairly well, does not review or format their materials or try to grasp the concepts of online teaching, the resulting classroom performance of that instructor is often disastrous. Students readily apprehend when an instructor seems lost in the online classroom. Renee Cicchino emphasizes, "it's so important for instructors to understand that it's not the designer's course, it's the instructor's course. Designers are there for support and guidance but instructors must take responsibility for their course, content and knowing the technology."

● ● ● ● ●

How to Best Approach a Course You Did Not Develop but Are Asked to Teach?

When you are asked to teach a course you did not develop but are asked to retain any major elements of that course, you are, in effect, still working with "others." That is, what you do in the way of design and development to modify that course must be done in the context of and with respect for what those before you have created.

In traditional face-to-face teaching, it is not at all unusual to be handed a syllabus created by another instructor and be asked to teach the same class. In some cases, one is expected to follow the syllabus very closely while in other cases, much leeway is afforded the new instructor. And in the traditional classroom there are courses, especially those of lower division, multiple section offerings, that go beyond a common syllabus to those in which particular class activities are mandated (ranging from specific lab and language exercises to writing and library assignments) or a common midterm and/or final are expected as well.

Online, because everything in a classroom may be preserved and observed, standardized elements of a course are even more easily replicated. This has led to the possibility of standardizing instructor lectures, activities, and discussion topics, as well as other class resources. Some have decried and fear what they derisively refer to as a "canned course," but most institutions have avoided such extremes of repurposing content ad nauseum and keep the courses "fresh" through constant revision and updating, as well as depending on instructor input and feedback, interpretation, and facilitation in the classroom.

Many institutions have rules governing what can and cannot be repurposed in subsequent sections of a course. In some cases, the originating instructor has created materials for the course as work for hire with the express idea that the subsequent instructors are required or permitted to reuse any portions they wish. In other cases, only certain basic course content modules and assignments are to be reproduced, and instructors must ask permission to reuse any other materials.

Therefore, upon being asked to teach an online course that you did not develop, it would be wise to quickly determine what must be retained, what you have the option to reuse, and what you can freely develop on your own to add to or replace elements of the course. For example, can you add your own lectures? Change all or some of the assignments? Is the textbook predetermined or can you substitute another or supplement it with other readings? And what about coverage of the content? Is it possible to eliminate, consolidate, or add other topics or shorten the chronological reach of a survey course?

Before making any changes, do consider the reasons behind existing course requirements and the expectations of students taking the course, as well as whether the course is part of a series or constitutes a prerequisite. For example, if the registration description causes students to expect the course to cover eighteenth-century European history or the course is intended to prepare students for advanced physics it would be doing a disservice to students to arbitrarily truncate the course.

Most instructors like to add something of their own to a course they have been handed. There is always a point of view and an approach behind every course developed, whether that development was in the hands of one instructor or a team of course developers. Being handed a course in which little or nothing can be changed may feel like being asked to wear a suit of clothes measured on another. There is seldom an exact fit and in any case, the instructor may find the style itself difficult to carry off.

When instructors are able to develop some part of the courses they are asked to teach, it is highly motivating—increasing their engagement in the class. Therefore, even if you are new to teaching a course, once you have determined the departmental or institutional requirements for altering the course, strive to enhance the course, whether through the artful shaping of discussion questions, the addition of new Web resources or ways to communicate, or subtle twists on the structure of assignments.

John Beyers spoke to his approach to motivating instructors who teach one of the many sections offered each semester of Developmental Math:

> It can be difficult for some who don't like any standardization. I created a model classroom for them to review and they can see my approach. I explain the benefits of standardization of certain elements—those that must be the same for all sections are the textbook, course module content, and learning objectives. The weight and content of the final proctored exam (worth 30%) must remain the

same, but how quizzes and the main project are approached can be handled differently by instructors and the way in which the discussion area is used can vary as well although participation weight remains at 10%. A few instructors will try to do everything based on my model, but if the fit isn't quite right, they can include additional software or develop a resource web site where students can get additional practice. I also encourage instructors to find their own creative ways to connect math to everyday life. For example, at the time of the 2008 Olympics, I posted a photo of the runner, Bolt, as part of explaining how to calculate the relationship between distance, rate, and time. That sparked my students' interest.

At Universitat Oberta de Catalunya (UOC), Open University of Catalonia in Barcelona, Spain, Christine Appel is English Coordinator, instructor of a Modern English 1 (intermediate English) course among other courses, and also served as the lead course developer for Modern English 1. UOC is a public institution whose mission involves using online delivery to serve their more than 37,000 students in 2008. Modern English 1 is offered in multiple class sections and each section typically has a ratio of 50 students to one instructor. UOC uses a standardized approach to course development and delivery, with multiple sections for courses that have been developed by an in-house coordinator/designer along with a content expert, and further supported by a department of multimedia experts. Group strategies and multimedia-rich resources permit a high quality of instruction and with about 95 percent of course materials standardized, instructors are free to concentrate on facilitating class activity, providing feedback at key points, and evaluating student work. They moderate discussions, clarify instructions, and intervene when needed in student group work. Although discussion topics are also standardized, instructors may add something from their own experience if the learning situation seems to demand it. They may also suggest other resources as student needs arise, either from the Web or selected by the instructor from among the collection of resources the university has made available for instructional purposes.

●　●　●　●　●

Suggestions for Approaching the Teaching of a Highly Standardized Course

If you are an instructor whose institution has determined that you cannot change *anything* in a standardized course, don't be disheartened.

First, make a point of carefully studying the course well ahead of the time you will teach and explore the points of view and approaches you find in the course so that you can intelligently help students do their best in the class. If you are uncertain about why a certain approach is taken, talk to other instructors, the course developers (if available), or your administrator. If, after sincere efforts, you cannot believe in the basic premises of the course, it will be hard to convince students of the same and you are better off not teaching such a course. If you find errors in the course, report these to the course developers or departmental administrator. Distinguish between a valid point of view and a mistaken one. While your own approach may differ from the former, only the latter is one that you cannot teach.

Once you have thoroughly absorbed the reasoning, approach, and principles of the course you will teach, you can look to providing feedback to the students as your main route to contributing to the course. Through feedback, you can contribute instructor commentary, encourage higher-level thinking, and point the way to additional resources. These should enhance, perhaps widen the scope, or provide clearer focus, but not undermine the course principles. For example, in responding to a student's posting in the discussion on some themes of the textbook, you may skillfully weave in commentary that you might otherwise have included in a lecture:

> *John, your response is a thoughtful exploration of the more subtle aspects of X. And you have noted some of the shortcomings of this theory. Some contemporary scientists have tried to explain some of these shortcomings. I have noted these with an asterisk next to their listing in the selection of recommended further readings for this week. This is also a topic that is possible for some of you to explore as part of your second assigned paper.*

Or, "Jack, Lorena—in regard to the difficulty you noted in arriving at the answer through this process—you may find that this Web resource which provides a visual simulation of the process is helpful to you."

While your feedback will necessarily be situational, dependent on the kinds of questions and comments arising during the class, you can also do some preplanned development. When familiarizing yourself with the course content, assignment directions, and other features of the course, jot down notes about any topical areas, issues, or assignment directions that you think are likely to require some further explanation or additional resources. If you are permitted to create additional discussion questions, draft these for each week of the course so that they enhance those discussion questions that already exist. Note any types of issues you anticipate might arise as a result of the existing discussion questions.

Another way you can make a contribution is through weekly announcements and emails which are usually left to the discretion of the instructor. Weekly announcements can be used to summarize the week's activities and point out areas that students successfully navigated or continued to have difficulty in comprehending. You can also preview the week ahead and draw attention to focal areas of upcoming course materials. If you feel that students may need more than the required texts are supplying, you may be able to suggest additional resources for background or further exploration.

Finally, if you feel that you have some ideas about how to improve the course, you might contact your administrator and signal your interest in joining the course development team assigned to the next update to the course. By articulating what you have found to be shortcomings in the course and suggesting how it might be improved, you may well persuade your institution of your approach.

5

•••••

Creating an Effective Online Syllabus

Whether working alone or as part of a team to develop a course, the syllabus is an important part of course development, regardless of delivery format—online, in blended format, or face-to-face. Defining syllabus broadly here, we assume the traditional syllabus should include not only a schedule of topics, readings, activities, and assignments, but also such elements as goals, objectives, or expected outcomes for the course, grading policies, procedures, and any other information necessary for students to succeed.

Some instructors separate these various elements and call them "Course Information," "Course Requirements," "Grading," "Schedule," and so on. For the purposes of this chapter, however, we'll cover all these essentials with the term syllabus.

Although the details of course requirements, expected outcomes, schedule, grading, and procedures are staple elements of any course syllabus, they are perhaps even more important for an online class. Students tend to feel somewhat disoriented without the familiar first-day speeches from the instructor, and they may wonder if any of the same old rules will apply in this new online territory.

It's typical for first-time online instructors to include too little detail in their syllabi. One instructor we know changed nothing in his regular on-the-ground course syllabus except to add the words, "This course is delivered completely online." Unfortunately, students had a hard time even finding his syllabus, as he posted no welcome at the "entrance" to his online course, and then they were puzzled by his schedule, which still listed "class sessions" as once a week. Some students reasonably thought this phrase referred to online, real-time chat. Others wondered if the phrase meant that their asynchronous communications should be posted only once a week, on the particular day named in the schedule. As a result of this lack of clarity, the first week's discussion forum was dominated entirely by questions about where, when, and how to do the assignments, and the main topics for that week were nearly forgotten in the confusion.

Even after the instructor's hurried explanations, students continued to experience confusion about dates and times, procedures and grading. They could refer back to the first week's forum and search through the various discussion **threads** in which these questions had been raised, but they had no clear reference document to which they could turn. One student even had a grade dispute with the instructor that arose from an ambiguity in the syllabus. In the syllabus, the instructor had declared that all late assignments would be penalized at the rate of one-quarter grade point each day, but hadn't clearly specified that the due dates for assignments were based on the instructor's time zone, not the student's. Thus, the student claimed that, when he posted an assignment at 11:00 P.M. Pacific time, on the due date, he was unfairly penalized because the server on which the course was housed, located (like the instructor) on the East Coast of the United States, had recorded the time as 2:00 A.M. the following day. These examples, both serious and trivial, illustrate some of the problems that can ensue if online syllabi (and, naturally, subsequent directions) aren't thorough and detailed.

In blended courses clear directions are equally vital. It's important, for instance, to explain to students how the mixture of different venues will be integrated. Which course activities will take place in the on-campus classroom, which in the online classroom, and what's the sequence of procedures students should follow each week? Imagine that, before the face-to-face class meeting on Wednesday, you want students to read the online lecture and post a preliminary report, but you want them to wait until after the class meeting to take part in that week's online discussion. In many cases, they won't understand that sequence unless it's carefully explained to them.

There are three aspects of an online syllabus we want to emphasize in particular: the contract, the map, and the schedule.

● ● ● ● ●
The Contract

Increasingly, the syllabus has come to be the contract between students and instructor, laying out the terms of the class interaction—the expected responsibilities and duties, the grading criteria, the musts and don'ts of behavior. Let's took at some features of the contract that are especially important for an online course.

Class Participation and Grading Criteria

What's meant by "participation" in the online setting won't be obvious to students. Participation should be defined. For example, is it posting, that is, sending messages to the classroom discussion board? Or is it just logging on and reading (an activity revealed to an instructor only when course management software has the capacity to track students' movements online)? Perhaps participation includes taking part in an online group presentation or showing up for a real-time chat.

Important! *Whatever kind of participation you expect in your course, you should make that explicit in the syllabus.*

If you're going to count participation toward the final grade, you should define how that will be calculated. We recommend, in fact, that you always give a grade for active participation in the class, that is, for contributing to discussions and asking or answering questions. The plain fact is that if students aren't graded, the great majority won't actively participate. For a blended class, you will want to decide whether students are given participation grades for both face-to-face meetings as well as online participation, and how the grade for one, the other, or both should be divided up. Besides judging the quality of students' contributions in the class, you may want to set a minimum level for quantity of participation or require that a portion of postings be responses to classmates.

Another consideration in asynchronous courses is the degree of self-pacing allowed. Must students follow a chronological order of topics in their participation, or can they go back and respond to previous weeks' topics?

Can they complete assignments at different times during the course? The answers to these questions really depend on the nature of your course. For example, if your course has a set number of tasks, which can be completed at any time or in any order within the twelve weeks of the course, then you may not be concerned about students' skipping about or restarting conversations about previous weeks' topics.

Managing Student Expectations

The task of managing student expectations is very important in the online classroom. Some students enroll in an online course expecting it to be much easier than a regular course. Others imagine that the course will be something like independent study. Still others think the instructor should be available for twenty-four real-time hours a day. Your syllabus as well as your introductory comments can help manage such expectations, correct false impressions, and set the stage for the smooth unfolding of your course.

It's also helpful if your institution has a general student orientation (or at least a student handbook or web tutorial) that explains how the online course will work, how much student–instructor interaction can be expected, and so forth. If your institution doesn't have such an orientation, or your class has a unique approach that goes beyond the typical online offerings at your institution, you may need to supply some of this information in your own syllabus. Michele Pacansky-Brock, now Director of Online and Hybrid Support with California State University East Bay, previously taught an online Art Appreciation class for Sierra College that was unusually rich in its use of technology and multimedia. In her syllabus she cautioned students about that fact, "Important!!! This online class is image intensive. Due to the visual nature of the content of this class, you will regularly download large files containing high resolution images and movies…"

A continuing-education instructor we know, who has a busy professional practice, complained after a few weeks of her online class that students had "unrealistic expectations." When pressed to explain this remark, she commented that if she didn't reply to each and every student comment in the discussion forum or if she appeared not to be in the online classroom every day, she would receive plaintive email queries or even classroom postings inquiring about whether she had read a particular message. She further explained that she had expected students to work on their own during the first part of each week and only then to post their thoughts in the discussion forum. Unfortunately, neither her syllabus nor her introductory comments ever mentioned these teacher expectations.

This case shows that managing student expectations can also require an instructor to communicate his expectations for himself to the students. This type of problem can be handled by a simple statement in the syllabus to the effect that the instructor will look in frequently during the week but may not be in the classroom every day, or that students should work on the week's assignments during the first part of the week (say, Monday through Wednesday) and then post their responses later in the week (Thursday through Sunday).

For her blended class, Isabel Simões de Carvalho of Lisbon's Instituto Superior de Engenharia expressed her availability online in the following manner,

> *Your teacher will be online with all of you at least every two days and will provide feedback within 48 hours maximum. However, if you have an urgent subject that you need to discuss with your teacher ... then you should send an email to the instructor and in this case, do not forget to fill in the course name within the subject line.*

Other information of a "contractual" nature that you might want to incorporate in your syllabus includes the following:

- your policy on late assignments;
- whether due dates are calculated by your time zone or the student's (or the server's, as that might actually be in a third time zone);
- your availability for real-time chat appointments (which some call "virtual office hours");

■ overall specifications for writing assignments (Formal essay? Informal journal? Of how many total words? MLA or APA style?);

■ your institution's policy on plagiarism and cheating.

● ● ● ● ●

The Map

In this new territory of the online classroom, students will seize upon your syllabus as if it were a map. Students will want to know how to proceed and where everything is located. So, one of the first things you must do, whether through the syllabus or in an introductory message, is to explain the "geography" of the course.

In fact, if the syllabus isn't visible on the first level of the course, but instead can be arrived at only by one or two clicks of the mouse, then this introductory set of directions must be given in an announcement area or even delivered prior to the course, by email. For example, an announcement with explicit directions to the syllabus might say,

> Welcome, please click on the Class Information tab at the upper left hand corner of this webpage to find the links labeled syllabus, and weekly schedule. These will guide your work in this course, so I recommend that you print these sections out for handy reference. If you have any questions about these documents, please post a question in the Q&A forum portion of the discussion area.

What else does "explaining the geography" mean? If your course consists of various web pages plus a discussion forum, you'll need to let the students know where to find the component parts of the course and under what headings: "Lectures will be on the page whose link says 'Lectures,' and these are arranged by weeks." If the discussion forum, a blog, or other software is hosted on an outside site, students need to be told that this link will take them off the university server, or that they must use a password given to them, and so on. If you've created a discussion forum dedicated to casual communications and socializing for students, let them know that the area you have imaginatively labeled "Café Truckstop" is intended to be the online equivalent of a student lounge.

This is particularly important when using course management software that has its own unique and not easily customizable category headings or when your institution or department does not have a common classroom template. Students will need to know what you have stored behind each of the online classroom headings or where a particular link might lead.

While not essential, a narrated guide to the syllabus can be created by an instructor to reinforce the importance of the syllabus and to draw attention to it from the very first day of the course. You can use a simple series of screen shots within a PowerPoint narration or use video capture software as you click about the syllabus to point out the various sections of the document.

In a blended course that combines face-to-face and online components, it's essential that you specify where to do each activity. For example, in Isabel Carvalho's blended Energy Production and Management syllabus she clearly stated, "Besides the weekly face-to-face sessions, this course has an online learning environment. The face-to-face and online components are not independent but instead are considered to be complementary." She added,

> We will be together face-to-face 4.5 hours per week and I will expect you all to spend at least 2 hours a week online using the discussion forum, viewing and downloading course resources and materials, and interacting with your peers.

Such general statements are then further detailed in the class schedule.

Other procedural and "geographical" issues you might want to cover in the syllabus include these:

- the URL for your home page, the companion web site for a text, or other resources;
- where to access and how additional technology tools will be used in the class;

- how emailed assignments are to be labeled in the subject line;
- which file types you'll accept for attached documents (for instance, Microsoft Word, Rich Text Format, PowerPoint, Excel);
- any contact information for technical and administrative support;
- the proper sequence for accomplishing weekly activities and assignments (for example, do the exercises before taking the quiz, post a message in discussion before emailing the assignment).

●●●●●

The Schedule

The course should be laid out by weeks for students, because this is commonly the unit by which students gauge their own participation and work. If your class starts on a Wednesday, then Tuesday will become the last day of your week unless you state otherwise.

We recommend that you think in terms of subdivisions of two- or three-day spreads. For example, if you post your lecture on Monday, allow students through Wednesday to read and comment on it rather than asking them to do so by Tuesday. Students can be told to log on every single day, but it is perhaps wiser to take advantage of the asynchronous flexibility of the online environment. Assume that some students will log on and read on Monday night, some on Tuesday morning, and others at midnight. The Monday reader may return on Tuesday night to reread and post. The Tuesday reader may respond with comments at once. This scheduling flexibility is even more important for those who have students in different time zones or in foreign countries.

It's also good to gauge your students' access to computers and their probable work schedules. This goes back to what we discussed in earlier chapters. If your students are accessing the course web site from a campus lab, the dorms, or branch campus libraries, then they'll follow a different pattern than will typical working adults or continuing-education students, who may want to use the weekends to do most of the time-intensive assignments. A Monday or Tuesday due date for assignments will allow working adults to make the most of their study time out of the office.

A Checklist for Your Online Syllabus

Here, in summary form, is a checklist for creating your online syllabus. You needn't include all of these items (some may be more appropriate for your class than others), nor do you have to include them all in one document called a "syllabus." You can distribute this information among several documents if desired.

- course title, authors' and instructor's names, registration number, and term information; syllabus web pages should bear creation or "last revised" dates if the term date isn't included at the top;
- course instructor's contact information, indication of instructor availability in classroom, for "office hours" and private communications. Contact information for technical support;
- course description, perhaps the same as the description used for a course catalog listing, but probably more detailed; should list any prerequisites or special technical requirements for the course;
- course objectives or expected outcomes; what students can expect to learn by completion of the course;
- required texts or materials: any books or other materials, such as software, not made available in the course but required for the course;
- explanation of grading criteria and components of total grade: a list of all quizzes, exams, graded assignments, and forms of class participation, with grade percentages or points; criteria for a passing grade; policies on late assignments. More detailed instructions for assignments should be included elsewhere but at the very least, the outlines and due dates of each major assignment should be listed first in the syllabus;
- participation standard: minimum number of postings per week in discussion and any standards for quality of participation. If a rubric will be used to evaluate participation, reference to the rubric and where it may be found can be provided rather than including the whole rubric in the syllabus;

- explanation of course geography and procedures: how the online classroom is organized; how students should proceed each week for class activities; how to label assignments sent by email; where to post materials in the classroom; any special instructions;
- week-by-week schedule: topics, assignments, readings, quizzes, activities, and web resources for each week, with specific dates;
- any relevant institutional or program policies, procedures, or resources not mentioned above. These may be available as links to institutional web pages.

Sometimes it's difficult to anticipate every issue that may arise during the class and to include that in your syllabus. There's obviously a balance between readable brevity and a syllabus so voluminous as to be intimidating. Whatever you do not include in your initial documents can be referenced for further examination—for example, "Discussion Participation is worth 20% of the grade. See the rubric for participation posted in the Major Assignments section of the online classroom"—or may still be introduced by means of announcements, weekly emails sent to all students, or postings in an appropriate forum. You will also want to use these means to reinforce important elements of your syllabus as the course progresses.

Using Specific Dates

Instead of simply listing the course schedule for "Week One" and "Week Two," your schedule should include the specific dates for each unit, week, or topic area covered. This is particularly important for asynchronous courses in which students may be logging on at diverse times and days during the week. It's quite common for students to lose track of the weeks in the term when following an asynchronous online schedule. (And it's not unheard of for instructors to forget the dates, either!)

If you don't want to include dates on the main syllabus web pages because you want to reuse it for subsequent terms, and worry about making mistakes in updating it, then send students an email version of the syllabus or post a downloadable document version with the relevant dates inserted. Some course management software includes a calendar feature that you may use to reinforce the dates for each segment of the course.

Supplying Information More Than Once

It's easy to lose track of where and when something was said in threaded discussions or by email. When you give directions, it may not be possible for students to simply link back to them at a later date. For that reason, you should provide important instructions in more than one location. However, to maintain consistency and accuracy, you will either need to *repeat that information in full* or *refer students back to the complete directions* in the syllabus or other central document. Be very careful not to truncate your instructions for an assignment—in posting reminders, always refer students back to the most detailed version. For example, an announcement can note an upcoming due date for an assignment mentioned elsewhere, "Remember, papers are due this week and must be a minimum of 1000 words and based on at least three scholarly resources. Please review the assignment details for this paper found in the syllabus and under Major Projects." Or you may respond to a question in the discussion area, "John, your paper must be on one of the topics listed and Wikipedia may not be one of the three scholarly resources. Please refer to the Major Projects area for full details on topics and resources for this assignment."

Important! In an online environment, redundancy is often better than elegant succinctness.

Although students in some course management platforms may be able to use a search function to find your instructions, in most cases students will have to waste energy and time to sift through materials before they can locate that one crucial sentence of direction. Therefore, even if you intend to explain assignments and procedures later in the course, it's best to state them up front in the syllabus as well. Then, if your course is laid out entirely in web pages, make sure that each page permits students to link back easily to essential information in the syllabus.

●●●●●

Sample Syllabi: Online and Blended Course Versions

The following is a composite syllabus based on courses in Modern China taught by Susan Ko at a variety of institutions. The first is a syllabus for the fully online version, followed by one representing a blended version of the same course. Both are designed as ten-week courses, but only the first five weeks of the course appear in the schedule.

Modern China: History and Culture

HISTORY 415

Delivered online, SomeUniversity Spring term, **** year

Course Description

This online course provides a survey approach to the history and culture of China in the modern period, from the mid-19th century through the year 2000.

Contacts and Communications

Instructor: Dr. Susan Ko, sko@someuniversity.edu

See my instructor's bio in the classroom link under my name. Please contact me via the email address above or feel free to use the classroom instant message (IM) tool when you see me among the names of those currently logged in.

I will log on to the classroom nearly every day and the discussion forum is generally the best place to ask most questions. But if you need to contact me on an individual basis, please use email and I will try to reply within 24 hours. Your communication is important to me! To ensure that I see your message among my email, please use the class name and number HIST 415 in your subject line. For those of you halfway across the world from the instructor's eastern US location, given the time differences you may have to allow up to 36 hours for a "prompt reply."

Technical support is available 24/7 by contacting tech24@7help.edu or calling 1-800-TECHELP.

Your Online Classroom and Procedures

Each class week begins on Monday and ends on Sunday.
Although all students will have taken the software orientation, at any point you may review the course management software features by clicking on the Guide link.

The **Announcements** area of the classroom that you see each time you log in will be used on at least a weekly basis to post updates and comments on class matters. The instructor will also email the class to remind students of important due dates. (If you prefer to receive text message versions of these emails, please let the instructor know by following the instructions posted in the classroom.)

The **Course Materials** area, arranged in folders by week, houses the content for the course. All materials for the course are posted and can be reviewed from the start of the class. There is also a folder within Course Materials labeled **Detailed Assignment Instructions** that provides full information, criteria, rubrics, and samples for completing each assignment.

The **Discussion area** contains at least one discussion forum for each week of the course. Each discussion forum will be opened for posting on the Saturday before each new week begins. There is a forum labeled "Student Lounge" for casual conversations as well as a general "Q&A" forum where questions about class requirements or other questions that do not fit into a weekly discussion may be asked.

The **Assignment Dropbox** is the place to submit individual assignments unless otherwise indicated in assignment instructions.

Remember that our classroom server is set to US Eastern time. Therefore all due dates are noted as of US Eastern time. Use the World Time Clock link available in the classroom to convert all times and dates.

Introduction

This ten-week course provides a general survey of Chinese history and culture in the modern period, from the Qing dynastic period through the founding of the People's Republic and post-Mao China through 2000. We will try to trace the continuing themes as well as changing conditions that mark China's tumultuous modern history.

This course is conducted completely online. To do your best in this course, it is recommended that you print out this syllabus to keep as a reference, log on frequently (at least 3–4 times a week) to the online classroom and keep up with all assigned readings and web work.

Course Objectives

- Describe the major cultural, political, and social elements of traditional China.
- Trace recurring themes and concepts in Chinese history.
- Identify the major historical figures and events that have shaped modern Chinese history.
- Analyze the underlying themes and issues in the modernization process, including those in the economic, political, and social spheres.
- Differentiate the characteristics of the Chinese state in the Mao and post-Mao era.
- Demonstrate an appreciation for Chinese arts or literature as a reflection of Chinese society and values in different historical periods.

Course Textbook and Materials

Main textbook: J. Spence, *The Search for Modern China*, 2nd edition only. See the link to **Buy Textbooks** in the classroom if you have not already obtained your book or check on Amazon. com for used copies.

If you are not already familiar with Chinese names and their pronunciation, you may find that in the beginning, you may have a little trouble remembering and identifying the names of people, places, and events.

I recommend that you take notes while you read and refer often to the Glossary contained at the end of the textbook. When referring to Chinese names, places, and events, I will try to include short identifications whenever possible. If you are ever in doubt about what I am referring to in my commentary or in the conference discussions, please don't hesitate to ask!

We will be using many web resource readings as well as periodical articles available through our electronic reserves of the library. The latter are labeled Library Electronic Reserve Readings and are also found under Course Materials for the week indicated. The instructor will also introduce numerous multimedia resources from the Web, especially during the last half of the course. (There will be alternative assignments for those who are unable to access the multimedia resources.)

Finally, the instructor will provide short commentary on a weekly basis to help elucidate the issues from our readings and provide additional perspectives. These commentaries are posted in the Course Materials area of our classroom.

Grading Information

Grades are based on a scale of 100 points and are distributed among major assignments as follows:

- Participation on a weekly basis: 30 points
- Group summary and question based on reading: 10 points for group work, 5 for individual contribution
- Short essay paper: 10 points
- Proctored exam: 25 points
- Final analytic paper or project: 20 points
- Grading scale:
  - A: 90–100
  - B: 80–89
  - C: 70–79
  - D: 60–69
  - F: 59 points or below

Timelines

Participation in discussions must be completed within the week assigned.

Other assignments are due according to the posted dates and as described in instructions, either submitted via the assignment Dropbox or posted in a designated discussion forum.

Unless otherwise noted, grades will be posted in the Gradebook no later than the end of the week following the due date of the assignment.

This university maintains a strict academic integrity policy. Please follow <u>this link</u> to read the policy related to plagiarism.

Assignment Descriptions

1. Participation

Students are expected to participate by responding to the instructor's questions as well as to ask questions or comment on the responses of their classmates. A good question is as valuable as a comment. See the Participation Rubric posted under Course Materials to understand grading criteria and expectations. There are ten graded weeks of participation.

2. Group summary and question based on reading

Each student will be assigned to a group by the beginning of the third week of class and group postings will begin in Week 5. You will work within groups of four or five to prepare a weekly summary ending in one or more discussion questions based on one of the weekly chapter reading assignments from the Spence text. The group will post the summary as pasted-in text and discussion question(s) in the weekly conference, creating a thread with the subject line, *Reading Summary, Chapter* ___. The group members will then be in charge of conducting the discussion.

Up to **ten points** will be awarded based on the criteria posted under "Group Summary" in the Course Materials, Detailed Assignments Instructions folder. This also includes some tips for organizing your group.

The summary and question must be posted in the online classroom no later than each Wednesday of the week assigned to your group. This will allow for sufficient discussion time. You will receive a grade of up to **five points** for your individual contribution. This grade will be based on the instructor's observation as well as a peer evaluation. See under Course Materials for the Peer Evaluation Rubric. You will be asked to evaluate yourself as well as your peers.

3. Short essay paper

This is a short essay, 2–4 pages in length, due at the end of week 4, February 20 of this course. Submit your assignment through the Dropbox and label the file **Firstinitial+Lastname+ShortE**.

The choice of topic questions and some guidelines are posted under the Course Materials area, Detailed Assignments Instructions folder. The style of this paper will be very much like the type of essay questions you will encounter in the proctored final exam.

4. Proctored exam

There is a mandatory proctored exam that must be completed no later than April 23. To schedule your proctored exam with an approved proctor near you, see the classroom link for "Exam Appointments."

Our exam will be short-essay and identification questions. Short-essay questions will ask you to reflect on what we have learned and draw connections between different events, themes, and facts. Identification questions require a short paragraph to explain the who, what, when, or importance of something we have studied. My own philosophy is that students shouldn't be surprised or "tricked" by what they encounter on the exam—if you have paid attention and kept up with your reading, discussion, and assignments, the questions should not be unexpected.

5. Final analytic paper or project

This assignment is an analysis of a continuing issue or theme that you have followed since the beginning of the course. For example, you may want to concentrate on economic development in China, the status of women, local officials versus central party control, China's relationships with its neighbors in East Asia, role of intellectuals and artists, etc. A full list of possible topics and issues as well as format and other requirements is contained under the detailed instructions for this assignment in Course Materials. This paper is due the end of the 9th week of this class but you must submit your topic for approval at the end of Week 5. There is a multimedia option for those students who may prefer to work in audio or video. See detailed instructions under Course Materials, Detailed Assignments Instructions folder for more information. Once you have submitted your project or paper, you are invited to share it online with your classmates during Week 10.

Other Resources

Need Some Review of Skills or Assistance?

For help in navigating the various types of writing assignments, follow the link to the Writing tutorial center in the resource list at the top right of the online classroom.

See the links in the classroom to **Library** and **Student Advising** for additional support if needed.

Schedule

Week 1, January 24–January 30

Traditional China under the Qing

Readings:

- Spence, Chapter 3, bottom page 53–top page 69, Chapters 5 and 6, pp. 96–137
- Instructor commentary under Course Materials for Week 1
- Visit web resources indicated under Course Materials for Week 1

Discussion forum:

Introduce yourself in the Introductions forum, then participate in Week 1 discussion forum.

Week 2, January 31–February 6

China's Dual Crises, External and Internal

Readings:

- Spence, Chapters 7 and 8, pp. 141–191, and pp. 202–214
- Instructor commentary for week 2

See list of topic questions for Short Essay assignment under Course Materials, Detailed Assignment Instructions folder.

Participate in Week 2 discussion forum.

Week 3, February 7–February 13

The End of Dynastic China

Readings:

- Spence, Chapters 10 and 11, 215–263
- Instructor commentary for Week 3
- Library electronic reserve reading #1

Participate in Week 3 discussion forum.

Locate and check in with your group in the designated Group area.

Week 4, February 14–February 20

The New Chinese Republic

Readings:

- Spence, Chapters 12 and 13, pp. 267–313
- Instructor commentary for Week 4
- Visit web resources for this week

Participate in Week 4 discussion forum.

Short essay due end of this week, via Dropbox. Label the file Firstinitial+Lastname+ShortE.

Week 5, February 21–27

Union and Disunion

Readings:

Topics under Course Content

- Spence, Chapters 14, pp. 314–341 and Chapter 15, pp. 342–374
- Instructor commentary for Week 5
- Library electronic reserve reading #2

Participate in Week 5 conference discussion. Group presentations begin.

Submit your final paper/project topic choice to instructor via email for approval by the end of this week.

Put HIST 415 and Final Topic in the subject line of your email.

Modern China: History and Culture

HISTORY 415

Delivered in blended format, SomeUniversity Spring term, ****
year

Contacts

Instructor: Dr. Susan Ko, sko@someuniversity.edu

Office hours on campus: Tuesdays, 3–5 p.m., Room 210 of Miller Building. Phone: 321-568-3987
Please contact the instructor via the email address above, or by phone, or feel free to use the online classroom instant message feature when you see the instructor among the names of those currently logged in to our online classroom.

The instructor will log on to the online classroom nearly every day, whether or not the class is meeting face-to-face in a particular week. The discussion forum is generally the best place to ask most questions. But if you need to contact me on an individual basis, please use email and I will try to reply within 24 hours. Your communication is important to me! To ensure that I see your message among my email, please use the class name and number HIST 415 in your subject line.

Technical support is available 24/7 by contacting tech24@7help.edu or calling 1-800-TECHELP.

Course Description

A survey approach to the history and culture of China in the modern period, from the mid nineteenth century through the year 2000.

Introduction

This is a **blended** course. That means we will meet face-to-face every other week and for the last class meeting in Week 10, but that we will only meet online during the other weeks. Attendance at the face-to-face meetings and participation in all online activities is required. You will find that the online and face-to-face elements of this course are interdependent and integrated. Online participation is required every week – you will be expected to go online, preferably within 72 hours of a face-to-face meeting, to continue discussion or complete other activities.

The dates during which we meet face to face are clearly indicated in bold font on the syllabus schedule.

This course provides a general survey of Chinese history and culture in the modern period, from the Qing dynastic period through the founding of the People's Republic and post-Mao China through 2000. We will try to trace the continuing themes as well as changing conditions that mark China's tumultuous modern history.

Course Objectives

- Describe the major cultural, political, and social elements of traditional China.
- Trace recurring themes and concepts in Chinese history.
- Identify the major historical figures and events that have shaped modern Chinese history.
- Analyze the underlying themes and issues in the modernization process, including those in the economic, political, and social spheres.
- Differentiate the characteristics of the Chinese state in the Mao and post-Mao eras.
- Demonstrate an appreciation for Chinese arts or literature as a reflection of Chinese society and values in different historical periods.

Information and Procedures

Each class week begins online on Monday and ends on Sunday. Our face-to-face on-campus meetings all take place on **Tuesday evenings, 6:30–9:30 p.m. in the Seely Center, room**

2009. The Center is equipped with wifi and you are welcome to bring your laptop to class.

Face-to-face meetings will be a combination of instructor lecture, discussion, and student presentations. If you miss a face-to-face meeting you will be required to do additional makeup work online.

Online Classroom

A brief overview of the online classroom will be given at the first class meeting. At any point you may review the course management software features by clicking on the **Guide** link. Here is a quick guide:

The **Announcements** area of the classroom that you see each time you log in will be used on at least a weekly basis to post updates and comments on class matters. The instructor will also email the class to remind students of important due dates. (If you prefer to receive text message versions of these emails, please let the instructor know by following the instructions posted in the classroom.)

The **Course Materials** area, arranged in folders by week, houses the content for the course. All materials for the course are posted and can be reviewed from the start of the class. There is also a folder labeled **Detailed Assignment Instructions** that provides full information, criteria, rubrics, and samples for completing each assignment. As noted below, read the instructor commentary before attending the face-to-face class.

The **Discussion** area contains at least one discussion forum for each week of the course, whether or not we are meeting face-to-face in a particular week. Each discussion forum will be opened on the Saturday before each new week begins. There is a forum labeled "Student Lounge" for casual conversations as well as a general "Q&A" forum where questions about class requirements or other questions that do not fit into a weekly discussion may be asked.

Important: Do not wait till the class meets face-to-face to ask a question! Post it online!

The **Assignment Dropbox** is the place to submit individual assignments unless otherwise indicated in assignment instructions. *Please do not bring assignments to the face-to-face class meetings to hand in to the instructor.*

Course Textbook and Materials

Main text: J. Spence, *The Search for Modern China*, 2nd edition only. See the link to **Buy Textbooks** in the classroom if you have not already obtained your book, or check on Amazon.com for used copies.

If you are not already familiar with Chinese names and their pronunciation, you may find that in the beginning, you may have a little trouble remembering and identifying the names of people, places, and events.

I recommend that you take notes while you read and refer often to the Glossary contained at the end of the textbook. When referring to Chinese names, places, and events, I will try to include short identifications whenever possible. If you are ever in doubt about what I am referring to in my commentary or in the conference discussions, please don't hesitate to ask!

We will be using many web resource readings as well as periodical articles available through our electronic reserves of the library. The instructor will also introduce numerous multimedia resources from the Web, especially during the last half of the course. If you are unable to access the multimedia resources from home, you are expected to use the campus labs to complete this work.

Finally, the instructor will provide short commentary on a weekly basis to help elucidate the issues from our readings and provide additional perspectives. These commentaries are posted in the Course Materials area of our classroom. During weeks that the class meets face to face, it is recommended that you read the instructor commentary **before** coming to class.

Grading Information

Grades are based on a scale of 100 points and are distributed among major assignments as follows:

- Participation on a weekly basis: 30 points
- Group summary and question based on reading: 10 points for group work, 5 for individual contribution
- Short essay paper: 10 points
- Proctored exam: 25 points

- Final analytic paper: 20 points
- Grading scale:
    - A: 90–100
    - B: 80–89
    - C: 70–79
    - D: 60–69
    - F: 59 points or below

Timeliness

Participation in online discussions must be completed within the week assigned.

Other assignments are due according to the posted dates and as described in instructions, either submitted via the assignment dropbox or posted in a designated discussion forum.

Unless otherwise noted, grades will be posted in the online gradebook no later than the end of the week following the due date of the assignment. This university maintains a strict academic integrity policy. Please follow this link to read the policy related to plagiarism.

Assignment Descriptions

1. Participation

Students are expected to participate by responding to the instructor's questions as well as to ask questions or comment on the responses of their classmates in the online classroom. A good question is as valued as a comment. See the Participation Rubric posted under Course Materials to understand grading criteria and expectations.

Additionally, during weeks in which we meet face to face, you may receive credit for participation in either the face-to-face class and/or the online classroom. This is detailed in the Participation rubric.

2. Group presentation and facilitated discussion

Each student will be assigned to a group during the face-to-face class meeting of the third week of class and will be able to hold their first organizational meeting face to face. Students will work online in the Groups area to prepare a five-minute presentation and at least three discussion questions based on an assigned topic from one of the weekly chapter readings from the Spence text, a Library reserved reading, or a web resource site. The group will present and facilitate a discussion (with help from the instructor) during a 15-minute period at each face-to-face meeting, starting with Week five.

Up to **10 points** will be awarded to each group for their live presentation, facilitation of discussion, and online preparation based on the criteria posted under "Group Summary" in Course Materials which also includes some tips for organizing your group. You will also receive a grade of up to 5 points for your individual contribution. This grade will be based on the instructor's observation of your preparatory work online, the presentation and discussion on-campus, as well as a peer evaluation. See under Course Materials for the peer-evaluation rubric. You will be asked to evaluate yourself as well as your group peers.

3. Short essay paper

This is a short essay, 2–4 pages in length, due at the end of Week 4, February 20, of this course. Submit your assignment via the Dropbox and label the file **Firstinitial+Lastname+ShortE**.

The choice of topic questions and some guidelines are posted under the Course Materials, Detailed Assignment Instructions folder. The style of this paper will be very much like the type of essay questions you will encounter in the proctored final exam.

4. Proctored exam

In Week 11 there is a mandatory proctored exam on campus in our regular meeting room. See the university website in February for the examination schedule for this course.

Our exam will be short essay and identification questions. Short essay questions will ask you to reflect on what we have learned and draw connections between different events, themes, and facts. Identification questions require a short paragraph to explain the who, what, when, or importance of something we have studied. My own philosophy is that students shouldn't be surprised or "tricked" by what they encounter on the exam—if you have paid attention and kept up with your reading, discussion, and assignments, the questions should not be unexpected.

5. Final analytic paper/project

This paper is an analysis of a continuing issue or theme that you have followed since the beginning of the course. For example, you may want to concentrate on economic development in China, the status of women, local officials versus central party control, China's relationships with its neighbors in East Asia, role of intellectuals and artists, etc. A full list of possible topics and issues as well as format and other requirements is contained under the detailed instructions for this assignment in Course Materials. This paper is due at the end of the ninth week, April 10, of this class but you must submit your topic for approval by the end of Week 4. Final projects will be shared with the class at the last face-to-face meeting. There is a multimedia option for those students who prefer to work in audio or video. See detailed instructions for more information.

Other Resources

Need some review of skills or assistance?

For help in navigating the various types of writing assignments, follow the link to the Writing Tutorial Center in the resource list at the top right of the online classroom.

See the links in the online classroom to **Library** and **Student Advising** for additional support if needed.

Schedule

Week 1, January 24–January 30

Face-to-face class meeting, January 25

Traditional China under the Qing

Readings:

- Spence, Chapter 3, bottom page 53–top page 69, Chapters 5 and 6, pp. 96–137
- Instructor commentary under Course Materials for Week 1
- Visit web resources indicated under Course Materials for Week 1

In-class overview of online classroom.

Online Discussion forum:

Introduce yourself in the Introductions forum, then participate in Week 1 discussions after the January 25 meeting, with your first posting by January 28.

Week 2, January 31–February 6

China's Dual Crises, External and Internal

Readings:

■ Spence, Chapters 7 and 8, pp. 141–191 and 202–214

■ Instructor's commentary for Week 2

Participate in Week 2 discussion online.

See list of topic questions for Short Essay assignment under Course Materials.

Week 3, February 7–February 13

Face-to-face class meeting, February 8

The End of Dynastic China

Readings:

■ Spence, Chapters 10 and 11, pp. 215–263

■ Instructor's commentary for Week 3

Participate in Week 3 discussion online after February 8 with your first posting by February 11.

Group work: On February 8th, assemble with your group, receive your topic and date for presenting.

Week 4, February 14–February 20

The New Chinese Republic

Readings:

■ Spence, Chapters 12 and 13, pp. 267–313

■ Instructor's commentary for Week 4

■ Visit web resources for this week

Participate in Week 4 discussion online.

Short essay due end of this week, via Dropbox. Label the file Firstinitial+Lastname+ShortE.

Week 5, February 21–27

Face-to-face class meeting, February 22

Union and Disunion

Readings:

- Spence, Chapters 14, pp. 314–341 and Chapter 15, pp. 342–374
- Instructor commentary for Week 5

Groups 1 and 2 present and help lead discussion on February 22.

Participate in Week 5 discussion online after February 22, with your first posting by February 25.

Submit your final topic choice to instructor via email for approval by the end of this week. Put HIST 415 and Final Topic in the subject line.

6

•••••

Building an Online Classroom

Now that you've done the necessary design, planning, and development work on your course and fleshed out your syllabus, it's time to actually build your course.

This means that it's time to put your work online—compose web pages, set up discussions, post assignments, create quizzes—in short, start learning about and working with the software you will be using to run the class.

As you move from the planning to the implementation stage, you may find that some of the features you planned to incorporate don't work as well as you thought they would. You may also find a few functions in your software that you didn't know existed. The fact is that this stage of preparation involves a bit of trial and error. As you experiment with sample units to create a prototype for your course, you will soon learn how to get the most out of whatever course management system or other software structure you are working in—whether it be a fully developed and integrated set of tools or some combination of web pages, discussion forum, and online testing. In fact, as you become more familiar with the particular software environment you will be using, you may find that you will want to go back and revise your course plan to reflect the opportunities or limitations that you have discovered.

In this chapter we will be discussing the various types of functions and features available in today's software and how best to exploit them. In doing this, we will use examples from a variety of different existing software platforms, both course management or learning management systems (CMS or LMS) as well as some of the standalone types of Web 2.0 tools. The good news is that those instructors whose institutions do not have a course management system will have little problem finding free tools and remote servers on which to set up their online and blended classrooms. And even those who have a course management system available may choose to supplement what they do with the use of some of these free tools. As you examine the features of course management systems or tools, be aware that this is a rapidly changing field. When we wrote the first two editions of our book, there was intense competition among many different course management systems. Since that time, there have been many acquisitions, consolidations, as well as new CMS programs, but there have also emerged more open-source systems like Moodle and Sakai and a wildly proliferating set of Web 2.0 tools that can be used for online education. Our descriptions of particular features for software correspond to the versions existing at the time of this writing. Our purpose is not to tout one software platform or tool over another, but to show (1) the opportunities presented by certain types of features and (2) how you can adapt and implement your favored teaching strategies.

This is not to say that a particular software or course management system may not be better suited to your pedagogical needs than another. But the trend in recent years is for an institution to be able to swap out one tool for another while still using the basic features of a course management system. For example, an institution might be able to substitute a different chat or discussion board for the one that comes with the system—either by having its own technical staff write a program or adopting a tool from a software vendor whose products are designed to be compatible with a particular system. This new flexibility may make it easier for your institution to find the right mix it needs for its online classrooms. However, we do recognize that many instructors will not have the final say (or may not have any say at all) about which system or tools are chosen for the institution, so our intention is to help you make the most of whatever you have. If you would like to compare and track the changes and innovations in software platforms, we suggest you visit the web site EduTools (www.edutools.info/course), now operated by the organization WCET (Western Cooperative for Educational Telecommunications) which builds on a resource originally created by Bruce Landon of Douglas College, New Westminster, British Columbia. This site is continually being updated as new versions of software debut; in addition to comparison and review charts, it provides links to the web sites of the different software platforms.

So, by all means take advantage of any special features afforded by your software system, but don't feel that your system must dictate your choice of teaching methods and approaches. Generally, if you have the desire to include a particular kind of activity, you can find a way to implement it in almost any system.

If you were fortunate enough to receive special training on the software system you are going to use, you probably learned some tips and techniques for exploiting that system. If you haven't received this type of training, we recommend that you join a user's group or mailing list, or find another online resource devoted to users of that software. You can also share information and strategies informally with colleagues at your institution who may already have had some experience with the system. You may discover that a colleague at your own institution—or at one half a world away—has found a new approach to solving the same problems that you face.

●●●●●

Dividing up and Organizing Your Material and Activities

In building your course, no matter which system you use, you will have to make decisions about organizing and dividing your materials.

For example, in terms of your overall organization, do you want to divide the course into units according to week or topic or some combination of both? As mentioned above, your ability to receive tracking reports might be one consideration. Other, more obvious factors include how many topics you will cover each week, how large your documents or media files are, and whether the portions you create will be easy to digest (and, if necessary, download) for your students.

Another basic question must be whether you want all presentation materials to be housed in areas apart from discussion and conferencing areas and, if so, what coordination you wish to have between these areas. For example, if you present a "lecture" in Unit 1, do you want to create a discussion forum that will match it and provide direct reference to it? Or do you want to post minilectures directly in the discussion forum thread, culminating in questions to which students must respond?

Similarly, do you want web resource links to be woven in among your assignments, discussions, and lecture materials, or do you want to house these in a separate area (when available)? How many assignments are to be delivered to you alone, and how many are to be shared with the class as a whole? Do you want students to work in groups? If so, you need to give them a space to work as a team and a place to present their work to the entire class as well if desired.

Important! *The overall guideline here is to create or make use of a space for every activity you devise.*

Timing of Access

Before you actually begin to build your course, find out exactly when students will first be able to access your classroom and whether they will have access to the entire course at that time. For example, will they be able to enter the course management software environment two days or even two weeks before the class officially starts? At that point, will they have access to an outer web page but not to the discussion area, or to the announcements and syllabus only?

Also, find out if your software allows you to work on a section of the course without making it available for students to see. Some systems allow you to set specific dates for the release of a section or document or simply to toggle an on/off switch to determine the availability of a specific area. If you have no way to control the timing of your students' access, you should consider laying out and arranging your course on paper or in a practice course shell, and making all changes in your word-processed and HTML documents prior to posting the final form.

This will prevent students from becoming confused if you need to revise your materials at the last minute. However, do post at least an announcement or syllabus for students to access on the first possible day, and remember to give detailed guidance about how and where to proceed. There's nothing more discouraging to students than entering an empty, unattended online classroom!

How much of your course materials should you actually make available to students at one time? This is a tough question to answer, because there is no one response that will suit all teaching situations and approaches. If you post all the presentation materials for all the weeks of your course so that students can review all content, this does offer two advantages:

1. Students can gain a more detailed understanding of what the course involves.
2. If they choose, students can work ahead.

The disadvantages are that, in an asynchronous class, even one with defined start and stop dates, you may be detracting from the sense that the class as a whole moves and learns together. If you also allow students to post in discussion forums as many as two or three weeks ahead, you further lose the sense of class cohesiveness. You may also prevent yourself from adapting to the class's needs by revising materials. You may find, too, that simultaneously keeping an eye on two, three, or four discussion forums adds significantly to your workload.

Often, a good compromise is to restrict the advance posting of materials and the opening of new discussion forums to no more than one or two weeks ahead of the time when you expect the class as a whole to be ready for them. Or allow students to see all materials and discussion questions, but if your system permits you to do so, set the discussions to read-only status.

Pacing Considerations

A final important consideration is the method of pacing your students in your course. Everything takes longer online. Even if your students all enjoy high-speed Internet access, you will still find that you must factor in the "click time"—the time it takes to open and close documents, to download and access documents and web pages, and to perform special tasks such as accessing large graphics, or **streaming media** and animations. If the class is a very active one, or one in which there are twenty-five students or more, it will take time for your students to pick through the postings that accrue each week.

Even though you want your course to be as rigorous as its on-the-ground equivalent, you don't want to overload students with materials and tasks for which the payoff isn't worth the time expended. Leave students enough time to delve deeply into the material. Presumably, you will already have factored in these considerations when composing your online syllabus. However, these matters often become more apparent once you begin to lay out the course within your course management software or web pages. In that case, don't be afraid to go back and make adjustments to your syllabus.

Presumably, if you have already done a particular activity in a previous face-to-face class, you will have some idea of the minimum amount of time needed to perform it. Then you need to factor in the additional time that might be needed to do the activity online. For example, students in a face-to-face class working in a group may be able to make the first group determinations in a few hours. Online, you will want to consider the asynchronous access and may allow two days for the back and forth it may take for all to register their opinions.

If you are unsure how long it will take for students to complete an assignment that involves online work, we suggest that you try out a discrete portion of it and time yourself. For example, if you want to ask students to visit a particular Web resource with a view to answering certain questions and then to write a report based on the visit, you can surely time yourself as you undertake each step of the visit and jot down responses to the questions. Given that you probably have more expertise or are more familiar with the resource than your students, you can factor in the additional time you think students will need to achieve the same results. In the end, beyond finding out whether you have calculated a correct estimate of the time needed for students to do this, you may also discover that your instructions should be revised for greater clarity!

If you have little experience with online discussion, you might ask to visit a colleague's class and time yourself on how long it takes you to read through and compose a meaningful response based on that class's weekly participation requirements.

Again, while you may have already factored in some of these considerations when composing your online syllabus, matters often become more apparent once you begin to actually lay out the course within your course management software or web pages. If you discover that your estimates were wrong, don't be afraid to go back and make adjustments to your syllabus.

Now let's look at some of the structures, features, and built-in functions that are available in course management systems and Web 2.0 tools.

Presentation Areas

Presentation areas are where you deliver your basic course content, lectures, and so forth. Web pages are the most obvious presentation format.

If you are using course management software, you will find that in some systems, presentation is clearly defined and set apart from other functions, while in other systems, multiple areas can be made to serve the presentation function. The presentation areas allow one to type or paste in text and to **upload** text and HTML files, PowerPoint slide shows, and so on, into what is, in effect, a document storage area. This storage area, which can be filled by instructors only, is entirely separate from the discussion forum and other areas where students can post or upload documents.

Course management software systems are increasingly sophisticated and most now offer the option of built-in editors or plug-ins that permit elaborate formatting and conversion to HTML without your having to know code. New versions of course management software also allow for the creation of course templates for uploading content. These make it easy to create sequenced learning content, and both templates and sequences are often able to be reused and replicated in subsequent classes. Free web site services like Google sites offer a good substitute for a CMS to present content, with the ability to upload many different types of files. For the many readers of this book who are not native English speakers, Google sites also support more than eighty different languages.

If, however, you are using software which has a limited number of areas in which you can present content, you may need to designate certain portions by name to serve as your presentation spaces. You might set these off by using special titles, bold text, or some other distinguishing marks, depending on what your software system permits. For example, if you wish to post materials in a discussion area, you might designate one forum for "Syllabus," another for "Lectures," and so on.

If you do not have course management software, the free web sites, as well as the wiki and blogging software highlighted in Chapter 1, can provide an adequate solution for your needs. All allow for copy-and-paste methods and include built-in formatting and templates designed to set your content off to best advantage. Some will allow you to set up discussions related to your content presentation.

Perhaps you want to present content via audio and/or video. Many course management systems will allow you to upload such content for presentation. In some cases, you may need to ask your technology staff to upload it for you. Perhaps your institution will allow you to upload a video lecture or demonstration to a site like YouTube and then you can simply provide a link to the video. Some free web sites, blogs, or wikis will also allow for the uploading of multimedia content.

If video is crucial to communicating your presentations, your first step is probably to contact your instructional technology or multimedia staff resources. It may be that video is easily inserted into your course management system or is hosted on a special institutional server. There may also be staff who can help you create your video. Many institutions now maintain a channel on YouTube to broadcast their video content.

However, instructors who have no support at all for creating or hosting video materials are increasingly able to find ways to do this on their own. Chapter 9 discusses some of the available methods for accomplishing this.

Podcasting has become a very popular option in recent years as everyone from politicians to radio broadcasters to self-styled experts on every subject have offered audio commentary and made it available to an audience who can subscribe to receive automatic downloads of these commentaries. Many educators have taken this approach to offering weekly lectures and commentary to their students who can download such materials to their mobile players for listening off-campus. Some course management software has built in podcasting tools, enabling instructors (and/or students) to easily create and publish such presentations. A growing number of institutions use iTunes U as a repository for their instructors' podcasts. For those who do not have such tools at their institutions, there are a variety of free or inexpensive services like Gcast (www.gcast.com) that also make the production and hosting of podcasts very user friendly, some services even allow allowing for production via phone (not always free) as well as uploading of files already created through a free recording program like Audacity.

Announcement Areas

Some systems have a marked-off announcement area, that is, a special form of presentation area that students see as they enter the online classroom. The announcement may appear on the main entrance page or it may simply be a link to a document storage area that can be named by the instructor and accessed by students.

For the instructor, the announcement area offers a quick method of typing in announcements and updates for the course. Even if it is set up as a separate document storage area, students will know to consult it each time they enter the classroom. If you don't have a course management system, a free web site, like Google sites, allows one to quickly make an announcement area set off from the rest of the web page, with formatting menus and other rich features already built in.

You can think of the announcement area as being like standing at the front of the room in a face-to-face classroom. Online, this is the stage upon which you call the class to attention, remind, cajole, encourage, and update students. Email, text messaging, and other communications may reinforce but cannot really replace classroom announcements. Therefore, plan to make full and regular use of this area if it is built into your software or to rig up an equivalent area in an online classroom to serve this function.

Syllabus and Schedule Areas

Depending on your software, you can post a syllabus and schedule in a document storage area, or you can create separate web pages for this purpose.

Important! *Make your syllabus available in a downloadable or easily printable document, because this is the "map" students will follow in your course.*

This means that, if you use graphics in your syllabus or if the syllabus is divided up into a group of hyperlinked web pages, you should also make it available in a text-only, scrollable document. This will permit students to print it out readily.

In some course management software, the syllabus area also serves as the chief organizing tool, the "home page" or outline for the course content. For example, each item on the syllabus may become a clickable link to respective sections of course material. If you have this sort of arrangement, make sure your headings accurately indicate the topics or content to which they provide links.

Discussion Forums

We will cover the management and facilitation of asynchronous and synchronous discussions in Chapter 11. Here, we will note that the asynchronous discussion areas in various software programs are structured in different ways, have different options for student use, and allow messages to be viewed or sorted in different ways.

Structure of Discussion Areas

Many systems have a hierarchical architecture. Forums, conference folders, or message groups form the highest level, with each containing a number of subordinate threads that together make up the discussion. In this case, it is important to decide how you want to divide up your forums—by week, by topic, by unit, or by some combination of categories. For example, you may decide not only to have weekly forums but also to create a forum that can serve as an open discussion or socializing area, a sort of "student lounge."

Take note of the arrangement of threads and responses within the system you are using. Within the limitations of a particular discussion software, the way you structure your discussion forums will probably affect your decisions about the number of topics you wish to introduce each week, whether to break down larger topics, and the instructions you need to give students about procedures.

User Options

In some discussion software, both students and instructors may initiate new topics; in other systems, only instructors may start new topic threads. Still other platforms may allow the instructor to set the options, using a switch that enables or prevents students from starting new topics.

Other user options in some systems include being able to add HTML files, use attachments, and change the subject line without having to create a new thread. Another user option you will need to investigate is whether or not students can edit or delete the messages they have posted and whether the instructor can intervene to do the same for student postings or their own. In some cases, a message may only be edited if a reply has not been posted to the message. In other cases, edits may be made but the system will indicate that an edit has been made on a certain date.

A feature that allows students to anonymously "rate" (for example, awarding a number of stars to a posting) and/or comment on discussion items of their peers has increasingly become available in many course management systems.

Therefore be sure to familiarize yourself with user options in discussion software. As indicated above, these may influence the design of course activities, facilitation of discussion, as well as record-keeping and even strategies for handling student netiquette problems!

Viewing and Sorting of Messages

How are conversations viewed in your software? Do the messages have to be opened and shut one at a time in order to be read? Is it possible to open and read all messages in a linear fashion, one following the other in a scrollable page? Many systems have moved to a dual capability, allowing conversations to be viewed as both individual messages in threads and continuous conversations.

Many systems also allow multiple ways for users to sort messages for their own viewing. For example, messages may be sorted by date, by topic, or according to the people who posted them. (This has some utility for classroom management, as explained in Chapter 11.) Some systems such as Moodle allow one to subscribe to receive email copies of new postings. While this can be useful for low-traffic discussion areas, it could obviously become overwhelming if one subscribes to email for a highly interactive forum.

VoiceThread (http://voicethread.com) is a free software tool that allows discussion to be centered on a visual element such as an image, video, or slides. (VoiceThread can also be thought of as a presentation tool.) Michelle Pacansky-Brock found this tool invaluable for facilitating discussion in her Art Appreciation course for Sierra College in California. Pacansky-Brock notes that before she began to use tools like VoiceThread, she had been "frustrated with my inability to truly engage my students with images. Their ideas and interpretations were distanced from the works of art. Using VoiceThread as a tool for discussions has changed all of this." Using VoiceThread, students are able to draw (called "doodle") on top of an image as they leave an audio comment, and the resulting "doodle" is sync-ed to the recorded comment in playback. Pacansky-Brock asks her students to "doodle" to circle examples of techniques or point out examples of key terms as she displays images of artworks. Comments can also be made as text or webcam, and

Format ?	HTML format
Subscription ?	Send me email copies of posts to this forum ▼
Attachment (Max size: 500KB)	I don't want email copies of posts to this forum
?	Send me email copies of posts to this forum

Figure 6.1 Discussion forum feature from Moodle, allowing one to subscribe to receive email copies of new postings to make it easier to monitor the classroom. Reproduced by permission from Moodle.

photos of students may be uploaded to display alongside their comments. Pacansky-Brock mentions that students often remark that their discussions using this tool "are more like f2f classroom discussions because they are able to see the pictures of students who have commented and hear the voices of those who choose to comment in voice form." She emphasizes that in teaching a visually oriented discipline such as hers, she previously felt as though she were "doing my students a disservice when I'd have them discuss an image in a discussion board without being able to simultaneously view the image. Such teaching lacks fluidity and doesn't allow students to fully engage with the images." (See a sample discussion with student comments from Pacansky-Brock's Women in Art class at http://voicethread.com/library/5.)

The explosion of Web 2.0 tools has meant that instructors like Michelle Pacansky-Brock who previously had access to little or no instructional technology support can easily find and apply tools that fit a specific pedagogical need. She comments about

Figure 6.2 Discussion of an image using text and audio in Voice-Thread. Reproduced by permission from VoiceThread.

her approach to using such tools in an effective manner without overwhelming students, "I find that, first, it's critical to be knowledgeable about using the technologies before I introduce them to my students. More importantly, it's critical to *explain* to my students *why* they will be using the technologies."

●●●●●

Other Communication Tools

Internal Email, External Email

Some systems allow for their own internal course email which is basically a private asynchronous messaging system which does not need to go to an outside email address. Students and instructors can use this mailbox exclusively for all correspondence within the course, sometimes by just typing in or selecting the name of the student or instructor. Another benefit of these systems is that instructors can maintain a full record of course communications. However, bear in mind that in many cases, students need to log in to the classroom in order to access this sort of message system. Unless there is an option for students to subscribe and receive these messages in their external email addresses as well, this sort of email can't be used to send reminders to students to log in to the class. Still other course management systems provide a convenient email roster, which allows students to send mail to all or part of the class from a central area that lists the addresses of all class members. These rosters also allow the sender to receive a carbon copy of sent mail at the sender's home email address.

Instant Messaging and Texting

Instant messaging (IM) and SMS texting are two ways of communicating that are particularly popular with younger students. IM may be a feature already bundled into your course management system but if not, you can incorporate instant messaging by asking all students to sign up for a free IM service like Yahoo or Google.

Be aware that you will need to set rules for interacting with students in this way—generally you can log in or out as you prefer, or you can leave it open on your computer but post messages indicating your availability status.

There are a growing number of tools that allow instructors to send an SMS text message to all their students' phones or email addresses. One of the best known is Twitter (www. twitter.com), a free "microblogging" service perhaps best known for its use as a way to send short 140-character updates for social networking purposes, which can also be used to send reminders and updates to students. Students can opt to receive your messages via cell phone text messages, email, or the Twitter web site. Many universities have been experimenting with software programs that allow them to send text messages in a crisis situation, while others have also enabled instructors to use such software for instructional purposes. Because SMS messages are generally limited to 140 characters, they are not useful for imparting instructional content, but can readily be used for reminder notices and last-minute changes or corrections to class assignments and schedules. Most such software allows students an option to subscribe via email or to log in to a web page if they choose not to use text messaging or do not have a cell phone or a suitably inexpensive text messaging package plan for their cell phone or other mobile device.

Chat, Whiteboard, and Other Collaborative Tools

Chat is a synchronous communication tool. There may be one or more chat rooms available for a particular class, depending on the software. As mentioned in Chapter 3, chat is sometimes combined with a whiteboard. There are also whiteboards that permit students to assume the role of presenter in order to share their work with classmates or that grant all students in a defined group the ability to collaborate on a project. If you have not included chat sessions in your course plan and syllabus, you still have the option to inform students that they are free to use chat for their social or group-project needs.

Synchronous tools like chat rooms and whiteboards are particularly appropriate for your class if your students live in the same time zone or are logging on from campus locations. If your students live in disparate time zones, careful schedule accommodation is required to make this a worthwhile and attainable learning experience.

If your software allows you to save and archive whiteboard and chat sessions, and make them available to view later, this can be a major asset. This feature enables students to refer to and reflect on chat and whiteboard activities, thus considerably increasing their value to your class.

Check, too, to see what options your software affords for student direction of whiteboard activities. If you can hand over the reins to students, this will allow you to arrange for individual student or group presentations in real time.

Depending on the nature of your course, you may find that past successful sessions that have been archived can be reused for future classes. For example, you may have used such software to demonstrate how to create a spreadsheet. Once you have archived it, you can share it with a new classroom as part of course content.

If you teach a blended class, you may have access to an in-class smartboard that allows you to save and upload content to the Web. Tools like those in collaborative software such as Adobe Connect and Wimba LiveClassroom allow instructors or students in online classes to meet in real time, using chat and/ or audio and slides, share and interact with documents on another's desktop, etc. These are sophisticated tool sets and it is essential that you get some practice and familiarize yourself with their workings before you decide to include them in your course plan. We recommend that you avail yourself of training provided by your institution or the software vendor if such instruction is available, and also consult with colleagues or even instructors from other institutions who may already have used the software.

For those whose institutions do not provide collaborative software tools of this nature, we recommend that you try out one of the free or inexpensive Web 2.0 tools that fall into this category such as DimDim (www.dimdim.com). The free version of DimDim allows one to hold an online real-time meeting with up to twenty students, and includes whiteboard, audio and video, application sharing, etc.

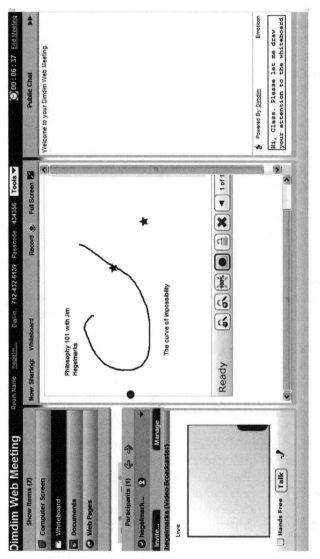

Figure 6.3 Professor Hegelmarks creates a presentation on DimDim (www.dimdim.com) free web meeting software. Hegelmarks has prepared the whiteboard for a synchronous presentation to his Philosophy 101 students. He plans to use chat but also has the option to use audio or a web cam to hold his talk. He has set the entire meeting to be recorded for the benefit of students who won't be able to attend in real time. Reproduced by permission from DimDim.

Group Activity Areas

Groups may be formed online when an instructor wishes to divide up the class for the purpose of certain tasks. Group activities may range from discussion to peer review to collaborative projects and cooperative learning activities, as explained in Chapter 7.

If you are using course management system software, you will probably be able to take advantage of its built-in group areas, each of which may contain its own asynchronous discussion, real-time chat, or document-sharing capabilities. This means that the members assigned to a particular group can engage in discussion and document sharing within their own small, private group environment, apart from other members of the class. Some course management software includes built-in blog and wiki options.

If you are using a software system that does not have built-in group functions, you can still find ways to carve out group areas. For example, you can simply designate and label particular discussion fora as group areas for asynchronous communication. To accomplish the document-sharing function, group members will attach or paste in documents in the appropriate discussion area. If you are using a system that consists mainly of web pages plus a discussion messaging system, you can assign topic threads within the system for use by particular groups. For example, you might name one threaded topic (or perhaps a whole forum) "Group A Discussion" and indicate to the class that this is only for a particular group of students to use. Students in that group can then post, read, and respond in that area.

Some software has additional special features, like randomization, that may be of value to you in setting up groups—such a feature has obvious advantages for trying to divide up students in large classes into small groups.

Again, if you do not have access to a course management system with group functions, many of the free software resources outlined in Chapter 1 can provide the ability to create such set-aside areas for small-group activity. A social networking site like Ning offers opportunities to create group sites that can include individual blogs, the ability to easily upload images and videos, and create a group discussion forum. Any of the free wiki software sites mentioned in Chapter 1 will allow you to create an area in which students can collaborate as a group. One advantage of using wiki software for group projects is that it provides the instructor with a clear "page history" of all edits made, in order of most recent to oldest, noting who made each edit and when the edit was made. This means that you will be able to track the contributions of each student to the overall group project and it also gives you a sense of the direction and decisions that the group took in their collaboration. Being able to review this history might enable you to give better guidance to students about errors, missed opportunities, or even suggestions for more effective collaboration. To get a clearer picture of how this works, call up any page in Wikipedia and click on the History tab. Wikipedia nicely demonstrates how to decipher history pages in its Help section at http://en.wikipedia.org/wiki/Help:Page_history.

Web Resource and Linking Pages

Some software provides places where you can organize a reference list of relevant web sites, making it easier for students to find and retrieve them as the course progresses.

Depending on the software's options, you may want to organize your links according to each week of the class or in a topical fashion. Some systems allow both instructors and students to add Internet links in the resource area, while others limit this capability to instructors.

Or, you may prefer to use a social bookmarking service like Delicious or Diigo, previously discussed in Chapter 3, which allow for tagging and sharing with "friends" or the formation of groups within which web resources may be shared.

Searching Capabilities

Some software platforms provide search capabilities. These can be very selective—for example, allowing users to search only in the discussion section. Or they can be comprehensive, allowing you to choose whether to search all sections of the course or to limit your search to a single area.

Search functions can be useful not only for your students but for you as well. They permit you to find that one passage or comment you only dimly recall.

Quizmakers

Some systems make available multiple-choice, short-answer, and true/false exams. Even if you don't normally use this type of test, you may want to consider creating some assessment instruments that make use of the feature. For example, you might create self-assessment quizzes to help students review the material at the end of each unit, or you might ask students to take a diagnostic quiz at the start of your course.

Important! *It is recommended that you rely on more than one form of graded assignment.*

From a security standpoint, it is better to be able to compare several different types of samples of a student's work than to base all the grades on a single type of assignment. Also, from the standpoint of multiple learning strategies, it is best to give students the opportunity to display their achievement and comprehension in a number of ways.

To increase security, find out the capabilities of your quiz-making system. As noted in Chapter 3, various features can help increase the security of an exam—for instance, timed, one-time access; password-protected access; and the ability to create pools of questions that permit individual randomization. There are many different approaches to quiz security issues. Some systems can limit access to a quiz to a certain IP address, thus allowing the instructor to control the student's point of access. Others may offer a posttest analysis that looks for similarity among student answers.

Another option available in some systems is the ability to give students automatic feedback. For example, in many quizmaking programs, students who answer a question incorrectly can receive automatic instructions for remediation: they can be told to review pages 10–15 in the textbook or to reread the instructor's Unit 1 lecture. Another handy feature of some software is the ability to postpone access to a quiz (for example, by withholding a password or blocking access) until the student has finished a particular section of the course.

Finally, there are options that permit an instructor to insert images or sounds into an exam. With these features, the instructor can pose questions based on graphs, charts, or bits of music and language. Depending on your subject field and teaching methods, these may be important features for you.

If you do not have access to a quizmaking tool, you may want to explore some of the free or low-cost (depending on the features you want, you may have to pay a small fee) online testing software sites. These sites allow you to create and will host the test-taking as well. As of this writing, some of the services include ZohoChallenge.com, SurveyMonkey.com (for surveys only), ProProfs Quiz School www.proprofs.com/quiz-school, ClassMarker www.classmarker.com and EasyTestMaker.com. Each service varies in features offered, and the free versions will usually include advertisements on their sites. Some services may allow one to circumvent this by embedding the quizzes on your own web site. In evaluating these quizmakers, you should consider the following:

- ease of use and reuse, templates available;
- types of quizzes one can make—multiple choice, fill in, essay, etc.;
- what kind of automatic feedback is it possible to add for test-takers?
- what types of media—images, video, audio—can be used in conjunction with test-taking;
- scalability—how many users can accommodate?
- can you create groups for each class of test takers?
- how scores are reported, what data is available;
- ability to embed the quizzes into one's web page or CMS;
- how readily quizzes can be saved;
- time limits or security measures that are possible;
- are the quiz products you create automatically made available to others to use?
- does the site include advertisements or non-educational materials that might be objectionable?

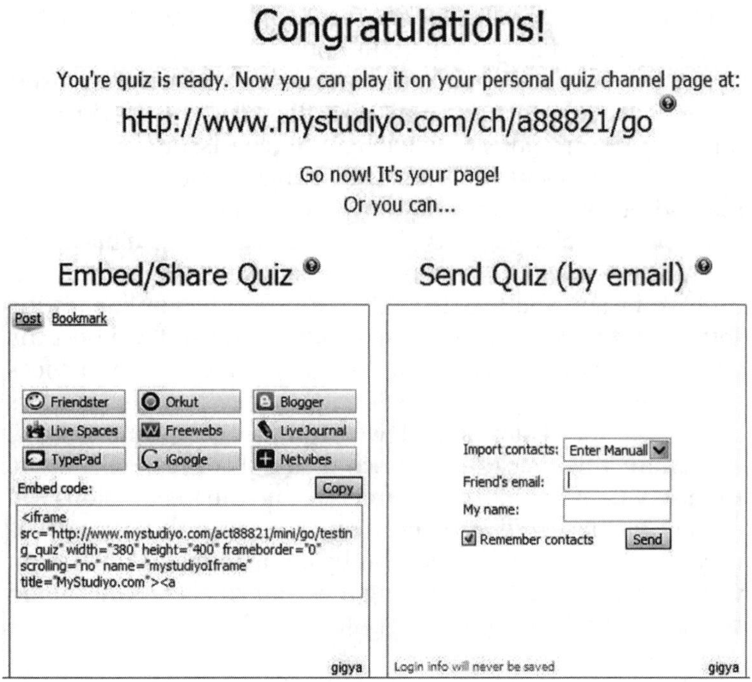

Congratulations!

You're quiz is ready. Now you can play it on your personal quiz channel page at:

http://www.mystudiyo.com/ch/a88821/go

Go now! It's your page!
Or you can...

Embed/Share Quiz   Send Quiz (by email)

Post Bookmark

- Friendster
- Orkut
- Blogger
- Live Spaces
- Freewebs
- LiveJournal
- TypePad
- iGoogle
- Netvibes

Embed code: Copy

```
<iframe
src="http://www.mystudiyo.com/act88821/mini/go/testin
g_quiz" width="380" height="400" frameborder="0"
scrolling="no" name="mystudiyoIframe"
title="MyStudiyo.com"><a
```

Import contacts: Enter Manuall

Friend's email:

My name:

☑ Remember contacts   Send

gigya   Login info will never be saved   gigya

Figure 6.4 After creating a multimedia quiz in MyStudiyo presented with choices and the code with which to embed the quiz. Reproduced by permission from MyStudiyo.

There are also delightfully creative approaches to self-assessment, low-stakes testing with programs like MyStudiyo (www.mystudiyo.com) that provide templates to create multimedia quizzes, allow instructors to create automatic feedback, and also feature scoreboards so that you can see how students have done. The quizzes can also be easily embedded into your course web pages.

Student Progress Reports and Tracking

Progress reports that can be accessed by the students themselves allow them to keep track of their own accomplishments. This is particularly helpful in courses in which the assignments may be accomplished in any order. If this feature exists, you won't have to be as vigilant in reminding students of their progress in the course.

Student tracking by instructors—that is, obtaining statistics about when students log on, how long they remain in a specific area of the course, which specific documents or messages they have read, and so on—is increasingly recognized as an important feature for any course management software suite. Some systems allow tracking by the number of browser "hits" in a specific area of the course. Some give the duration of time spent in each area or reveal whether an area or item has been opened. These tracking abilities can be valuable data in helping you assess participation.

Bear in mind that these indicators are not always accurate, because they can be manipulated by students. For instance, a student can open an area of the course and simply let the clock run. This will give the appearance of the student having spent a great deal of time studying that section of the course.

However, if statistics reveal that the student hasn't even entered a certain area of the course, that will tell you that he or she hasn't read the material contained within it. Or, if the student has spent only five minutes in an area of relative complexity, this is a sure sign that he or she hasn't dealt adequately with that portion of the course.

Finally, data may be relatively meaningless without analysis and evaluation of quality. Thus the best way to use tracking functions is as a contribution to a more comprehensive evaluation, including student assignments, student postings in discussion, student presentations, and objective quizzes and essays. Online courses do permit you to know a great deal more about a student's attendance and participation than is possible in an on-the-ground course but a true picture can only be compiled in the context of the student's entire record and with regard to the actual content of the activity being tracked.

Adapting to Your Software's Tracking Functions

If tracking is available in your software system, it's important to find out exactly how it functions, For example, if you can track the responses a student makes in discussion but can't tell whether the student is reading the topic messages you post, you might want to require a specific number of postings in specific threads each week. As another example, assume you can track students' access to your presentations, but only on a unit basis; that is, you can't tell whether students have read individual documents within a unit. In this case, you might want to place the most important documents in their own individual units.

If you have little or no tracking capability, then student work submitted to you directly by email or posted in the classroom will assume greater importance, as will quiz questions that test comprehension and familiarity with material.

Online Gradebooks

An online gradebook is a tool that allows you to record and compute grades for students and permits students to access their own grades. Just a few of the course management systems that offer such gradebooks are Blackboard, Moodle, Desire-2Learn and eCollege. If you have an online gradebook available to you, we highly recommend that you consider using it. Online students really appreciate being able to track their own progress. Make sure that you take the time to access a gradebook in your CMS from the student perspective so that you will be aware of how much students can perceive of the record. There are often different options available to the instructor, such as setting a due date that will not permit late submissions without notification of the instructor, or areas in which feedback may be offered to the student. If the software permits, it is a good idea to build out your entire gradebook at the beginning of the course so that students are able to get a picture of the whole that complements what they will learn from the syllabus.

Whether or not you have an online gradebook as part of course management software, you can create your own electronic gradebook in spreadsheet form for your own benefit. Even though you may feel that you can always refer back to the online classroom for a record of activity, it is easy to lose track of individual students in a busy class. Thus it is no less important to keep detailed records of student activity in an online setting than it is for the traditional on-the-ground class. See Chapter 11 for more information on record-keeping strategies.

● ● ● ● ●

Other Course Areas and Features

If your course is conducted completely online, think about creating an asynchronous "student lounge" discussion area—a place where students can socialize. Another useful discussion area is one in which students can address questions to you throughout the course, questions that either are "off topic" or concern ongoing procedural matters. These two types of messages can be combined into one area or separated, depending on your wishes. Having such areas available benefits the students, many of whom need the added interaction and feeling of camaraderie with classmates, as well as one central place where they know they can address urgent questions about the course.

Other helpful devices for personalizing a class include a discussion forum where students introduce themselves during the first week of class and student web pages where students provide some brief biographical information about themselves. Besides helping to break the ice, these areas provide an important service by allowing students to refer back to identifying details about their classmates as the course progresses. When using blogs or web pages for this purpose, always inform students whether web pages are open only to the class or can potentially be accessed by the public on the Web.

Most course management systems, blogs, and social networking spaces make it easy for students (or you) to upload a photo to the classroom. This should always be voluntary. There are many reasons not to push this option. Although it does help give each student an identifiable face in the classroom, it undercuts the egalitarian advantages inherent in an online classroom. Not knowing the race, ethnicity, attractiveness, or even gender of a student—except by that individual's own choice in self-identifying—often allows students (and you) to pay more attention to the ideas and words of class members without all the assumptions and subtle biases that we all harbor.

Another desirable area to carve out is a technical support area or help link. For instance, you may set up an area of the classroom or web pages that contain downloadable programs and **plug-ins** (or hyperlinks by which one can access software), plus either a simple FAQ for the course management software or a full instruction manual. If support staff are available, they may monitor this area. In the absence of a full student orientation, the area plays a vital function in providing self-help to students or a connection to support materials or staff. As a backup to these technical support areas, provide, via an initial email or letter, some instructions for getting started and any other relevant information, such as phone numbers for support in the event that students have trouble logging on to the class.

Connecting to Social Networking Sites

While many students might prefer to keep their MySpace or Facebook pages as a private realm apart from their classmates and schoolwork, many institutions have been taking advantage of the popularity of these social networking sites to give students an option to link up with what is happening in a course. Surmising that many of their students spend more time at these sites than they might be consulting their email, some institutions have arranged so that students who desire to use applications like CourseFeed (www.coursefeed.com) or Blackboard Sync to receive updates and reminders or links to course content from the class may do so from within Facebook.

Some instructors have also encouraged students to use MySpace and Facebook as a way of presenting their self-introduction at the beginning of a class (or have presented their own self-introductions in this way) or to encourage social interaction among the entire class or small groups engaged in projects.

Finding the Right Web 2.0 Tools and Keeping Informed

An assortment of Web 2.0 tools has been mentioned in this chapter in conjunction with various course areas that one can utilize or improvise.

Because these tools are constantly in development, appear and disappear, it is necessary to find a way to keep up with the appearance and availability of these tools, as well as to take advantage of critical commentary on such tools from an educator's perspective so that you can quickly evaluate their suitability for your needs. A selection of blogs and other resource sites by educators devoted to evaluating new tools are included in the Guide to Resources.

Once you find some sources that you value, you may find it convenient to add some of the tools you use to the bookmarks toolbar of your Internet browser for easier access. Most recent versions of browsers also have built-in **RSS (Really Simple Syndication) feed readers**, also known as **aggregators**. These permit you to subscribe to a blog, podcast, or other resource site so that you can receive the latest news or installment from that site without having to actually visit it each time. You can also use a browser start page like Pageflakes.com or Netvibes.com that allow you to create a home page that includes all your feeds—that way, each time you open your browser, your feeds will automatically be updated and you will have them all in one place.

Virtual Worlds

Educators have been experimenting for many years with various types of **virtual worlds**, that is, online 3-D immersive environments that simulate reality and in which participants interact by using avatars, that is, representations of themselves (these can take the form of animals, cartoon-like characters, or images more closely based on their own appearance). Nearly ten years ago, at the time of the first edition of this book, the authors researched educators who were using Active Worlds, while in recent years, Second Life has become perhaps the most widely known program for virtual-world educational use.

Despite great strides in the development of such software, virtual-world software still presents a fairly steep learning curve for the majority of instructors to perform even simple tasks and for many students as well. (Those instructors and students who have grown up playing multi-user games will be generally more comfortable in this environment.)

Reasons for using the virtual world for educational activities range from simple curiosity, the coolness factor, and the desire

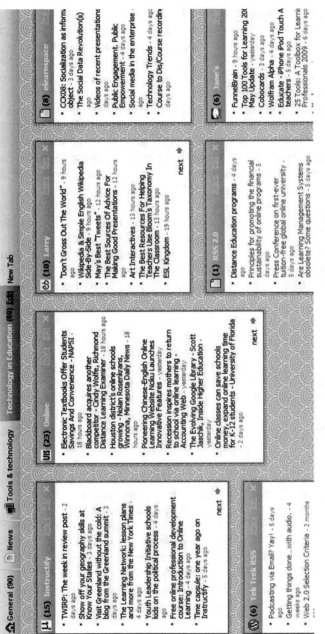

Figure 6.5 Susan Ko's Netvibes.com start page within Firefox browser, illustrating her collection of RSS feeds to blogs and other resource sites on technology in education and Web 2.0 tools. Reproduced by permission. Source: Netvibes.com.

to inject some fun into education to exploiting the virtual environment for role playing, interaction with objects, or complex simulations which involve danger or would incur prohibitive expense in the real world.

Many institutions have now staked a claim on "property" in Second Life, and have small cadres of staff and instructors who have become quite skilled in moving within the virtual world. Universities have found ways to sequester their educational activities from the greater commercial environment by creating private spaces and some virtual worlds have been dedicated solely to educational uses.

There is an active community of educators involved in virtual worlds, and there are many resources and papers available on the Web to advise instructors how to use virtual worlds in an effective manner as well as voluminous materials in different media, offering tips and tricks. (See the Guide to Resources for some of these.) If your university is involved in using a virtual world, and your subject matter seems to lend itself to this type of environment, we recommend the following steps as part of the planning, design, and development cycle:

■ Assess your students' likely ability to access the virtual-world environment. Students who do not have access to the latest computer equipment are unlikely to be able to access these environments.

■ Allow sufficient time to practice your own skills in the virtual-reality environment before you even decide to use the environment for instructional purposes. Clearly the time needed will vary according to the individual instructor but the estimates we use here are based on our average reader of this book. Even if you are not creating anything within the virtual world, allow up to five hours practice time to feel comfortable in mastering the basic skills that enable you to move and communicate, and up to another twenty hours to be able to facilitate activities for your students. If your own institution does not offer the training you need, consider taking a workshop from the Sloan Consortium (www.sloan-c.org), which provides excellent training in this area in the company of other educators.

■ Find out what materials are available from your university to assist students and run a required orientation for students to practice before you initiate any instructional activities in the virtual world.

■ If you decide to use the virtual-world environment, draw up a detailed explanation of what students are expected to do there. Be prepared for the eventuality that some students may have difficulty participating, and offer an alternative activity that might accomplish the same goals.

7

●●●●●

Student Activities in the Online Environment

What kinds of instructional activities are most effective for an online or blended course?

In this chapter we suggest some rules and guidelines to help you find the most suitable student activities for your course. We also present some concrete examples of activities that instructors have found to be effective, and we suggest how these might be organized and assessed.

You may well be familiar with theories of "learning styles," and perhaps you have applied these ideas in your on-the-ground classroom. An example of the learning style concept would be the idea that a visual/verbal learner prefers to read information, while a visual/nonverbal learner might learn best when there are graphics and pictures to supplement the text. There's nothing to prevent you from designing your online course with the concept of learning styles in mind. We know of at least one online instructor who gave students a learning style assessment within the first week of class and then followed through with this approach in devising weekly assignments. Students were allowed to choose one question from an array of exercise assignments, each question choice having been designed according to a different learning style.

In this book, however, we won't attempt to define online activities in terms of any of the complex learning style matrixes that have been developed. (See the Guide to Resources section at the end of this book for some guidance on this subject.) Rather, we think it may be better to approach the subject from the standpoint of the desirability of incorporating different types of learning opportunities and recognizing that there is more than one way to approach learning. Variety is as important online as on the ground, and using multiple approaches will both reinforce student learning and allow students to address the subject matter from different perspectives.

●●●●●

Group Activities

Group activities constitute an obvious strategy for large online classes, but they can be equally effective in classes of fifteen to twenty students. A mixture of individual and group-oriented activities can help provide a variety of contexts within which students may learn skills and concepts and demonstrate their mastery.

Group activities can range from the most informal small-group discussion to a highly structured and scripted arrangement. A group may include three or four students, or it may be just a pair of students who work out their own consensus about how to approach a mutual assignment. Some of this range of possibilities is illustrated in the discussion here that follows.

To organize group activities, you need to provide guidelines for each group's collaboration, set reasonable goals and objectives, and provide both a place for the group to work and a place or method to present its work. These matters often depend to some extent on the course management system or other collaborative software you're using, a subject we discussed in earlier chapters. Here, rather than going into the mechanical details of setting up a communal online working space, we'll focus on general principles and on examples from actual courses.

You may have already learned a hard fact about collaborative activities in your on-the-ground classes: collaboration doesn't just happen. Many students have no idea how to collaborate on a task in a course. Thus it is vital to provide detailed guidelines on the responsibilities of each member of a group, as well as explanations of how groups are to proceed with their task. As mentioned earlier, you may want to define such roles as group recorder of the activities, group manager or leader, and group spokesperson.

It's also necessary to define clearly what the end product of each group's project should be, what it should include, and where in the online environment it should be presented. Timing may be critical here, if you want the entire class to have the chance to read and critique what a group has produced. Make sure you clarify the deadlines for each stage of the process.

Icebreaking Activities

As we mentioned in earlier chapters, online students need opportunities to get to know each other. By an icebreaking activity, we mean any activity that allows student to begin to form some sense of community online.

We recommend that every online class—and every online component to a web-enhanced or blended course that includes a discussion forum—begin with an exercise in which each student introduces himself or herself to the class. This can be accomplished by a discussion thread or through the creation of student blogs or web pages. If you carve out a separate area for this activity or create a page of links to students' own blogs or web pages, your students will be able to refer back to the biographical information throughout the course.

It's best to keep the requirements for introductions simple: "Please say a few words about yourself and your reason for taking this class," or "Let us know from what part of the world you are logging on, and tell us a little bit about your background in this subject." Begin the process by introducing yourself to the class. Generally, you should include both the formal details of your career and academic interests and some informal information. How much of the latter you offer is up to you. You can also include information about how you prefer to be addressed, either explicitly ("call me Dr. Ko") or implicitly (for instance, signing off your introduction with just your first name).

In addition to these initial icebreaking activities, many instructors find it helpful to have the members of small groups engage in some sort of icebreaking team-building activity. This may involve asking each person for initial comments about how he or she visualizes the common project. It may include questions about people's typical online schedules and times when they might be available for a real-time chat. The more concrete and specific the icebreaking questions, the better, because specificity allows students to respond without worrying about whether they have stayed within the expected boundaries of the activity.

Some instructors encourage students to add photos, either by uploading them or by attaching an image file to a discussion thread or email sent to the entire class. This is also an option for the instructor. Photos personalize the biographical information and help classmates form a clearer image of their fellow students. However, photos also have disadvantages as people naturally form impressions based on the images posted. Members of minority groups, older or disabled students as well as others may feel that preconceptions or even biases may result. Our only recommendation is that, if you encourage the use of photos, you always make it a voluntary matter. Students may end up using **avatars** or other alternative representations (images, icons, symbols), and in some cultures, it is not uncommon for students to post photos of themselves accompanied by family members, boyfriends or girl-friends. Again, instructors and students should feel able to post whatever representation (or no representation) of themselves they choose.

Dividing Students into Groups

Generally speaking, it's best for the instructor to play a role in dividing students into groups. It can prove difficult, confusing, and irritating for students when they are simply left to their own devices to form groups. Many online instructors don't realize how clumsy it can be for all but the most outgoing and determined students to join or form groups on their own. In addition, if the task will involve synchronous activities, the time zone in which each student resides becomes a major factor, and the instructor is often in the best position to take this into account. Also, depending on the nature of the group task, you may want a mix of students of differing characteristics or skills in each group. For example, you may want a mixture of male and female students in each group or those from diverse disciplines, or to combine students with relatively weak communication skills together with those who demonstrate a more fluid writing ability.

Nonetheless, you may want to include some measure of student volition in the process of setting up groups. Student choice may be desirable under three circumstances in particular:

1. The group activity involves a diversity of choices, and you would like as many students as possible to choose the area that truly interests them.

2. There are already "natural" groupings of students in the course that you would like to incorporate in your assignments in order to promote group camaraderie.

3. In the case of students in blended courses, it is more likely that they already know each other, especially if you have first given them the opportunity to get to know each other in one or more previous face-to-face class meetings.

An example of the second situation would be a course in which three students enroll from the same corporation, and all of them have an interest in working together. Other examples might include mothers and adult children in the same course, or a husband and wife studying together. However, in some cases, you might want to break up these groupings to make it easier to distinguish the individual contributions or because you want students to work within groups of the greatest diversity possible.

When you would like to give students some measure of choice in forming their groups, one method is to ask students to email you their preferences. Tell them simply, "I'll try to take into consideration your preferences in forming the groups, but please be aware that it isn't always possible to satisfy everyone."

Stephen Rowe teaches an advanced accounting course at Southern Cross University in Australia in which students address a case study and carry out their work in a group wiki. Each group represents the issues of a different character in the case study and must address a different question. In order to form groups, Stephen instructs students that after they have read the case material they should "nominate which of the case characters you want to play." He then tries to match up students as much as possible with their preferred role, but lets students know that it's "first in, first served—a maximum of five per group."

If you have strong beliefs about students forming their own groups, there are a few ways to facilitate this. One method is to create a discussion area where this formation can occur, and ask students to share some additional information that might assist them in making an appropriate selection. For example, Christine Appel of the Universitat Oberta de Catalunya notes that time availability is often a factor for her students who will use both real-time chat as well as asynchronous discussion to communicate. With a large percentage of working students, those who work days versus evenings are able to sort themselves out fairly quickly in selecting a group.

In the case of blended classes, we recommend that you take advantage of the opportunity to meet face-to-face to enable groups to conduct their first meeting in the on-site setting.

Size and Duration of Groups   Don't make the groups too large. The ideal number will vary based on the task. A group formed only for the purposes of discussion can easily accommodate ten or more, but when the group members must collaborate on an assignment, a group of four or five is probably the optimum size. For online collaboration, any number larger than that risks creating problems of organization and communication that will consume valuable time.

Try to maintain the composition of the group for the duration of the course. It takes time for groups to develop a working dynamic. Changing the groups just as members are getting familiar with one another leads to needless waste of time as students adjust to their new circle of collaborators.

Group Roles   Assigning and rotating roles within each group is an effective method of ensuring true sharing and cooperation in the work. For example, assign one member of the group to summarize, another to record the group's conclusions, and another to lead the discussion or allocate portions of the work. Then request that these roles be rotated during the duration of the course. Make the rotation frequent enough to give each member a chance at several roles, but not so frequent as to interfere with group continuity.

To some extent, the frequency of the rotation will depend on the length of the course. In a course of eight weeks or less, more than three rotations would be an unnecessary bother.

Supervision and Assessment of Groups

Although some instructors like to give groups complete privacy—from the instructor as well as from other class members—we don't advocate excluding yourself from the groups unless they are completely informal in nature or their work product is not intended to be assessed.

Important! You need not participate in group activities but your supervision will encourage participation by all group members and ensure that an individual's contributions to the group are recognized.

The question of whether groups should observe the activities of other groups when all are working on a common problem raises a different issue. We tend to feel that groups need the assurance that the instructor knows they are coming up with solutions as a result of their own efforts and will be given credit accordingly. If you provide a forum for presentation of group work to the entire class, there is no need for the class as a whole to examine earlier, preliminary stages of a group's efforts. However, if your course management software or other software program you are using for group work does not allow for private areas, you may have no choice but to permit everyone to view the work of other groups. In this case, the instructor's review of group work throughout the process is doubly important.

Students are often concerned either that they will expend effort not matched by others in the group or that they will be unduly hurt by uncooperative or inactive group members. An instructor who directly supervises groups can assign grades based on both the whole group's output and the work of the individual members. Combined assessment of this sort is reassuring and encouraging to well-intentioned students.

If you perceive that a student isn't holding up his or her end of the group assignments, you may want to email that student privately. Some instructors also ask group members to privately evaluate each member of the group, using a well-defined set of criteria. This provides additional input that can aid the instructor in discerning what each student has contributed to the group effort. A very simple, stripped-down rubric for final peer evaluation of group work used by one of the authors, Susan Ko, for a variety of types of classes and training courses consists of the following:

1 = *member participated at minimal levels*

2 = *member's individual work, participation in discussion, organizing, editing, or presenting role was significant*

3 = *member's individual work, participation in discussion, or organizational/editing/presenting role greatly influenced for the better the quality of group interaction and product.*

Jonathan Mathews has a different approach to factoring in individual contribution and group efforts. He teaches an Energy and the Environment course online for Pennsylvania State University through their World Campus program. He has a very large class of 500 students formed by combining as many as fifteen sections of students enrolled in the World Campus, main campus, and other campus locations, and has support from at least two teaching assistants. Given those numbers of students, trying to discern individual contributions throughout a group project is too time consuming. Instead, he precedes the group project with an individual short research paper on one of two topics. This is then worth 3 percent of the grade. Students are then assigned to a group of four or five students based on the topic selection they chose and the quality of their two-page paper. The group project is on the same topic as the individual paper, but is a greatly enhanced study worth 13 percent. Both individual and group projects use the same interactive evaluation rubric, available online, which permits students to calculate their own scores and get feedback as they check to see that their papers are in the best order possible before submitting them to their instructor. Table 7.1 is a sample portion of the rubric and its corresponding feedback. The highlighted right-hand column represents how a sample student might have performed when judged by two of those criteria:

The corresponding additional automatic feedback returned by the interactive online rubric on these two categories would

Table 7.1 Interactive Evaluation Rubric, Sample Portion

Introduction	Paper had an introduction that addresses the title of the paper, and the introduction also raises readers' interest in reading the rest of the paper	Paper had an introduction that was both applicable and well-written	Paper had an introduction, but the introduction did not enthuse the reader or provide a clear indication of the papers direction	Paper did NOT have an introduction
Well-developed Argument	Paper presented well-developed arguments to support the conclusion, and showed an exceptional analysis and evaluation of material	Paper presented arguments that were supported by research and evaluation of material, and that supported the conclusion	Arguments support the conclusion partially. Paper showed some incoherent or incomplete arguments	Paper demonstrated no flow of argument. Argument is weak, unsupported and cannot directly support the conclusion

be as follows. Note that the feedback addresses the particular performance while it also reiterates the general principles to follow for those criteria:

Introduction: Papers require an introduction! An introduction is essential in terms of introducing the topic and background and, in general, sets the scene for the rest of your writing. The simple way to write an introduction is to introduce the importance or background of the topic, and then how you organized your writing.

Well-Developed Argument: The arguments used are weak and cannot directly support the conclusion. Outline the main findings in your paper, and then reorganize the ideas. Probably one direct way to develop strong arguments is to organize the ideas in a logical and cohesive way. Then use different transitions to strengthen the flow of ideas. Data and statistics can when used appropriately strengthen the paper. The foundation, however, is quality research; without that you have a "house of cards."

A Problem-Based Learning Approach: Pete Mikolaj uses a problem-based learning approach for a group project in his Commercial Property Risk Management and Insurance course at Indiana State University. He explains to his students that problem-based learning is an instructional strategy in which "problems form the organizing focus and stimulus for learning and are the vehicle for development of problem solving skills," with he, the instructor, functioning as a facilitator or guide. The group project is intended "to provide an opportunity for application of problem solving principles to an actual commercial property situation," as Pete explains to students, and to "make it as real world a situation as possible," with the resulting report "intended as a recommended action plan to top management," while "management looks to the report as a source of critical thinking and problem solving to support difficult corporate decisions."

With the help of instructional designer, Sharon Guan, Mikolaj devised a Project Reporting Log to provide documentation by each team of their weekly activities, both as a group and of individual contributions. A sample of the Project Reporting Log looks like Table 7.2, with each member of Team A recording none, one, or multiple entries for work accomplished in the group project for that week.

Mikolaj treats the Project Log as part of the real-life model that he is trying to convey through this assignment, telling students "it is important to keep management informed on the status and on any problems or issues that are being encountered," and that one purpose of the Project Log is to "assure management that progress is being made and to document this progress." Mikolaj also hopes through this activity to impart to students a hands-on experience with project management. The final project as well as the team itself is evaluated using the rubric in Tables 7.3 and 7.4 which reviews both the process and work product of the group:

Mikolaj provides for individual accountability through an individual contribution grade that is computed from peer evaluations from each group and a self-evaluation, with the peer evaluation counting two-thirds and the self-evaluation comprising one-third of the individual contribution grade.

A Team Marketing Communications Plan Penny Ittner teaches an undergraduate course in marketing principles at University of Maryland University College, providing an introduction to the field of marketing. Students in the class are usually business or marketing majors, but are generally neophytes on the subject of marketing. Ittner's course features a "new product development" group assignment in which students work in a simulated "marketing team" to develop an effective marketing communications plan for the introduction of a product. Each group picks a product to work on from those developed in an earlier activity in which each person in the class was asked to come up with a product idea.

Ittner assigns students to groups of four or five who work in the private "Study Groups" area of the university's course management software. She makes the assignments to groups based on a combination of factors:

> *I try to put a core of the early active students together (and group the late-to-the-task students together in the same way)—this is designed to reduce frustration. But then I salt the groups as evenly as I can, sprinkling those who make the highest quality discussion postings among the groups and making sure the relatively lower performers are also evenly distributed.*

Table 7.2 Example of a Project Reporting Log

Name	Date	Time	Activity/Notes Attachments Can Be Added	New/Modified File Name
Whole Team	6/16 – 6/22	Multi Hrs.	Problems/Next Period Plans: Group Discussions have continued to go well by communicating through posts. Members have checked board frequently and responded in a timely manner. Parts of the report are beginning to be posted so other members can review and add their suggestions – With the multitude of threads, a small glitch in communication on a change in second hazard has been cleared up. We changed from employee theft to food contamination/spoilage – For the next period, team members will continue to work on their assigned project roles, finalizing their contribution, and communicating with members through the discussion board and collaboration chats. All material is at this time being collected by Student5 to compile the final report into one document. Student5 will then submit on July 2, the report and the PowerPoint slides after Janet has emailed the oral report to her	
Student 2	6/26	2.5 hrs	Searched the web for possible solutions to reduce food spoilage loss and fire hazards	
	6/29	0.5 hr	Called Student5 to talk about her part over food spoilage and tried to get some assistance with the Cost/Benefit Analysis	
Student 3	6/23–6/27	4 hrs	Read and replied to posts. Rec'd XYZ company logo and incorporated that into the rough draft of the presentation and formatted more slides	

Student 1	6/24	2 hrs	– Did some editing and revisions to rough draft – Replaced the previous file (rough) draft with progress so far as Business Risk Updated 6/24	Business Risk Updated 6/24
Next week	6/29–7/2	–	– Will be doing the Weekly Team Project Logs – Continued communicating with team on group discussion board for final changes made to project and other final compiling of oral report (power point project)	
Student 4	6/29	2 hrs	– Working with Student5 specifically for the two hazard risks of fire and food spoilage/contamination – Has posted file to file exchange for Fire Analysis Final Copy	XYZ Fire Analysis Final Copy
Student 5	6/29–7/2	3 hrs	– Continues to work with Student4 on relative information from XYZ – Volunteered to compile the project parts into one document for the team to review before submission – Plans on submitting assignment for the team on the due date, July 2	

Table 7.3 Rubric to Evaluate Process

Process (Team Activity)	Below Avg.	Satisfactory	Excellent	Score—50 Pts. Possible
1. Team has clear vision of the problem(s)	1, 2, 3	4, 5, 6, 7	8, 9, 10	
2. Team is properly organized to complete task and cooperates well	1, 2, 3	4, 5, 6, 7	8, 9, 10	
3. Managed time wisely	1, 2, 3	4, 5, 6, 7	8, 9, 10	
4. Acquired needed knowledge base	1, 2, 3	4, 5, 6, 7	8, 9, 10	
5. Efforts communicated well within group	1, 2, 3	4, 5, 6, 7	8, 9, 10	

Table 7.4 Rubric to Evaluate Product

Product (Project Report)	Below Avg.	Satisfactory	Excellent	Score—50 Pts. Possible
6. Meets minimum project requirements per syllabus	1, 2, 3	4, 5, 6, 7	8, 9, 10	
7. Well-organized, logical sequencing	1, 2, 3	4, 5, 6	7, 8, 9	
8. Shows creativity, solves the problem(s)	1, 2, 3, 4	5, 6, 7, 8	9, 10, 11, 12	
9. Demonstrates knowledge, conclusion(s) reached	1, 2, 3	4, 5, 6	7, 8, 9, 10	
10. Distinguishes between fact, opinion, and value judgments	1, 2, 3	4, 5, 6	7, 8, 9	

Ittner explains to students that she "will be observing your group discussions, but I will not be participating in them unless you need my help." In addition to presenting the students with detailed instructions for the group project, she also draws attention to documents that are intended to assist students with their group assignment, "One is entitled Team Development and its purpose is to help you and your team work productively and with satisfaction together." The Team Development document discusses the stages of development in terms of the "forming, storming, norming and performing model." She also asks them to review the Group Project Rubric that shows the grading criteria for their assignment. The Group Project Rubric evaluates the resulting project on the basis of demonstrated knowledge of subject matter (40 percent), critical thinking and problem-solving skills (30 percent), fulfillment of assignment requirements (20 percent), and writing skills (10 percent). Finally, Ittner also has students file a peer- and self-evaluation form at the end of the project, scoring each team member and themselves on the criteria of participation in group discussions and meetings, the degree to which each contributed to helping to keep the group focused on the tasks, contribution of useful ideas, amount of work done, and quality of work accomplished. Group members are all given the same grade for their actual project, but these peer and self evaluations, she tells students, are "to assist me in assessing individual participation levels" since participation in the group project counts for 25 percent of the overall participation grade for the class.

● ● ● ● ●

Role Playing and Simulations

Role-playing activities have been used to great advantage in such subject areas as human resources, business, counseling, international relations, and economics, as well as in history and foreign languages. The same kinds of role playing can take place in an online instructional environment. The examples from Penny Ittner and Pete Mikolaj are themselves a type of role-playing exercise whereby their students take on the role of a team in marketing or insurance to practice real-world skills.

Online role-playing exercises can be carried out in small groups, with each member taking a different role. For example, in a human resources class that is studying hiring interviews, one person becomes the interviewer and the other the interviewee. Alternatively, an exercise can be designed for teams: for example, one team playing the role of Germany in World War I and others representing Britain, the United States, and France.

A third alternative might involve an individual student making a presentation in which he or she assumes a particular role.

Pam Taylor teaches nursing informatics at Middle Tennessee State University. She uses the discussion area of her online class to provide for a role-playing exercise related to an assignment in which students design a data-collection tool for a particular group of hypothetical employees. Taylor poses as the Chief Information Officer and students then ask budget-related and technical questions of this CIO. In yet another role play, Taylor plays the part of an employee who will be using the data-collection tool and students again address questions to her as a potential user. Taylor notes that in these types of role-playing exercises,

> students can see each other's questions and tag off these questions to create additional knowledge about the problems posed. This type of activity is very effective in connecting the classroom with actual application in the real world. It also improves students' ability to ask meaningful questions related to a problem.

Online Debates

In an online debate, students may be asked to defend their views in a public venue or to argue a point of view different from their own. Online debates can involve some of the same activities as role playing, such as preparatory research of the position the student is assigned and post-activity reflection and discussion. Yet debates can also be more pointed and more focused on a specific issue: For example, students might be asked to debate the question of whether the states should be able to tax Internet commerce or whether intervention in Darfur is justified.

You can arrange students in pairs, with each student taking one side of an issue. Or you can divide students into groups, with each group doing the research and consultation necessary to represent a particular point of view. Each group would then appoint a spokesperson to debate another group's spokesperson on the issue. To encourage objectivity on sensitive issues, you might require students to sign up to represent the point of view with which they actually disagree.

If conducting the debates in asynchronous discussion forums, provide students with a carefully paced schedule for each stage of the debate. You can also create a rubric for evaluating each stage of the arguments.

As each stage of the argument is presented, you as moderator will want to stop and address some questions to the presenters or to point out fallacies in logic. For example, "Team A, your point about X seems to be in contradiction to your earlier statement saying Z," or "Team B, is there any data to support your claims?"

There are quite a few web sites that feature rules for debating, sample debates, and actual debates held completely online or represented by transcripts. You can review these sites to find possible models for students to follow or to find debates on the same subject as those your students are debating—in this case, you might wait till your own debates have concluded before asking students to compare their arguments with those available on the web sites, all as part of their reflection, debriefing, or summing-up activity. See the Guide to Resources for these debate web sites.

In order to make the role-playing process work online, students need to be given the information or scripts necessary to play their roles, or they need to be directed to research the relevant material. In the first case, you need to make sure the preparatory materials are posted online or sent in course packets to students. In the second case, you need to provide adequate time and proper guidelines for students to research their parts.

To provide an exciting learning activity online, role playing can be combined with a simulation of a changing situation. Such simulations usually start with a scenario and evolve with planned or unplanned actions, news bulletins or other interventions supplied by the instructor. These role-playing simulations, while carried out online, are not to be compared with computerized simulations which most faculty cannot create on their own. The latter are described later in this section.

Two well-known and influential online scenario simulations illustrate some of the possibilities.

Mark Freeman from the University of Technology in Sydney, Australia, devised an award-winning role-playing online activity for his graduate school course in business finance, "Securities Markets Regulation." Students were anonymously assigned the roles of real Australian figures who were involved in the deregulation of Australian securities markets (such as the prime minister, the finance minister, and tycoon Rupert Murdoch). Students then had to respond to "events" announced to them online in a "public forum" over a period of ten days. The responses could be posted in the public forum (read by the whole class), or the students could approach each other privately via the course management system's internal email.

The anonymous role players were unmasked only at the end of the simulation, when students were asked to reflect on their experience. The anonymity and asynchronicity provided by using the Web, rather than face-to-face meetings, meant that attributes such as ethnicity and gender (and even language proficiency) were less likely to interfere with the role playing.

At the Center for Middle East and North African Studies at Macquarie University in Sydney, Australia, a Middle East politics simulation experience on the Web devised by the late Andrew Vincent with software created by John Shepherd has been used for more than a decade for several courses and in collaboration with universities outside Australia. Each class taking part is divided into small teams, and each team is assigned the role of a prominent Middle Eastern figure. Each team must prepare a comprehensive role profile that is based on research into the background, the figure's long-term and short-term objectives, and other characteristics of the assigned role. These role profiles are shared with all other participants. A scenario is proposed to the students to begin the simulation, and students communicate by email, chat, and the Web, as well as by telephone or face-to-face (if participants are in the same location). Although students are expected to operate under the simulation guidelines, they must submit any major actions (such as a military attack) to "controllers," who are appointed to monitor activity, resolve disputes, and grade the teams. The simulation ends with a teleconference of all participants that may be enhanced by videoconferencing. Each team must also produce a final report.

A detailed explanation of the simulation with links to pages that offer additional information about structuring such simulations can be found at www.mq.edu.au/mec/sim.

One key to the success of these types of role-playing simulations is adequate preparation by students. Students need to understand the concepts and issues of the subject matter, the roles they are playing, and the instructions and guidelines for carrying out the exercise. The instructor must not only create these guidelines, but also give a great deal of forethought to the simulated events so that they will evoke relevant and worthwhile student responses.

Equally important is the time spent afterward in reflecting on the role-playing experience and integrating what one has learned into an assignment. Reflection can be prompted by individual papers or by whole-class discussion. Integration can be accomplished by having students contribute their newfound understanding to a work in progress or a final project.

Computer-Based Simulations and Animations

Computer-based simulations attempt to recreate an actual process or activity or, on a broader scale, model complex real-life circumstances. There are simulations that might be available through your institution's subscription to an external supplier or perhaps there is programming support at your university to create simulations for use in some of your courses. But beyond those in-house solutions, there are many free web sites providing computer simulations that can be used in a class. A quick search on the Web will lead to numerous free sites that offer simulations in your subject area, for example, NASA's Jet Propulsion Laboratory at http://space.jpl.nasa.gov allows a student to look at Jupiter as seen from Earth and compare that view with Jupiter as seen from Uranus.

Animations use simple representations such as cartoons or drawings to illustrate processes, how things work, motion over time, or to offer a 3-D perspective. The Multimedia Teaching Objects site http://tlt.its.psu.edu/mto at Pennsylvania State University is a repository of royalty-free animations in many disciplines that illustrate such varied items as the time value of money, the measurement of blood pressure or the electron flow in lightbulbs.

The SERC portal, http://serc.carleton.edu/index.html, based at Carleton College, is an excellent collection of resources for the sciences, including computerized simulations and simple animations. A visitor to this site can not only find links to simulations and animations but also guidelines, lesson plans, or assessments from instructors that can help provide context for the use of such multimedia objects. Similarly, the MERLOT (www.merlot.org) collection offers a number of links to simulations and animations, with commentary about how they might be used in teaching. Many Merlot materials are accompanied by peer reviews of the resource, pointing out the special features of an item or suggesting ways in which it can be incorporated into a course activity. They will also report concerns about a site such as a high percentage of broken links. To find the gold among these resources, you will need to set aside some time to try them out on your own. However, the advantage of sites like SERC and MERLOT is that they bear the traces of other educators who have searched before you and can often give you a head start in evaluating whether they are appropriate for your own class. Keeping this in mind, we suggest that if you discover a resource and devise a way to integrate it into your course, you take advantage of the opportunity provided by MERLOT to leave your own comment for others to find.

There are also CDs and DVDs offered by publishers and web sites that provide simulations on a low-cost subscription basis. You may want to consider these resources in the same way that you would a traditional text that you might order for your students. By integrating computer-based simulations into your readings and structuring an assignment around a simulation, you can provide a resource so that online students can participate in a hands-on activity.

Finally, if you are lucky enough to have your university create computer-based simulations or animations that you can use in your course, be mindful that it still rests with you to devise a meaningful activity to take advantage of that multimedia object. Whether it is as uncomplicated as an animation demonstrating a single chemistry process or as complex as a criminal justice crime scene involving multiple decisions, you will still want to introduce and have students reflect or apply their experience in regard to one or more specific learning objectives. It may also be possible for you to gather data or observe how students use the simulation to pinpoint difficulties in grasping the material, diagnose problems, and provide additional instructional activities to meet those observed student needs.

Virtual-world simulations, like those conducted in Second Life or Active Worlds, previously described in Chapter 6, are often called immersive environments in that they contain features like 3-D, realistic graphics, or interactive elements which can help sustain the illusion and deepen involvement in a simulation. Again, in these environments, the instructor can begin with a scenario, but arrange for the role playing to take place in the virtual-world environment. This form of simulation does require considerably more planning, training, and preparation on the part of both instructor and students even if the instructor is not building a new area in the virtual world. For example, if you want your students to visit a virtual Istanbul, is it for the purpose of speaking Turkish while referring to objects in the environment of that virtual city? If you are running a public health emergency simulation in a virtual world, what are the roles, objectives, rules, and other details students need to know before entering the virtual world? Once having entered a virtual world, it can be very awkward and disruptive if participants are not properly oriented to the purpose of the activity.

But the sophistication of a virtual world or specially created software is not a necessary prerequisite for instructors to create simple but effective simulations through the use of text alone or text and graphics, with the addition of documents, audio or video, and other resources available on the Web. For example, a simulation involving American history could easily draw on the wealth of materials made available through the Smithsonian's American Memory site at http://memory.loc.gov/ammem/index. html while contemporary classes in political science, economics, and the sciences might use archived news stories and videos to provide the scenarios and bulletins needed to set the stage or provide dramatic turning points within a simulation.

For all these sorts of simulations, whether low-tech or high-tech in nature, it is advisable to provide the following:

- ◼ an introduction to the simulation, setting the stage for the simulation through background information, identification of the issues or problems, readings, research, discussion as appropriate. Provide technical preparation or practice if needed when software is used in a simulation;

- ◼ an initiating scenario that "kicks off" the simulation;

- clearly defined roles for those taking part in the simulation, with opportunities for those participants to research and prepare for their roles;

- "time out" periods if needed to discuss the activity or, at the very least, a clear indication of how to ask questions or obtain information during the simulation;

- a debriefing exercise at the end in which the results and experience of the simulation can be discussed and, if desired, a follow-up assignment.

● ● ● ● ●

Summaries, Consensus Groups

A very uncomplicated but effective online activity is to ask students, either individually or as a group, to summarize some aspect of a course's activities, discussions, or readings. This process reinforces the material and provides additional perspectives from the students themselves about the course's themes and foci. It also serves to help students synthesize the discussion and topics of study in a busy online classroom. This can be particularly important in a classroom that is highly interactive, one that has many students, or one in which students are divided up into smaller groups for a portion of their work.

When you have an online class with fifty or more students, it's usually necessary to divide it up for discussion. But students need to know what transpires in the rest of the class, as well as what they can learn from their own group activities. Having small groups of students present their summaries to the entire class forum allows students to analyze and then synthesize a wide variety of material. It permits students to feel involved in the larger class while maintaining the interaction and focus of the smaller groups.

A variation on this procedure is to ask each small group to appoint a spokesperson who not only will present a summary of findings to the entire class but also will lead a discussion. Or one person from the group can present the summary while another from the group responds to questions and comments from the rest of the class.

Yet another version of this activity is to ask small groups of students to meet and discuss an assigned topic with the goal of coming to a consensus on that issue. Each team can then be asked to present their group's findings to the whole class. Consensus groups may work particularly well when you find that students do not feel comfortable openly disagreeing with other individuals in the classroom or in conjunction with problem-based learning or the use of case studies. Consensus groups can collaborate within group areas of CMS software, in a discussion forum dedicated to a small group, by using wikis to compose their thoughts, or by means of a group blog. A consensus group might also create an audio or video to present their ideas.

●●●●●

The Experience-Based Practicum or Lab Assignment

The online class that includes a practicum or similar activity can not only provide all the advantages of traditional field-based exercises but offer some additional benefits as well.

A practicum by its nature involves the organizing and accomplishment of an individualized plan of action. Even though the practicum may rely mainly on the student's performing some activity in the real world, the online environment allows opportunities for peer review and exchanges with classmates, to help the individual reflect on his or her experience. The feedback might occur in response to obligatory weekly or monthly reports. Or students involved in a practicum could make occasional postings whenever they needed feedback from the instructor or from classmates.

In an education course, for example, a practicum or field-based exercise might involve the student's observation of a classroom situation, the creation of a lesson plan, an internship situation, or the conducting of an interview with an educator or administrator. Reports of that experience might then be shared with others in the online classroom, and classmates might be asked to critique or pose questions to the presenter.

Lab work presents unique challenges to instructors who are teaching online classes although institutions with the means to do so are increasingly using lab simulations to provide these resources to their online students. In regard to computer science studies, it is becoming increasingly easy to find reasonably priced online computer learning arrangements through subscriptions. But for those instructors who do not have access to these online lab simulations, some instructors devise lab kits that students can use to do simple science experiments at home in introductory courses. Others arrange for students to work in labs at nearby campuses or to use videoconferencing to observe lab experiments. Still others rely on a combination of these methods along with DVDs and the types of computer-based simulations discussed earlier in this chapter. For some institutions whose online students reside within a well defined geographic area or who may even be residing on campus, the blended course may be the ideal solution. Whatever the methods used to integrate lab work into the online classroom, the lab component needs to be carefully thought out and arranged well before the course begins.

● ● ● ● ●

Reflective Activities

Reflective activities such as journaling encourage thoughtful, focused consideration and critiques of a topic, and are generally carried out on an individual basis. The great thing about these activities is that they allow a student to measure his or her progress in learning over time. Sometimes, it might be helpful for the larger class to also offer feedback to the journaler, depending on the nature of the reflective exercise. Journaling already has a long history of use in online classes, especially those in teacher education. In the past, this was usually carried out through the submission of word-processed documents or written in the spaces of online workbook-like CMS areas. Sometimes this was accomplished by asking students to create personal web pages, combining text, images, and links to web resources to create a reflective piece. Often students had to learn a bit of HMTL unless a WYSIWYG-type interface was available to them, and because it was not always convenient for students to make updates, this sort of web page journal was often limited to a single concerted effort, in the form of one assignment or project.

The arrival of blogging software has made the blog one of the easiest methods to accomplish this sort of reflective journal, allowing quick and easy updates and the addition of multimedia. Many educators worldwide, from K–12 teachers to university instructors, have found the blog a good fit for students to reflect on their development throughout a course. Writing instructors in particular have found the blog to be an effective format for the showcasing and sharing of writing assignments. Students can maintain individual blogs or a class blog can be created by which all students contribute their reflections.

Les Pang teaches an undergraduate course in Information Technology Foundations at University of Maryland University College, and uses blogging for the purpose of what he terms "reflective learning journals." He has students use free blogging software which is external to their course management system to create their own reflective journals. Students have three major categories of assignments related to these journals. First, students post an introduction on their blog at the beginning of the class. Next, they are assigned a weekly blog response, addressing three questions:

- What did you learn in the preceding week—not a list of facts, but what can you take away from the lesson, what has value to you?
- How do you connect what you learned this week with your personal experience or with what you already knew?
- How could/would you apply your new knowledge?

Finally, students are assigned a reflection at the end of the course, an overall summation.

Les Pang connects all the student blogs by an index page so that students have potential access to all the journals of classmates. He is quick to point out that if your journaling activities involve more personal issues, it may be desirable to have blogs kept private, open only to the instructor's gaze. Students are free to post comments in response to their classmates' blogs, but are not required to do so. Pang adds a unique element to this reflective exercise by maintaining an instructor blog. The instructor's blog affords a way to reinforce points, reassure, and sum up issues. The instructor's blog functions in some ways as an announcement section of a CMS might be utilized, but allows for more elaboration and detailed explanations than does the relatively abbreviated announcement area.

Pang notes that some of the benefits of reflective blogs to the instructor include the enhanced ability to monitor student progress, to garner continuous student feedback rather than waiting until the end of the semester, and to quickly identify challenges related to weekly class activities before serious problems set in. He concedes that it does involve increased workload for instructors to find the time to read and respond to the student blogs, but Pang has found it relatively painless to keep up by using an aggregator, Google Reader, and subscribing to each blog. This means that he can simply open up Google Reader each week and follow all his student blogs without having to separately log in and check each one.

To make the reflective blogs a more meaningful activity, Les Pang emphasizes developing a rubric for grading the blog contributions, encouraging students to find creative ways to reflect on their class lessons—whether by text, audio, video, or other means—and establishing minimum requirements as to minimum length and structure, as well as what to include or avoid (for example, avoiding blog posts or photos of a too personal nature, making impolite comments about another's blog, linking to resources that are not pertinent to the class subject matter).

Michelle Pacansky-Brock made the creation of "artblogs" by students a significant form of assessment in her Art Appreciation class at Sierra College, comprising 20 percent of the final grade. But rather than simply leaving students to jot down their impressions, she assigned blog entry topics each week as homework, providing detailed instructions for each assignment. Some were open-ended "reflections" while others were more directed—for example, requiring that students visit a local museum or gallery opening. She asked that students demonstrate an understanding of course concepts and a deep reflection on what they saw. Students were also encouraged to make extra blog entries about what they observed in daily life that related to class. As Pacansky-Brock explained it to her students,

> *share your perspective about a current art controversy occurring in your community, comment about a painting you saw in a doctor's office that resembles the work of an artist you read about in your book, reflect on the form and content of a movie you saw. The ArtBlog will reflect how deeply you've internalized the concepts from our class and have begun to apply them to your own daily activities.*

Pacansky-Brock encouraged students to be creative, using color, images, and other decorative elements that reflect their aesthetic preferences and to show their own artwork as well. She further encouraged students to post comments on their classmates' blogs and even had a competition whereby she asked students to nominate an ArtBlog of a classmate that they think is worthy of being called a "masterpiece." Students who received at least three nominations could be awarded ten extra credit points.

There is a large global community of educators who use blogs to communicate their ideas about teaching and learning and many of these offer tips on the use of student blogs that may have a special relevance to your own teaching. See the Guide to Resources for a few of these.

While blogs are an obvious format to set the stage for journaling activities, Rich Cerkovnik, who teaches Introduction to Physical Science to undergraduates at University of Maryland University College, uses the discussion forum structure within his course management system as a means to the same end. In weekly "concept conferences" students are asked to choose from a selection of topics on which to focus their writing and reflection. As Cerkovnik expresses it in the course syllabus, "the purpose for the concept conference is for you to personally process the information from your reading, activities, and discussions to make your current understandings visible and helpful to your classmates and me." Cerkovnik clearly lays out the requirements for the concept conference postings, with each entry comprising 50–300 words and each addressing either an occasional instructor-set topic of the week or one of the following:

- Makes Sense—discuss one thing related to this week's readings, activities, or discussions that makes sense to you. Use enough detail to convince me that you understand.
- Does Not Make Sense—discuss one thing ... that does not make sense to you. Discuss which aspects of the concept confuse you.
- My Life—discuss how a concept related to this week's readings, activities, or discussions relates to an experience from your own life.
- Change in Thinking—discuss how a concept you now understand related to this week's readings, activities, or discussions is different from what you had previously thought.
- Resource—identify a concept (i.e., gravity, inertia, balancing chemical equations, etc.) that you feel it would be of benefit to you to understand better. Identify a resource that accomplished the goal of deepening your understanding of the concept in question ... perform a search using a Web search engine and at least one University of Maryland University College database ... for resources on your selected concept ... describe your personal understanding of the concept prior to finding and using the resource and then afterwards. Report on how the resource accomplished the goal of deepening your understanding of the concept in question.

With students posting questions to another forum each week, Cerkovnik notes that these concept conference postings will necessarily contain incorrect concepts that need to be modified but that students are not assessed for correctness in these postings but for relevance and engagement. The instructor and the class, he says, "can then work to modify and expand the understanding of these concepts." Students are credited up to one point for each of their weekly concept conference postings, while they can earn twice that amount for responses that provide "useful assistance to other students." Students are asked to assess their participation three times during the semester in the form of a report in which they review their postings and assign a score. The instructor then either agrees or disagrees with the self-assessed score and provides feedback. The student therefore must provide evidence and the rationale for a particular score.

In a basic science class designed for non-majors, Cerkovnik points out that this type of participation activity not only helps create a non-threatening environment to facilitate student reflection, but also minimizes frivolous postings. Students feel they have been fairly assessed and, beyond that, there is an increased level of incentive to produce responses that assist the learning of classmates, resulting in a "shared responsibility for learning" and a strong sense of community within the classroom.

Finally, ordinary word-processed essays still provide an effective means for quick reflective pieces. Jonathan Mathews teaches Energy and the Environment online at Pennsylvania State University both through its World Campus and to resident students. For each of the course's lessons, he asks his students to write an informal reflective essay in response to a specific question. Mathews characterizes these as "brain-dumps," casual pieces that compel students to think of each topic in personal terms. For example, students studying a lesson on pollution will be asked to rate their individual impact on pollution caused by their own travel. Mathews guides students with a set of simple criteria, provides some examples, and emphasizes that they should spend no more than five minutes on "unrehearsed," casual responses.

●●●●●

Just Discussion

People often refer to online discussion as a given, but as suggested in Chapters 3 and 6 there are many activities beyond "just discussion" that can take place in a discussion forum—it is a logical area to base the ongoing question-and-answer sequence of a course, for demonstrations of problem solving, to provide a place for students to present their work, and many of the activities previously described such as debates, scenarios, and role-playing can be carried out there as well.

But in regard to the category of "just discussion," there is still a lot of variation in what the objective might be for such an activity. As indicated in Chapter 3, this is something that should be planned during the design of your course but one should also remain open to spontaneously occurring opportunities for a discussion. In Chapter 11, we discuss how to set up and manage an asynchronous discussion. Here we want to set out a few rules for "just discussion."

1. *Coverage:* All major content areas need a corresponding forum for discussion or, at the very least, an opportunity for questions. If you are asking students to read or research a topic area, you should provide some way for them to address issues that arise with that topic.

2. *Objective:* Determine the level of thinking or instructional objective you are aiming for in establishing the discussion. (Bloom's Taxonomy might come in handy here.) Is it associated with both recall and identification, to make sure that students are actually reading the material? ("After reading X, what two or three major trends did you discern concerning labor in the early industrial period?") Or are you asking students to analyze the material, and perhaps question the assumptions as well? ("What were the author's underlying assumptions about X, what evidence does he cite, and are there any flaws in his logic?") Or are you asking them to share and query each other about ideas synthesized from more than one of the readings? ("Author X identifies the following as the main abuses of our globalized economy. Please share with us any results from your research that would tend to affirm or refute author X's assertions and post at least one response, comment, or questions to a classmate whose reply differs from your own.")

3. *Spur of the moment:* While you will have likely established a regular pattern for discussions, don't be afraid to create a new topic thread when indications seem to call for it. It is impossible to anticipate every teaching situation, and the particular student mix and ensuing dynamic in our classes may change from term to term. For example, if you find on the basis of the results from the first writing assignment that

many students fail to comprehend the finer points of providing evidence for their arguments, you may want to go beyond simply referring them to an external resource, and hold a discussion on the topic before they start work on the next paper. You might post a negative example of an argument and ask students to identify the missing elements in the evidence or to find the point in the reasoning when logic went awry.

Or perhaps an event in the news might spur you to create a topic thread to discuss the ramifications that event might have for one of the issues in your course. Since such news items are timely and may spur the interest of students, you might well want to take advantage of such an event that provides a teaching opportunity.

● ● ● ● ●

Scenarios and Case Studies

Scenarios present concrete situations that can be used to stimulate analysis, requiring students to imagine how they might respond to a particular set of circumstances. In an on-the-ground classroom, scenarios typically involve hands-on activities. Online, scenarios can be used to provoke responses related to matters such as procedures and planning. They can constitute a type of problem-based learning in which a specific challenge is presented and students are asked to find approaches to resolving the issues. Scenario questions can transform an abstract or theoretical discussion into one in which students demonstrate concrete problem-solving skills in a particular context. Scenarios may also stimulate debate on a variety of approaches, thus acting as a valuable tool for bringing multiple perspectives to a problem. In either individual assignments or group activities, scenarios are a particularly good vehicle for stimulating students' thoughts about step-by-step planning or the process of reaching a solution.

Scenarios have proved to be popular approaches in health and medical education, in ethics training, in teacher education, business, and criminal justice. Handling these online within an asynchronous communication environment can actually provide conditions more conducive to the success of such approaches as students are afforded more time for reflection and collaboration with others on a problem.

Case studies, similar to scenarios but typically less open-ended, are easy to transfer to the online environment. They are basically stories that present a specific situation or a set of facts, either real or hypothetical, and there is little difficulty in posting them online. Case studies call for analysis or for the application of principles learned in the class. For example, a case study in an accounting class for CPAs might describe the financial profile and statistics of a business and ask questions about its tax status. Problem-based case studies may either present a clear-cut problem or set up a situation in which students must identify both problem and solution.

Case studies can easily form the basis of a written assignment, questions for a quiz, or a series of questions that you pose for a discussion forum. Like scenarios, case studies may be used for both individual assignments and group assignments. Online, case studies provide enriched opportunities over their use in face-to-face courses, with the rich variety of online resources readily accessible for research. Students can be assigned case studies as individual work, but online, the small group structure can provide increased opportunities for interaction and expanded learning through the sharing of ideas by a team.

Al Turgeon teaches an online course in Turf Management, "Case Studies in Turfgrass Management," for Pennylvania State's World Campus that uses this case study approach as its main organizing principle. Turgeon explains his approach: "We begin with an orientation case in which I attempt to teach them how to analyze the case using concept mapping, and how to come up with appropriate solutions or amelioration strategies using decision trees."

Students work together in teams of five or six members each. Each team member is responsible for contributing responses to a total of three cases, and for posting their reports, concept map, and decision tree to the team's discussion forum. Members then pose questions and respond to questions posed to them by others on the team. Finally, they revise their individual reports in preparation for grading and feedback from Turgeon. Turgeon applies a grading rubric developed for each case. After the completion of these three cases, students are asked to develop a case from their own real-world experience.

There are many resources now available that provide examples of case studies that you might use or adapt for your own classes. For example, in the sciences there is the National Center for Case Study Teaching in Science collection by the State University of New York at Buffalo. The Center not only provides cases but also includes instructor guideline notes at http://ublib.buffalo.edu/libraries/projects/cases/ubcase.htm.

For those involved in management studies, through the MIT Sloan Teaching Innovation Resources site at https://mitsloan.mit.edu/MSTIR/Pages/default.aspx, instructors can download and freely use case studies in such areas as industry evolution, sustainability, and global entrepreneurship. Public Health Games (www.publichealthgames.com) provides links to simulations and games in which scenarios such as a bioterrorism attack or a natural disaster striking a community are presented, with the participant choosing a role to play and decisions to make in response. The ChemCollective (www.chemcollective.org) hosts a variety of simulations, virtual labs, and scenario-based activities for chemistry courses.

Beyond those available on the Web, you can create scenarios and case studies on your own using simple video and slide show tools. Situations can be demonstrated through photographs, video already available online, your own staged dialogue, or narration over text and images. While purely text-based case studies and scenarios work well online, it's increasingly easy to enliven cases for your students with the use of multimedia even if you cannot create more sophisticated online applications on your own.

● ● ● ● ●

Peer Editing and Review

Peer editing, review, and evaluation are marvelous activities from the standpoint of workload management, enabling an instructor to provide students in a large class with additional opportunities for feedback. Several examples have already been provided of peer-review evaluation rubrics. These activities are also intrinsically beneficial to students, for at least two reasons. First, they require students to view the criteria for an assignment with fresh eyes. This helps them critically review their own work. Second, students get the benefit of a perspective other than the instructor's, and sometimes that can provide added insight.

Whether on the ground or online, peer-review activities are most effective when instructors provide specific questions or defined criteria to use in evaluation and editing. For example, an evaluation rubric sets the criteria for each grade designation, explaining what "100%" or "5 points" or "B+" indicates. If a student is evaluating an essay, the rubric may state that five points are to be awarded only if the essay contains certain specific elements; if two of these elements are lacking, the essay rates only three points. Similarly, a series of guideline questions, coordinated with the original guidelines for the assignment, can focus the peer reviewer's attention: "Did the paper summarize the main thesis of the article? According to the author of the paper, what evidence was given in the article that supports the conclusions of Dr. X?"

For peer-review to be most effective, students should be graded as much on their work as reviewers as on their classmates' reviews of their work. Students often worry about being unfairly appraised by the inexpert eyes of their fellow students. But if they are graded on how well they review others, students will exercise more prudence and care in their reviews, and they will be assured that at least one portion of this peer assignment is receiving the attention of the instructor.

●●●●●

Student Activities Involving Guest Speakers

You can bring in a guest "speaker" for a period of several days or a week, during which time he or she will post some material and be available for questions. Or you can simply post the material from the speaker in the asynchronous class forum. The material may be plain text, or it may take the form of a Power-Point lecture or audio presentation.

In some cases, a guest speaker may be available only for a live, real-time chat experience. Because chat is at best a fast-paced activity that demands quick thinking, you should make sure that students are familiar enough with the speaker's material that they can make informed comments and frame relevant questions. We recommend that you ask the guest to submit some materials in advance for you to post before the chat date. Students can then read the materials and prepare themselves for the chat. On the basis of this asynchronous posting, you may also wish to ask students to submit questions to convey to the guest prior to the chat date.

During the chat, in addition to introducing the guest speaker and setting some ground rules, you may want to act as moderator. We recommend, too, that you save and post the transcript of the chat for the benefit of students who cannot attend. Then, if it's possible for the guest to make him- or herself available later for a set period of time, students can pose their questions in the asynchronous discussion forum and have the guest reply to them there.

Generally, then, the keys to making guest appearances serve as valuable learning experiences are:

1. providing an asynchronous channel for questions and answers, as well as for the presentation of the guest's main material;

2. budgeting adequate time for students to prepare themselves for any real-time activities.

One advantage of a guest speaker is that it provides students with another expert voice apart from their instructor. This brings fresh perspectives, and a series of speakers can add to the diversity of such views. If you teach a blended class, you can use the online environment to help students prepare for the guest speaker at the on-site meeting, or to continue the conversation online after the speaker has presented. Some guests will be available to take part online, through a guest account in your CMS that permits the guests to post materials and engage with students in the discussion area. If your guest has very limited time, at the very least you can take questions from the students and relay these to the guest. And perhaps the guest can prepare a PowerPoint or audio presentation that you can provide to students. Another option is to record an audio interview with a guest speaker via online chat software. If you cannot record and save it within the program, there are free third-party software applications available that can allow you to do this (you can search for the latest of these on the Web as they change from week to week). Or you can use an inexpensive piece of hardware to connect a phone to a recording device, or make you call using an Internet telephony service such as Skype along with recording software. See more about recording audio in Chapter 9.

If you do not have a guest speaker readily available to meet with your students online, with the ubiquity of YouTube videos or iTunesU podcasts of distinguished speakers in a variety of subject matter, you may be able to find a virtual guest speaker through the medium of video and audio resources existing on the Web. While you may not produce a live performance or customized presentation in this way, you are still providing your students with another voice and dimension to a subject. In his course Introduction to Philosophy and Critical Approaches to Literature at University of Maryland University College, Richard Schumaker found that by referring his students to podcasts on iTunesU by an eminent philosophy professor, he was introducing them to an approach in philosophy that was quite different from his own, and that this contrast in approach stimulated students to explore the reasons for that difference. While Schumaker might have achieved the same result through a series of diverse reading assignments, listening to the podcasts likely provided students with a much more immediate and lively illustration of contrasting approaches, which more closely approximates a presentation by a guest speaker.

● ● ● ● ●

Cross-Cultural Exchanges

When a course involves students from two or more countries, it can be an exciting learning opportunity. Naturally there are also many barriers to overcome.

First, assuming the countries have different languages, which language will be used to communicate? If one is chosen as the common language, will the students for whom it is not a native language be able to receive some assistance when communication is not clear? At each principal site, it is helpful to have an instructor or assistant who is bilingual and who can intervene or redirect conversation when communications become garbled or strained.

A related issue is whether the main texts will be available in one or both languages. Even when one group of students is fairly proficient in speaking the other's language, it may be a strain for them to keep up with the pace of reading challenging texts in that language.

One barrier that needs to be dissolved before the exchange begins is that of conflicting schedules. Students in one country may be just about to embark upon vacation when students in the other country are midway through a semester. Overall terms may vary greatly in length and prolonged holiday periods may not be observed in both countries. So the cooperation may need to be confined to a particular period during which both classes are in session or it may be arranged so that certain stages of a project are carried out at some periods within one country's own group, with other stages of the project planned for times when the two countries' schedules coincide.

Another potential challenge relates to cultural patterns of learning. If students are used to an instructor-centered classroom where there is little student-initiated participation, they may need specific guidelines about when and how to volunteer their comments and questions. In some cases, students' habits of learning may not be readily apparent until the course begins. You may need to rely on your co-teacher to play the role of informant for his or her culture.

It may be best for organizers or leaders at each site to develop a set of guidelines for both instructors and students, covering communications in the classroom as well as expectations for written assignments. The latter would involve guidelines for writing as well as rules about plagiarism and originality. For example, in many Asian countries, modeling one's work on that of an authority or expert has long been a traditional study method, whereas in Western countries this might be interpreted to some degree as plagiarism. To avoid misunderstandings, you can develop mutually agreed-upon policies that are posted for students to read.

Make sure, too, that the forums for discussion are clearly established and that file-exchange methods and file formats are all made explicit. Place, time, method, and the rules of engagement should be clearly delineated in every online class or online component of a class, but these are even more crucial for classes involving two different countries.

Cross-Cultural Teams

In cross-cultural courses, one question that often arises is whether to form teams composed of a mixture of students from both countries or to have each country's students form their own team. The latter setup is easier to organize, but the former may lead to better cross-cultural exchanges and greater opportunities for new perspectives. Again, the ability to form cross-cultural teams will depend a great deal on whether or not the two countries have concurrent time periods during which collaboration will be possible.

If you choose to create teams that mix students of different countries, do prepare specific guidelines about times and frequency of communications. Remind students about the time differences. Ask your counterparts about details such as ease and frequency of Internet access. Students in many countries have only limited Internet access at the campus site, and Internet service providers and phone connections in many countries are not stable. Find out how often students are likely to suffer broken Internet connections midway through their work. If Internet connections are unreliable, you would want to avoid scheduling many real-time activities, and you should probably build in more time for asynchronous activities to be coordinated.

Another potential difficulty arises when students in another country observe different religious and secular holidays than those at your site. Keep in mind that students who do not have reliable Internet connections (or even computers) in their homes will be unable to communicate online during those periods.

Jon Rubin is head of the Center for Online Collaborative Learning (known as COIL) of the State University of New York (SUNY) system at Purchase College. The center promotes online, international learning collaborations. Rubin himself has been teaching a Cross-Cultural Video Production course for several years, partnering with institutions and team teaching with instructors in a variety of different countries, beginning in 2002–2003 with Belarus, and thereafter with Mexico and Turkey. A detailed description of the development of this course exists on the COIL site at http://coilcenter.purchase.edu/index.php?option=com_content&task=view&id=22&Itemid=141.

Rubin emphasizes the importance of getting to know the partnering instructor in some depth before beginning the teaching and learning collaboration. He suggests that partners:

> *Meet face-to-face first if at all possible, at least three months before the course is to begin. Otherwise, spend some time on the phone or even better in video conference so you can establish real rapport. Your relationship will be the basis of what happens in the course.*

Other recommendations from Rubin are:

- Go over carefully all possible scheduling conflicts: academic calendars, time zone differences, university holidays, etc.

- Discuss each teacher's experience with the CMS/LMS or other software that you plan to use for collaboration. Make sure that some form of tech support is in place and that adequate technology and access is in place.

- Consider carefully the goals of the shared course. Make sure that key terms are mutually understood.

- Make each participating instructor's responsibilities clear from the outset. Teaching for some instructors may consist mainly of lecturing and such instructors may not be familiar with assuming a more facilitative role. Also, an instructor might assume that he or she will take a back-seat role, as if the course mainly belongs to the other, with himself as a participant in the grand scheme. The instructors on both sides need to commit to doing certain things such as alternating in their leading of discussion.

- When developing your syllabus, dedicate time to exploring cultural aspects of the exchange and provide time for trust to develop so that collaboration is possible. Cross-cultural courses can range from those that are more discipline-centric to those with more focus on the cross-cultural aspects.

Rubin says that collaborative exercises work well "if they are about sharing ideas rather than doing something correctly." He explains, "I think that what you learn is that what seems so evidently correct from one perspective can seem wrong or just curious from another perspective." He suggests that the tenor of questions should be oriented toward "what is your perspective on such and such?"

Rubin uses an icebreaking activity involving creative writing wherein two to four students pass a story back and forth, each side adding a paragraph to the story. This serves as a warm-up for his main video production activity in which duos of two students from each country collaborate on a theme to create a video. There are four scenes to be produced based on a chosen theme, with one side taking the first two weeks to make the first scene, then passing it to the second group to respond with the second scene and so on.

The Challenges and Rewards of Cross-Cultural Courses

In regard to the potential for misunderstandings, Rubin has a unique perspective on this issue. "Misunderstandings," he says,

> were the central thread of the experience. Because students were asked to continue or respond to a video scene made in the other culture, and because their own egos were invested in their own productions, they almost always found their expectations confounded by the work of their partners. Finding a common path through this conceptual thicket was the real key to a satisfying collaborative experience.

For example, he notes that American students often tend to be ironic or flippant in attitude and assume that others from the partnering culture will get the joke, but often that is not the case. At one point during the back and forth of creating a video on the theme of "A Day in the Life," an American student, noting the rather melancholy mood of the other side's scene, gave a teasing title, "My Life is Better than Your Life" to his video response. None of the American students took the title seriously but the partnering students were offended by this seeming deprecatory comment on their work and Rubin notes that "it then took weeks to work through the source of this misunderstanding, but this was an important learning experience for both groups." Students ended up discussing the concept of irony and what it means to be "serious."

Even seemingly trivial assignments can reveal surprising cultural differences. For example, Rubin notes that when students in a class composed of students from the United States and Mexico were asked to post "a photo that represents yourself" the American students posted frontal facial shots or somewhat humorous, very individual shots, but almost always of themselves alone. However, at least one-third of the Mexican students portrayed themselves by posting photos of them accompanied by family or girlfriends/boyfriends.

Rubin also reminds us that cross-cultural courses constitute a nexus of both cultural and personal perspectives. For example, he says that when a group views an image and tries to address the question of what is of importance in the picture, the responses will "vary by individual as well as by culture."

In Rubin's case, while the cross-cultural experience is conducted online, the context is that of a blended class, with each country's class also meeting face-to-face on their own. He points out that the question of how to share what happens in the face-to-face meetings with the other side is one that needs to be carefully considered, or there is a risk that the face-to-face sessions can become "a place for withdrawal from the interaction," with each side "talking about the other side." Rubin suggests that one way to handle this challenge is to designate a student to take notes on each face-to-face discussion to share with the other side when they again interact online. He emphasizes that this approach raises the question of whether the note-taking consists merely of minutes of the meetings, with sensitive issues omitted, or whether the purpose would be to convey the essence of what was discussed, including a framing of the possibly controversial points? In any case, Rubin recommends that a template and some rules be established to ensure that the reporting follows along the lines of agreed-upon conventions. Instructors may also want to agree on an overall approach for integrating the online activity into their own face-to-face meetings.

Even though cross-cultural international courses present complex issues, the rewards can be enormous. There is an opportunity, not unlike studying in a foreign country, to encounter another culture on its own terms. There is the possibility of creating knowledge through collaborative activities that draw on the strengths of individuals as well as the diverse perspectives of different cultures. Cross-cultural collaborative assignments, notes Rubin, mean that "students have to build on others' work and also anticipate what will be workable and of interest for the other side."

Rubin notes that only a small percentage of students anywhere will ever study abroad, but "A structured interaction with a group of students in another country can really open students up to the world," while for faculty, "encountering the learning styles and new perspectives of international students is always a challenge, but one that can also be transformative, especially in a class that is focused on the value of cultural exchange."

● ● ● ● ●

Using the Web as a Resource

One often-overlooked aspect of planning course activities is the use of the Web itself as a basis for assigned work. The frequent neglect of this option arises, in part, from the sheer vastness of the Web. To most of us, it is like an immense sea of information. There are so many documents, databases, archives, and collections to be examined that looking out at it is somewhat like standing at the edge of the ocean. It seems safer to stay within the confines of our own web sites, with their more familiar course materials and tools.

But when you do limit student activities to your own course site, you and your students are totally dependent on information that you provide, and this inevitably restricts the course's breadth and scope. We hope, therefore, that you will make use of the Web's rich potential for student activities. In this section we will suggest how you can do so without allowing yourself or your students to become inundated in a sea of minutiae.

Preparing the Way

Whenever you use the Web as part of an assignment or activity, you should take care to examine the material yourself before assigning it to your class.

This point may seem obvious, but it is all too often ignored. Instructors often prefer to employ something that might be called the "treasure hunt" approach. They tell their students that somewhere out there on the Web sits a valuable nugget of information yearning to be found. They arm the students with either a list of possible sites where this precious nugget might be found or instructions for using a search engine to hunt it down. The students then spend more time than they can afford clicking through links that lead nowhere or scrolling through pages of irrelevant text until the desired information is found, copied, and bookmarked, and the requisite posting is made on the course discussion board.

It's fun to explore and rewarding to make discoveries, but the treasure-hunt approach is often both impractical and unsound. Spending an inordinate amount of time hunting and tracking through link after link can become a frustrating experience for students—one that is even more bothersome if it seems irrelevant. If the task is to examine a given piece of information, why not simply direct the students to it rather than require them to ferret it out?

There is a place for such web exploration, of course. If a student is trying to refute a given piece of information—or to affirm it—he or she may very well want to search out applicable material to make the case. Similarly, when researching an essay or a project, students often will scour the Web on their own, because they feel it is effective to do so and because they feel confident they can assess the material they find. Or if the assignment is basically one to help the student attain some level of information literacy, it may be that learning how to do a search is itself the goal.

For most situations, however—such as a homework assignment or a question on a quiz—you should probably do the hunting yourself and let the students spend their time learning instead of searching.

Evaluating Web Sites

What criteria should you use in choosing web sites for your course? You should evaluate each site for quality, just as you would any other resource.

First, you can apply the same guidelines you would use in choosing a book or article for a reference list supplied to your students. For example,

- check the site's sponsorship;
- check the authorship of any articles or sections on the site;
- assess the relevance of the material to your topics. Does it bear only a tangential relevance to what you intend to examine or discuss, or is it closely connected?

Second, you can apply some additional scrutiny to the web material that you probably would not need to apply to books and articles. You can ask questions like these:

- How well is the site designed?
- How difficult is the site to navigate? Will students be able to find the most relevant material without wading through extraneous details or unnecessary links?

Varieties of Useful Web Sites

Once you begin exploring web resources, you'll find that articles are not the only web materials that will prove useful for your course. Equally valuable choices are sites that provide graphic examples, documentation, or illustrations of your main topics and principles. Works of German Expressionist art from the 1920s might provide a good starting point for a discussion of the impact of World War I on Germany. Photographs found online might provide the basis for an essay. You may also base a research project on students' exploration of a web site. In that case, you would want to provide some questions or pose specific problems for the students to tackle during their visits to the site. Some sites specifically categorize themselves as open educational resources (often called OER) and these can often be used within your own course. These usually carry a permissions statement that declares that the material on the web site may be repurposed or copied for educational use as long as proper attribution is made. Other sites have more restricted terms of use posted that allow for educational reuse but not for distribution outside the class or repurposing or combining with other content. We discuss OERs in more depth in future chapters, but at this point, we want to make you aware of the different types of public sites that exist.

Here are some of the different types of potentially useful sites you can expect to find on the Web:

Collections and Portals   Some sites on the Web offer collections of photos, speeches, essays, art, documents, articles, and recordings. These provide raw materials with which you can fashion a focused and relevant assignment or discussion. Others are portals to suggest pathways of links to find resources. Finding all of these is no more difficult than conducting a simple Google search. Some examples that demonstrate the range of these are:

- The National Geographic Map Machine: http://maps.nationalgeographic.com/map-machine allows one to search for maps worldwide, with street, birds-eye, satellite, and 3-D maps available. Google Maps and Google Earth can similarly allow one to interactively explore the globe and the oceans.

- The Atlas image database of the Louvre in Paris at www.louvre.fr/llv/oeuvres/bdd_oeuvre.jsp?bmLocale=en offers views of 35,000 works in the museum. Many of the major world museums offer databases of art works or at least samples of art from their collections.

- The World Radio Network, which carries "on demand" audio programs and podcasts from radio stations all over the world: www.wrn.org/listeners/#stations

- World Wide Internet TV, http://wwiTv.com, a portal featuring direct links to live online streaming from television stations worldwide, in the languages of diverse countries but also sometimes in English. Both this and the World Radio Network provide access to material that can be used in courses on language, culture, and contemporary affairs.
- The Internet Archive, www.archive.org/index.php, is a free library resource of web sites and other digital content.
- Free Music Archive, http://freemusicarchive.org, a curated collection of music as well as a social networking site.
- Europeana, www.europeana.eu/portal, is a portal that provides access to digital materials from different sources in Europe, including text, images, video and sound.
- UNESCO's World Digital Library, www.wdl.org, launched in 2009 and available in seven languages, offers primary-source cultural materials from all over the world—manuscripts, recordings, photographs, drawings, etc. It has a handy quick-browsing feature wherein one can browse based on a time period—so you can choose the period from 8000 BC to AD 499 and you will see a variety of artifacts ranging from an oracle bone from ancient China to rock art paintings from South Africa to various antiquities from ancient Egypt.

Online Magazines and News　Online magazines and news sources include the major news sources published online in nearly every language. There are also specialized sites for those interested in finance, literature, art, photography, and science. The Public Broadcasting Service (PBS) of the United States offers a wide array of multimedia resources on contemporary society, going back a decade. These can provide the basis of a single assignment or research project, or a continuing series of such assignments. However, not all of these offer open access to all sections of the site, and some charge if you want to access anything but the most recent issue. Others require registration even though they may be accessed free of charge. So, always research the access policies of online magazines and news sources if you intend to ask students to use them.

Commerical Sites   Maintained by major corporations for the purpose of promoting their products and services, such sites often contain valuable information but should be carefully identified and used in conjunction with targeted objectives. The same is true for sites maintained by nonprofit organizations.

Personal Sites   Maintained by individuals with a particular passion for Mozart, bamboo, or World War II weapons, for example, are often quirky (and sometimes verge on the crackpot), but they can provide valuable collection points for hyperlinks, photos, and documents. Some of these sites are in the form of blogs. These sites do not always provide the necessary citations and references to evaluate their material, so their inclusion in a course should probably be supplemented with warnings or commentary from the instructor to put the material into proper perspective.

Online Classroom Materials   Posted on the Web by educational institutions, materials associated with a specific course may prove worthwhile for your own class, especially if they cover topics similar to the ones you teach. But beware! These materials are notoriously ephemeral and may not last beyond next semester. If you want to use such materials, take note of the dates they were posted and contact the instructor listed to determine how long the site will remain available. More stable are the collections of opencourseware made available by institutions like MIT, Yale, and the Open University in the UK.

Annotated Collections of Links   Some sites provide annotated collections of links to other sites in a particular field. These are often hosted by universities. For example, EcEdWeb, the Economic Education web site hosted by the University of Nebraska, offers links to resources and lesson plans incorporating web resources on economics and related topics that are geared to K–12 as well as university-level instruction (http://ecedweb.unomaha.edu/home.htm). But these may also be hosted by individual educators—Larry Ferlazzo's Websites of the Day at http://larryferlazzo.edublogs.org is a valuable blog that is aimed at educators like himself teaching English as a second language, but his recommendations are often equally applicable for those teaching in other fields, from K–12 through university level. If you find a blog that provides worthwhile resources for your subject area, you will profit by subscribing to that blog through your RSS reader, start page, or email so that you can regularly review items of interest without having to schedule visits to multiple sites.

Image Collections   Beyond the many museums offering digitized views of artworks or photography, there are other sites that allow for inclusion of images in your own instructor-generated content or that can be used in conjunction with student projects. These range from amateur but often very good collections on sharing sites like Flickr (www.flickr.com) to the New York Public Library (www.npl.org). In Chapter 9 we will discuss how to find images that you or your students can use for free.

Sites Specializing in Sharing Video   The ubiquitous YouTube and YouTube EDU (http://youtube.com/edu) as well as the educator site, Teacher Tube (www.teachertube.com), permit users to upload and share video. Such sites can be valuable resources for course-related topics. YouTube presentations can be embedded (the code copied and pasted into your own classroom) so that students need not leave your course management system to access the video. Instructions for embedding content can be found on the YouTube site handbook and if you need more directions, a simple search at YouTube for "how to embed video" will produce a large selection of instructional videos made by users on the subject of how to embed YouTube videos into blogs, PowerPoint, web sites, etc.

Podcast and Vodcast Collections   Educational podcasts and vodcasts (video podcasting) on iTunesU have already been mentioned in this book but nearly every news source features podcasts on contemporary news and culture, including music. These have application for a wide variety of different courses whether as a single recording or a series of recordings.

Wikis on a Variety of Subject Areas   These are often most easily discovered through a simple search with Google or other search engine. Simply use the search terms for the subject matter (e.g., biology) plus "wiki."

There are some other excellent methods for finding resources in your field. You might consider joining a mailing list (listserv) or discussion forum in your discipline that shares information about web resources or subscribe to a blog that specializes in your field. This is a great way to quickly accumulate some solid leads. Second, you might look for professional association or academic web sites in your area of study that provide annotated links to web resources. Finally, there's no substitute for visiting and evaluating sites on your own. Try to budget short periods of time a few times a year that you can use just to search the Web for resources in your field.

However you decide to use the Web, whether as a resource or as part of a group activity or exercise, think twice before making a specific site optional rather than required. Often instructors post a list of links (or resources) and encourage students to use these for valuable supplementary information. But when students learn that they aren't required to visit a site, they usually won't. This doesn't indicate a lack of intellectual curiosity on their part. Rather, it indicates that students have other priorities: jobs, families, lovers, friends, finding an apartment, fixing the plumbing, walking pets, not to mention handling a full load of coursework from other classes. So, when they see the word optional attached to a given item on their syllabus, their natural instinct is to pass it by.

Using the Web as a Resource: Two Examples

Let's look at two examples of how web resources can be used as the focus of an assignment.

For a course on modern China, one of the authors, Susan Ko, made use of a number of publicly available web sites to give students added insights apart from the somewhat dry textbook readings and her own commentary.

For one assignment, she sent students to review original documents from the US National Security archive (www.gwu.edu/~nsarchiv/NSAEBB/NSAEBB66/#docs) on the "Shanghai Communique" of 1972 that led to the reopening of US relations with mainland China.

Students were asked to respond to questions in the discussion area,

> *Based on the NSA documents, what was most surprising to you about the way that relations between the US and China were reopened? What did you discover that you did not already know from your textbook readings and how would you characterize the discussions that took place between the two parties? Please give an example from one of the documents to illustrate your points.*

Another site used was a series of video interviews on a PBS video site, focusing on the years 1998–2001 in China, highlighting the great changes in the economy at this time (www.pbs.org/wgbh/pages/frontline/shows/red/view).

The interview segments were conducted with real people and their struggles to adjust to change. This site proved very popular because the students really liked being exposed to this more personalized view of change as revealed through the video interviews.

The corresponding discussion requested that students respond to one or more of the following questions:

1. What was the situation for state-owned, state-run industries in the late 1990s? Why were workers afraid for their futures? What happened to such workers? Use examples from the video to represent the different fates workers experienced.

2. Judging from these videos, what characteristics and circumstances do you think made a person more likely to thrive or fail in the new Chinese economy and society?

Another example is provided by Pam Taylor during her time as a nursing instructor at the University of Tennessee at Chattanooga. She built a series of seven online exercises that employed guided web search for specific information related to disease processes. Explaining the design of these exercises, she says they "provided for the increasing sophistication of the student's understanding of the pathophysiologic processes and web search skills."

In several cases, Taylor combined a case study method with the guided web research, asking students to apply the information learned to answer questions about a hypothetical patient. For example, she directed students to a series of web resource sites on hematology and cardiovascular topics. She then posted a case study of "John Smith" and asked students to answer a series of questions about Mr. Smith's health, based on the knowledge gleaned from the web sites. This was an individual assignment, in which students input their responses into an online form. The case study included graphic elements, such as a diagram of Mr. Smith's heart, as well as questions related to the graphics: "Mr. Smith is diagnosed with an inferior myocardial infarction. Use the following diagram to locate where the infarction occurred in Mr. Smith's heart." The student then had to check one of three boxes showing the location of the infarction.

What were Taylor's goals in using this approach to teaching? Taylor noted that she hoped to "present students with increasingly complex technology-related skill-building situations related to their course of study," as well as to "provide students with increasingly complex opportunities to apply their growing knowledge base of pathophysiology to situations which also require critical thinking skills."

● ● ● ● ●

A Grading Rubric for Every Activity?

A rubric is an assessment tool that offers a defined range and set of performance criteria for meeting learning objectives. While most instructors probably have a mental set of guidelines and criteria that they use to guide their assessment of student work, creating and posting a rubric makes this internal set of criteria more explicit, benefiting both students and instructor. The student knows what to expect and uses the rubric as a guide in carrying out assignments, while the instructor finds there are fewer questions from and challenges by students and that students are more responsive to the clearly enunciated objectives.

We have featured a number of rubrics in this chapter in conjunction with instructional activities. But it is possible to create a rubric for almost any sort of online course activity. We mentioned in Chapter 5 the importance of clearly defining your grading criteria when shaping the syllabus for an online class. In addition to including a concise description within the syllabus, you might want to consider creating a detailed grading rubric for one or more of your assignments

An effective rubric should be detailed enough to cover all the complexity and different aspects required to complete an assignment, but simple enough that an instructor has little trouble deciding between the higher and lower parts of the grading range. We recommend keeping rubrics to no more than five or six different scoring categories. This will help ensure that you have an efficient process that avoids unnecessary hair-splitting and time-consuming deliberations.

You may overlay a late policy onto your rubric (for example, deduct one or a partial point from any score when postings are made within a specific number of days after the due date) or build your late policy into the rubric itself.

In writing rubrics for assignments in an online class, you should also address some general expectations about what constitutes quality work for undergraduate or graduate students, including coherent and largely error-free writing, adequate documentation, and your institution's policy on plagiarism. These are no less important for an online class than for one delivered face-to-face, and such criteria help reinforce the principle that online courses should be held to the same (or higher) standards as those delivered on campus.

Although writing a good rubric requires some initial investment of time, you may find that the process of constructing one, by requiring thoroughness and attention to each aspect of the assignment, helps produce a more carefully considered and effective assessment of student work.

A Rubric for Online Discussion

Since online participation in particular often presents a challenge to students who are trying to judge their own performance, you might find a rubric that helps set standards for online participation in discussion very useful. Here is a simple rubric for judging online participation on the discussion board that can be adapted and revised to fit a number of different circumstances:

Three Points

- Participant made at least two postings on the discussion board, one of which was a response to that of a classmate.
- Participant's comments were responsive to the discussion threads posted by the instructor.
- Participant made substantive comments or questions that significantly enhanced the discussion and served to help move the conversation forward. These included follow-up questions, examples, or new perspectives.
- Participant's comments provided evidence that the participant had read a substantial number of classmates' postings.
- Participant referred to or showed evidence of having read, viewed, or completed the relevant assignments.
- Participant's postings were constructive, and differences of opinion were expressed in a respectful manner.

Two Points

- Participant made at least two postings, but none was in response to that of a classmate.
- Participant was responsive to the greater part of the discussion threads posted by the instructor.
- Participant made comments or asked questions that contributed to the discussion and helped move the conversation forward. These included at least a few follow-up questions, examples, or new perspectives.
- Participant's comments provided evidence that the participant had read at least a few classmates' postings.
- Participant showed some evidence of having read, viewed, or completed the relevant assignments.
- Participant's postings were constructive, and differences of opinion were expressed in a respectful manner.

One Point

- Participant made at least one posting of a substantive nature.
- Participant was responsive to at least one discussion thread posted by the instructor.
- Participant's comments provided evidence that the participant had read at least a few classmates' postings or had read, viewed, or completed one of the relevant assignments.
- Participant's postings were constructive, and differences of opinion were expressed in a respectful manner.

We hope that this chapter has helped you realize that the types of instructional activities that can take place online are not only as varied and potentially engaging as those that can be achieved in the face-to-face class, but in many cases offer possibilities far beyond traditional on-campus classes. In the next two chapters we will consider how to enrich your content and opportunities for deepening the learning experience for your students.

8

●●●●●

Copyright, Intellectual Property, and Open Educational Resources

In the last chapter, we discussed the use of the Web as resource and focus of online course assignments. Instructional use of the Web has been greatly enhanced in recent years by the growth of open educational resources (OER). OERs by their very nature permit instructors to freely use, adapt, or even add to their content. However, many other potential materials that you may want to include in your courses are those governed by copyright and **fair use** laws. Finally, instructors who create their own content may be concerned with the issue of intellectual property. This chapter deals with these three related issues of import to the online instructor. Copyright and fair use and intellectual property are but two sides of the same coin. These three issues are treated here as follows:

1. *Copyright and fair use.* Do you have the right to use other people's materials in teaching your course?

2. *Intellectual property.* What happens to the intellectual material that you create once you've posted it online? Do you still own it? What can you do if an unauthorized person makes use of it?

3. *Open educational resources* (known as OER) are generally free materials that are available under terms of use that encourage sharing, reproduction, and, in some cases, even repurposing by educators. In most cases, while the materials

are freely reusable, the user is required to attribute the resource to its original creator.

While there exist international copyright regulations, specifics in copyright law differ from country to country. Here we will discuss copyright and fair use as well as intellectual property as it relates to the United States, and touch on possible significance for other countries. We are not legal experts on these matters so our intention is merely to set out some guidelines that faculty can reasonably follow in approaching these issues. After discussing copyright, we will then discuss open educational resources, a truly international movement.

●●●●●

Copyright and Fair Use in the United States

No matter what country you are in, you need to be aware of the copyright laws where the material originates. In using materials you find on the Web, you need to know what material you can use, under what circumstances you can use it, and when you are breaking the law.

The simple answer to all of the above is that copyright law, as it is written, states that if you're using material that belongs to others without their permission and the material you're using goes beyond "fair use" and is made openly accessible (either on your public web site or via a DVD you've distributed to your students), then you're probably breaking the law and thus vulnerable to a suit by the material's rightful owner.

If you are an educator, the powers that be (a consortium consisting of representatives of industry, publishing, education, and other areas in the United States convened to advise Congress on the creation of a new or amended copyright law) have made a few grudging exceptions. If you are teaching in a classroom or online, you may make use of materials that you don't own, as long as you do not make them freely available for distribution and the amount you use does not exceed certain fixed limits. These exceptions have been collected in a document known as the Fair Use Guidelines for Educational Multimedia which emerged in the mid-1990s. They are "guidelines" rather than legal code because they did not constitute a formal amendment to the basic copyright law. Nevertheless, an educator adhering to the Fair Use Guidelines is likely avoiding the risk of liability to a suit.

Kimberly Bonner is an expert in intellectual property who heads up the Center for Intellectual Property at University of Maryland University College. We asked her about the most common misconception that faculty have about fair use and she replied, "I think many faculty really think that fair use is automatic for educational purposes and it is not."

So how do you determine if what you're using falls within the fair use criteria? The copyright law itself specifies four overall determining factors:

1. What is the *character* of the use? Put simply, is it for commercial or noncommercial purposes? Noncommercial use is much more permissible. If you are a teacher at an educational institution, you will have no problem satisfying this criterion. But if you are assembling courseware for distribution—say, via a DVD—you may not qualify for the fair use exemption because you have copied information that does not belong to you and made it available outside the confines of your classroom.

2. What is the *nature* of the work to be used? If the work is in the public domain—that is, out of copyright or never copyrighted (created for public use or older than the copyright laws)—then, of course, you're fine. If the work is copyrighted, the "nature of the work" may include how original or creative it's considered to be. Original or creative work often requires the permission of the owner. Strictly factual material is less likely to require permission.

3. *How much* of the work will you use? Large amounts and large percentages of the original work do not qualify as fair use.

4. What effect would the use have on the *market* for the original work? Use that would significantly damage the work's market value does not qualify as fair use. This is the key provision for online educators. If you are teaching using a password-protected site, to which only students or other invited guests

may gain access, you probably qualify under this part of the fair use rules. In essence, your site may be deemed the equivalent of a traditional classroom bounded by four walls. But if your class is accessible by anyone on the Internet, you are, in effect, making the work available for anyone who wants it, and this presumably damages the work's market value.

To these four original factors, the consortium that developed the Fair Use Guidelines for Educational Multimedia added the following stipulations:

1. Students may incorporate portions of others' works into their multimedia creations and perform and display those creations for academic assignments.

2. Faculty may incorporate portions of others' works into their multimedia creations

   a. to create multimedia curriculum materials;

   b. to teach remote classes where access and total number of students are limited and where technology makes copying impossible. (If materials can be copied, they may be made available over the network for only fifteen days and then must be placed on reserve for on-site use only.)

3. Faculty may demonstrate their multimedia creations at professional symposia and retain them in their own portfolios.

4. Time limit on fair use by faculty: two years from first instructional use of the multimedia work.

5. Copies limit: Generally only two copies are allowed, but joint work creators may each have a copy. In an electronic sense, a copy is a file you have saved on a disk.

6. Portion limits:

   a. motion media (including video and animations): up to 10 percent of the original work or three minutes, whichever is less;

   b. text: up to 10 percent of the original work or 1,000 words, whichever is less;

   c. poems: up to 250 words, but further limited to:

      i. three poems or portions of poems by one poet, or

ii. five poems or portions of poems by different poets from a single anthology.

7. Music (including lyrics and music videos): up to 10 percent of the original work or thirty seconds, whichever is less.

8. Photos and images: up to five works from one artist or photographer; up to 10 percent or fifteen works, whichever is less, from a collection.

9. Database information: up to 10 percent or 2,500 fields or cell entries, whichever is less.

The Technology, Education, and Copyright Harmonization (TEACH) Act of 2002 is a copyright amendment that did serve to broaden the conversation to explicitly include distance education and digital creations. But the TEACH Act is complex and is not something individual instructors can be expected to interpret on their own. In some ways it has confused as much as elucidated the rules for educators and it often addresses issues that must be handled by institutions as a whole. However, if you are seeking to use text, video, or audio without paying a fee, you are probably on solid ground if you observe some of the same limits we have already noted. To sum up:

■ Limit amount—do not attempt to make available an entire work (see fair use guidelines above).

■ Limit time—do not make the work available for an entire semester.

■ Limit access—make available only to enrolled students in your class; use a password-protected site such as your course management system.

Is Anyone Really Watching?

Some readers may find the foregoing fair use guidelines somewhat excessive. After all, you might argue, with so much material available on the Web, who could possibly monitor it all anyway?

Think of the matter this way: It is just as easy for those who own material to find it on the Web as it was for you to secure it in the first place. Sophisticated search tools now exist, and are continually being improved upon, for tracking down pirated material. As the market for distance education grows, so do the economic incentives for people to protect any material that rightfully belongs to them.

Thus, you must be especially conscientious about materials you post on the public Web. If you aren't, the institution you work for will no doubt encourage you to revise your behavior, because it is usually the institution that bears the heaviest liability in a copyright suit. But you personally are not immune.

Finding the Rightful Owner

Ascertaining the rightful owner of copyrighted material can sometimes prove quite complex, particularly when ownership may have changed hands several times since the work was first published.

There are a number of ways to track down authorship using the Web. Services such as the Copyright Clearance Center (www.copyright.com) can help with searching out the ownership status of a given piece of material and can often give you price quotes as well.

What to Do If You Aren't Sure Whether You Need Permission

First, we recommend that you consult your institution's library to see if they are able to assist you with licensing or securing permission. They will also be able to tell you what costs, if any, are associated with licensing. Such costs are not easy to calculate in advance—they can range from inexpensive electronic rights to a short article or an exorbitant price for one poem. Once you know what the costs incurred might be, you (and your institution) can make a choice about whether or not to use particular material. Your institution may have a specific form that they want you to use in applying for permission or to enable them to make that determination for you. If you do not have access to such a service and you think the work you are using does not qualify for the fair use exemption you should write the owner and ask for permission.

State who you are, what you plan to do with the material, and how long you plan to use it/when you plan to remove it from your course site. Some publishers have their own forms for permissions posted on their web sites. But in other cases, you may

---

A Sample Letter Requesting Permission

The following general template can be can adapted as necessary when you need to secure permission to use someone else's work. In the paragraph where you explain your intentions, be sure to note the key features of the proposed use, such as who will have access to the site and how long the material will be made available. If the material is to be sold as part of a coursepack, you should indicate that as well.

[Letterhead stationery or return address/email/phone or fax numbers]

[Date]

[Name and address of addressee]

Dear [title, name]:

I am [describe your position] at [name of institution]. I would like your permission to [explain intended use in detail—e.g., reprint, incorporate into lectures, post in online classroom, distribute via DVD] the following [insert the full citation to the original work or attach a copy of the image or graphics if needed]. The material will be made available to # students as follows [e.g., through password-protected web site, on DVD] for the expected period of [time period intended].

Please indicate your approval of this permission by signing the letter where indicated below and returning it to me as soon as possible, by mail, by fax, or [by scanned image] via email. Your signing of this letter will also confirm that you own [or your company owns] the copyright to the above-described material.

Thank you very much,

Sincerely,

[Your name and signature]

PERMISSION GRANTED FOR THE USE REQUESTED ABOVE

[Type name of addressee below signature line]

[Date]

need to write the owner directly. (See the box "A Sample Letter Requesting Permission.") Keep a copy of all your correspondence, whether by letter or by email. If no one responds to your request, you can then probably use the material, relatively secure that you have made a good-faith effort to contact the author and secure his or her permission.

In most cases—probably about 95 percent of the time—you will receive permission to use the material without having to pay any fee or royalty. In those rare cases in which you are not given permission free of charge, you can either pay the fee or use other material instead.

Important! *If you are not sure whether or not you can use someone else's content, the rule is—when in doubt, ask.*

What about Links and Embedded Resources?

Linking to someone else's public web site, whether as part of a course assignment or as an addition to a page of course notes, does not contradict the copyright strictures. However, as a matter of courtesy, it may be advisable to let the owner of a personal page know that you are linking to the site, particularly if it is a personal site housed on a hosting service that might incur additional costs if more than a prescribed number of visitors "hit" the site. Very often, when you notify the owner this way, he or she may return the favor by letting you know when the URL for the site has changed.

An increasing number of Web 2.0 sites like VoiceThread, YouTube, and TeacherTube allow for the copying and **embedding** of code within your course management system, blogs, PowerPoint, or web page, permitting your students to play the video or other multimedia from within your own course site. This is particularly helpful for those whose institutions have blocked access to the YouTube site or for those who do not want students to wade through all the other potentially inappropriate or distracting links surrounding a video. On the other hand, the video in question is still being hosted on the other source's external server, so the instructor does not need to worry about possible overload on a university or personal hosting server. Instructions for embedding a video and its player from YouTube are supplied at www.youtube.com/sharing. When the embed code is automatically generated by the external party as is the case with YouTube, you, the instructor, do not need to write any of your own code to embed the video, so it is a real boon to instructors who do not know how or do not have easy access to support to create code. Embedding, when it is made freely available in this manner, may be thought of as a sophisticated way of linking.

Figure 8.1 Auto-generated code for embedding a VoiceThread item within your web page, blog, or course management system. YouTube and many other Web 2.0 tools offer this option which allows your students to access the application without leaving the classroom. Reproduced by permission from VoiceThread.

● ● ● ● ●

Intellectual Property in the United States

It's one thing to borrow someone else's work to help teach your class—you know your intentions are good—but it's quite another thing if someone borrows your work. Among instructors who are leery of using the Web, one persistent fear is that their intellectual property will be stolen by some enterprising student, or worse still, by another educator.

This fear is not unfounded. Students do reproduce course notes and even sell them, often supplementing them with notes they have written themselves. This practice has been going on since long before the advent of the Web (surely no one has forgotten the dreaded copying machine). But the practice is significantly easier when lectures and other course materials are posted online, because all one needs to do is to copy the materials electronically and save them as a file.

A more sinister scenario involves other educators, or even for-profit publishers of educational material, "borrowing" your lectures and using them for their own purposes, either reworking them or reformatting them to suit their own needs. In a world in which tenured positions are becoming less commonplace and many instructors find themselves teaching for various universities at one time or another, intellectual theft of this sort may not be as rare as you suppose.

Let's look first at your legal rights and then at some practical steps you can take to protect your work.

The Legal Status of Your Work

Believe it or not, legal ownership of material you create is a very gray area at most institutions. Most faculty members are under the impression that the intellectual work they produce or publish automatically belongs to them. Not so. It is simply the accepted custom of most universities, particularly those involved in research, to cede rights to such intellectual property to their faculty members, because the administrators realize that work thus produced will bring the institution revenue in the form of grants. But institutions do not *have* to cede these rights. They merely choose to.

The same has been historically true for course content, including syllabi, lecture notes, and course outlines. Departments, however, often retain copies of these materials to make available to new instructors or TAs who are teaching the course for the first time. Of course, in this situation the new instructors may be expected to *adapt* rather than copy the original syllabus. A departing instructor is also usually free to take his or her courseware to a new institution.

Teaching online often means creating original material in the form of electronic files or web pages enriched with multimedia elements such as graphics, sound, video, and animations. Instructors who create such material may assume it belongs to them, but when a university or other institution is intent on marketing its courses and programs online, ownership of these materials may not be quite as clear-cut. From the institution's point of view, such material may not bring in revenue in the form of grants, but it can help create revenue in the form of increased tuition. Hence the institution may be less willing to cede rights to the instructor. The institution may consider what the instructor has created as work-made-for-hire, that is, work that was done in the context of fulfilling job responsibilities. Or, the institution may "unbundle" the rights, permitting themselves to continue to use the material while allowing the instructor to use all or a portion of the material at another university or in some other educational context.

As Kimberly Bonner notes, faculty,

> need to understand the "works made for hire" doctrine in copyright law that makes the employer the copyright owner of a work if the work was done within the scope of employment or pursuant to an independent contractor relationship. And they need to know that course ownership policies may not be enough to alter a "work made for hire" arrangement.

It is a good idea, therefore, to find out—in writing—your institution's policy with respect to online materials you've created to teach your course. If there is no established policy, come to some agreement with the administrators about your material. This is especially important if you're a nontenured adjunct or lecturer and expect to use your courseware at several different institutions, either online or as part of a blended course. As Bonner explains, "faculty should either have specific language in their contracts that support them retaining ownership in their works or incorporate copyright policies in their teaching contracts (particularly if the policy permits faculty retaining ownership rights in course materials)."

If you can't secure clear ownership rights to your own material, you can always copyright the material yourself before making it available to your institution or class. Although most faculty members aren't aware of this, you automatically hold the copyright of your intellectual property the moment you commit it to paper or to any fixed medium. If it came to a court case, however, you would have to prove the date you created the material. One way to do this is to send yourself a registered envelope or package with the material inside and then keep the package unopened. A second way is to submit a claim for copyright to the Library of Congress.

As online instruction becomes more lucrative for universities and private institutions alike, the question of who owns the rights to material and who benefits from revenues derived from it will become more and more important, especially since the percentage of instructors in contingent rather than secure, full-time permanent positions has also increased.

The field of copyright law and intellectual property is rife with legal experts. We do not pretend to a special expertise. What we do suggest is that you take nothing for granted when it comes to material you have created and that you make the effort to learn in advance the specific policies of the institution you are working for.

Practical Steps for Protecting Your Work

A copyright notice prominently displayed is like a scarecrow in a field. It will scare away some of the crows, but some will come pecking all the same. So it pays to be both vigilant and practical.

Various instructional materials are pilfered from ordinary classrooms every day, and the Internet makes it even easier to steal material and repurpose it. With a little care, however, most instructors who post material online can avoid serious problems.

Begin with common sense. Say you have an essay you've been working on. It hasn't yet been published, but you have good reason to think it may be published. Meanwhile, you'd like your class to read it. If you're fearful that one of your students may copy it or send it to someone else, then post an abstract or description of it instead. Or, you may affix a notice that clearly cautions students that the essay is not for distribution—this is a milder approach, but surprisingly effective: most students will be respectful of this and it suggests to all that you are consciously setting up some controls on this content.

There are also some technological strategies you can use to help ward off potential thieves.

Technological Methods The first, and probably the most obvious, technological stratagem to reduce theft is to use a password-protected web site. Most course management systems possess encryption tools that prevent unwanted visitors from viewing the course. If you aren't using a course management system, tools exist that will permit your computer support personnel to password-protect your web site with various computer programs. Even if you're essentially on your own, with no support, a number of easily accessible programs will allow you to password-protect your site (refer to the web sites listed in the Guide to Resources).

There are also some technological methods for protecting unlawful copying or downloading of your work. Some software programs permit you to limit the way your work can be copied by others online. Take the case of a lecture you have created using Microsoft Word. If you save this document as an HTML file or post it to your web site as an attachment, your students will be able to open it or download it exactly as if they had copied it from your hard disk. What you might do instead is to use a program such as Adobe Acrobat. This is the program that permits you to create the Acrobat file format that you see everywhere on the Web, and it provides options that can help limit unauthorized use of your material.

Using Adobe Acrobat

With Adobe Acrobat, you can use any program you normally would to format your material: Microsoft Word, PowerPoint—any program that permits you to print. When your document is ready, you "print" it in a format known as **PDF (Portable Document Format)**. You can then make this PDF file available via your web site, permitting any student who possesses the ubiquitous Adobe Acrobat Reader to read, download, and even reprint your file exactly as you originally formatted it without having to own the software program that created it.

However, if you do not want your students to reprint your material or save it, Adobe Acrobat permits you to restrict how the material is used. You can remove the ability to reprint text and graphics or even to select and copy them once they reach a student's home computer. You can restrict printing out the document so that no printing out is allowed or only in low resolution. You can require a password to open. Similarly, assuming you are operating according to the fair use guidelines, you can copy articles or material culled from other sources and "print" them as PDF files, then limit your students' rights to repurpose them by taking advantage of the features just mentioned. (Note: Adobe Reader is a free program, but Adobe Acrobat is not. If it is not available on your computer, check to see if your institution can install it for you. Once Acrobat is installed, the PDF option should appear as one of the printing options available in your print setup (dialog) box or in the "Save As" option.)

Another way to protect your intellectual property is to convert it into streaming media format, particularly when it involves the use of multimedia. Streaming media, such as narrated slide shows and recorded audio files, are housed on the server and streamer to the user. They exist in temporary memory on the user's computer. A particularly clever student hacker might figure out how to retrieve this material from the temporary memory cache, but most users will neither want to nor know how to. The same may be said for the PDF restriction detailed above—a determined student may be able to evade the restrictions, but sending out information in this format is like building a fence around your fields. It will keep most, though not all, intruders from pillaging your crops.

Checking for Unauthorized Use

Finally, if you are worried that your intellectual property is being stolen, or even if you are just sensibly concerned, try conducting an online search every six months or so. Choose a unique sentence or phrase from one of your lectures and use a search engine to search online. If the phrase pops up, and it looks as if it was borrowed from your notes, drop the author of the offending page a warning note or query, as the case may demand. Be gracious—it may often be inadvertent on the part of the offender.

● ● ● ● ●

Open Educational Resources (OER)

The term "open educational resources," mentioned in Chapters 3 and 7, derives from a 2002 UNESCO forum on open courseware for developing countries. Since 2005, the OER community has grown to encompass organizations and individuals worldwide who are interested in sharing resources and creating new digital resources that can be made available to all on the Internet. The definition of OER not only includes the notion that the content of OER is free for use but also that sharing of knowledge is actively encouraged. A useful handbook for OER educators is available at www.wikieducator.org/OER_Handbook/educator_version_one—the handbook and the Wikieducator site itself are both examples of OER.

OER content ranges from small learning objects, images, quizzes, lesson plans, syllabi, or discrete modules to larger collections of modules and entire courses. OER can usually be freely reused, adapted to new uses through mixing with other content, and freely distributed in their new form. The terms of use for OER can vary but most require attribution to the original creator and are offered free for use by nonprofits and educational institutions. Look for terms of use on each OER site. For example, the MIT Opencourseware site clearly sets forth its own rules as (1) noncommercial, i.e., the content can only be used by non-profit groups and educators; (2) attribution must be made to MIT and the professor whose work you are using, whether the content is used as is or mixed or repurposed; and

(3) "share-alike"—anything created with their content must be offered as an OER to others.

They also give explicit guidelines concerning how to affix an attribution.

You can find OER content through a number of different ways. Obviously, you can search your library databases or the Web for such resources, and while this may turn up articles on OER rather than the materials themselves, there may be links to the actual OER as well. There are some well-known sites that provide collections of OER, such as the OER Commons (http://oercommons.org), or that have more discipline-specific collections such as the previously mentioned Chemistry Collective (www.chemcollective.org). (See the Guide to Resources for more collections of OER.)

By making use of appropriate OER, you are often able to enhance your course while avoiding the issues and costs associated with copyrighted material. Another approach to using OER is to incorporate or adapt the OER with your own materials. For example, you might add to your own lecture in introductory physics by using some materials from a lecture by one of the professors featured on the MIT Opencourseware site. By mixing OER with your own materials in this way, you may find that you are able to add diversity of perspectives and approaches to your own content.

● ● ● ● ●

Creative Commons License

Do consider whether or not a particular piece you have created is something you want to protect for whatever reason—e.g., it involves expected income or because you fear another educator may reuse it and claim it for their own. If you simply want acknowledgment and attribution of your work, then especially for publicly available web sites, blogs, wikis, or other sites where you may share your work, the Creative Commons license (http://creativecommons.org/license) may be a good approach. When you sign up for a free license with this organization, you can decide what limitations you wish to put on what you publish online—this can range from no restrictions to no modifications

License Conditions

Creators choose a set of conditions they wish to apply to their work.

(i) Attribution	(o) Share Alike	($) Noncommercial	(=) No Derivative Works
You let others copy, distribute, display, and perform your copyrighted work — and derivative works based upon it — but only if they give credit the way you request.	You allow others to distribute derivative works only under a license identical to the license that governs your work.	You let others copy, distribute, display, and perform your work — and derivative works based upon it — but for noncommercial purposes only.	You let others copy, distribute, display, and perform only verbatim copies of your work, not derivative works based upon it.

Figure 8.2 Creative Commons Licensing Conditions, from http:// creativecommons.org/about/licenses. Image licensed by Creative Commons.

or use by commercial entities; the Creative Commons site has a very helpful series of questions to take you step by step through this decision. By affixing one of the six main Creative Commons notices, you can let others know that you are encouraging the propagation of your ideas, but that you do want credit for originating those ideas. Deliberately making some portion of your work available as an OER can actually benefit you in many ways—you may create a demand for your work that might not have otherwise transpired, find potential collaborators among the world of educators, and find yourself quoted, invited to present at conferences, and other unexpected benefits.

If you want to mix the use of OER materials along with some non-OER materials that are not covered under fair use, you will want to request permission from the copyright holder. The OER handbook discusses how to handle this situation and provides a sample letter requesting permission for clearance at www.wikieducator.org/OER_Handbook/educator_version_one/ License/ Copyright_clearance.

● ● ● ● ●

Special Issues Related to Free Web 2.0 Sites

Many of the free Web 2.0 sites mentioned in this book and the many others not explicitly mentioned here may invoke terms of use that, while granting that what you blog, record, or otherwise create using their tools and hosting service remains your intellectual property, may yet contain provisions that entitle them to display and reveal your content as part of their publicity, demonstrations, or other possible uses. This is especially true for any content that you choose to make public, but may also potentially include your "private" areas. While you should not overreact to this sort of use (which, in effect, is part of the bargain, like advertisements, in exchange for free use and seldom exercised), it is a reminder that you should hesitate to post anything or create content—such as something incorporating private contact info, personal details, photos, etc.—that you would feel uncomfortable having revealed to the world. It is a good idea to make your students aware of the terms of use for the sites and encourage them to use similar discretion outside your course management system. There is also the fact that a Web 2.0 site may be hosted on a server in a country that does not hold to the same privacy provisions as those of your own country, so that is yet another reason to carefully read the terms of use and privacy policy posted on a site.

●●●●●

Assuring Academic Integrity among Your Students

In Chapter 3 we discussed the need to devise assessments in such a way as to make it more difficult for students to plagiarize essays and papers. For instructors who suspect that the elegantly worded phrases they suddenly encounter in their students' essays may have been borrowed from something the students discovered online, a simple search on Google will often result in the identification of the plagiarized portions.

But again, as students spend more and more time online and students themselves increasingly engage in production on the Web, assurance of academic integrity and guarding against plagiarism is something that should start well before the work is produced. Here are some other tips for encouraging academic integrity when developing an assignment:

■ Make sure that paper or essay topics are sufficiently specific, rather than so broad that any borrowed text could meet the requirements.

■ Include an element that requires students to refer to discussions or other content specific to the class activity.

■ When allowing for choice in picking topics, either provide a set of choices or require that students provide an outline, bibliography, and rough draft of their papers so that you can monitor the development of the work.

■ Make sure that rubrics or listed criteria for grading the assignment include responsiveness to the assignment requirements and questions. While you may not be able to prove plagiarism, you can easily see what's relevant and what is not.

■ Ask students to give examples and evidence to support their arguments and theses.

■ Insist on clear citations and a reference list that matches those citations.

■ For group work, ask students to clearly label each person's contribution.

■ If students are creating multimedia products, ask them to read about fair use guidelines and document what they have borrowed from elsewhere.

■ Remind students at the beginning of the course of your institution's policy on plagiarism, and give examples, if not provided by your institution, of what constitutes plagiarism.

There are some excellent web sites such as the Virtual Academic Integrity Lab (VAIL) site (www.umuc.edu/distance/odell/cip/vail/home.html) at University of Maryland University College that offer tutorials on academic integrity for both instructors and students. (See the Guide to Resources for additional resource sites.) Requiring students to take such tutorials or devising other exercises as part of the introductory materials in your course can help students get off on the right foot. Students do not always realize that they have plagiarized or otherwise offended the rules of academic integrity. Exposing all your students in a systematic way to such resources, creating a short assignment around such a resource, or simply discussing the rules are frank, non-threatening ways to raise awareness of the issues before any offense occurs.

Having looked at the subject of content ownership, in the next chapter we shine a light on the ways in which lively content for online courses can be created, assembled, or enriched by those with limited technical skills as well as those who are more technically proficient.

9

•••••

Creating Courseware and Using Web 2.0 Tools

If you are lucky enough to have access to instructional technology staff who can create your every wished-for simulation, beautifully displayed web pages, and videos with high production values, then you may not care much about creating course content beyond the usual text-based materials on your own. But even the most fortunately equipped and staffed institutions may have some limitations as to time that can be expended on just your course. So if the course you are teaching is not already fully supplied with superb multimedia and beautifully crafted modules, you will want to think about how to enhance your courseware through the use of multimedia, additional resources, and tools that add interest and enhance interaction in your class. By the term "courseware" we mean all the software tools, digital materials, and resources used as course materials to deliver an online class. Courseware thus includes both text-based and multimedia-enriched materials. We also include applications and tools that are inseparable from the communication of course content.

This book has always promoted the use of low-threshold, low-barrier types of software solutions for instructors to create course materials. Low-threshold, low-barrier means those technologies that are easily learned by you (and perhaps by your students) and that can be used to easily accomplish your instructional objectives. When considering what constitutes the category of Web 2.0 tools, our definition includes "easy to learn and easy to apply" tools that have built-in sharing and collaboration features.

The course management system or virtual learning environment software still serves for most online instructors as their main stage. Within your CMS, it may be that you can already create HTML pages via WYSIWYG ("what you see is what you get") editors, and perhaps even generate audio clips, PowerPoint slides, and images within this system. If you have a CMS, it makes sense to fully exploit the capabilities that reside within it to create enriched content. So find out what the capabilities are in your CMS and experiment with the various document formats available to you. Beyond that, you can easily link out to open educational resources, web resources that incorporate media, and perhaps connect to textbook-publisher-supplied multimedia.

But what if you have no CMS, or want to consider some options not available in your CMS? In the past, if you wanted to go beyond enlivening your course with just a few relevant graphics or charts to creating a narrated slide show with the sound of your voice synchronized to the display of images or a video lecture, there was a substantial learning curve to accomplish these things. Some technical staff and instructional designers might have told you that this was beyond your reach, that creating "really good" learning objects and web pages required knowledge of complex software programs in order to make really cool web pages, the ones with text flying around like swarms of locusts and colors undulating like the northern lights.

But the great news about software is that every year it becomes easier and easier to use. The obstacles that formerly impeded instructors have been removed. In fact, there are a number of low-tech tools that cost very little, or even nothing at all, that are easy to learn, easy to use, and easy to remember when you use them again a month or so down the road. Better still, much of what you may need to do can be accomplished using software that is menu-driven, freely available to use, and that requires no programming ability at all. Web 2.0 tools in particular may not even require a download of software but may instead allow you to accomplish everything you need to do through your browser.

To fully appreciate the possibilities that come with using Web 2.0 tools to create multimedia, just look at some of the educators' blogs available on the Web. A great way to start is by viewing some of the blogs by educators nominated or awarded by Edublogs (http://edublogawards.com), which not only recognizes educators but also class blogs by students, best educational use of wikis and social networking sites, and best resource-sharing blogs. The use of multimedia on these blogs, especially through the use of Web 2.0 tools, is impressive and can open your eyes to the possibilities now available to ordinary instructors.

Let's look at some of the options for creating courseware and the use of Web 2.0 tools, beginning with the simplest means.

● ● ● ● ●

Creating Text for Course Pages

To write text for your course pages, you can generally avoid having to learn HTML at all. In most cases, there will be a WYSIWYG editor incorporated into your CMS or you can create pages outside that CMS using the built-in blog or wiki or free web site software of your choice. If you still need to create a web page on your own, we recommend using a free web page WYSIWYG editor.

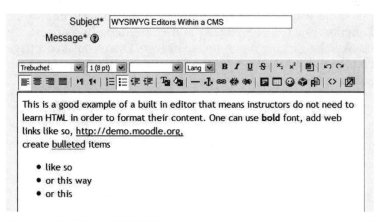

Figure 9.1 Built-in WYSIWYG Editor within Moodle, from http://demo.moodle.org. Reproduced by permission from Moodle.

While you can use a word-processing program like MS Word to create a web page, it does add proprietary code or can result in problems like strange spacing that needs to be cleaned up in an HTML editor, and presumably, if you knew how to use an HTML editor, you would be likely to use that in the first place. However, if you are looking to create some very simple pages, you can certainly try it out in whatever format you intend to place it—with Word 2003 and 2007, you can simply choose to save as "Web page." With Word 2007, you have an additional choice, to save as "Web Page, Filtered" instead. This filters out additional Word code, makes for a smaller document, and should generally work better within a browser, but the best thing to do is experiment and see how it works in your particular setup.

Creating Web Pages in a Web Editor

A more reliable way to produce a web page is to work directly in a web page-editing program. One of the most popular commercial editors is Dreamweaver and your institution may well have a license for it or a similar program. However, this may be way beyond what you need and there are several free, cross-platform (for Windows, Mac, and Linux) editors like KompoZer (www.kompozer.net) and SeaMonkey Composer (www.seamonkey-project.org) that will do the job for you. Most web editors work the same way and are not unlike standard word processors. Functions such as boldfacing and centering a line of text are invoked by clicking on an image or icon. Once you save a page created in a WYSIWYG editor, it is automatically saved as a web page complete with all the requisite code.

Designing Web Pages for Instruction: A Few Tips

Keep the background simple. The fact that you can add a background color or design doesn't mean you ought to. Your students are visiting your page in order to get information they need. What's important to them is seeing the information clearly. So, if you must use a background, make it very light so that dark text will contrast with it.

When choosing fonts, don't overdo it. Too many fonts, sizes, or colors confuse the eye rather than guide it. Look at any published book and notice the relative simplicity of the layout. One size of font (generally between 10- and 12-point type) defines the body text. It is usually a font with serifs—the fine strokes at the top and bottom of letters—because serifs help make a visual connection between one letter and the next. Headings tend to be printed in either bold or a sans serif (that is, nonserif) font. Sans serif fonts tend to look stolid and important—or so our brains have been trained to think.

Never use light text against a light background, such as yellow text against a white background. It's usually unreadable. Always use very light against dark, or very dark against white.

Don't force your readers to scroll down the page to follow the main text. Reading on a screen isn't the same as reading a printed page. Many people don't like to read too much text from the screen, because of eye fatigue. On the other hand, it isn't particularly enjoyable to follow links from one short page to another short page. Usually the best compromise is to create one long page and then provide some way, other than tedious scrolling, for your reader to navigate through it. This means creating a table of contents somewhere (usually at the top of the page) with links to "anchors" you set up on the page.

Don't stretch your text completely across the page. Leave a little white space on the left and the right. The white space contains the text and makes it easier to read on the screen. The easiest way to achieve this format is to create a table with two columns. Type in the right column and leave the left column blank. Format the table so that it has no lines defining the columns. Using a table, in fact, is one of the most effective and efficient ways to format both text and graphics on a web page and to make sure they will display evenly no matter what the resolution and size of the monitor on which they appear.

Don't overload your page with web links. Your students are visiting *your* page; they should be able to see or get to the information they want to find immediately. Even links to other pages within your own site can easily be overdone. Try to make it easy for students by listing the main topics on the front or main page, with links to related pages. On the related pages, make sure you provide them with a way to get back to the main page. That way, your students can move back and forth with ease.

The How and Why of Images

Images include everything from drawings, charts, and maps to photographs, fine art, and cartoons. Building on the examples noted earlier, here are some of the ways that images can enrich your course:

■ to illustrate an abstract or unfamiliar concept, object, or phenomenon. For example, a Japanese woodblock print from the late nineteenth century showing the Meiji emperor dressed in a western suit and viewing cherry blossoms might reinforce a lesson on the concept of modernization of Japan.

   Photos or artworks of the trenches of World War I might remain in the mind of students long after a text description has faded from memory.

■ to provide more vivid detail than possible with text alone—for example, maps documenting the changes over time in the course of the Mississippi River, a drawing or photo showing the past practice in China of footbinding for women, or a diagram clearly marking the parts of an animal or the stages of digestion in a biology lesson will provide more information than from the student's reading alone.

■ to enliven and emphasize points in a lesson—for example, photos and artwork capturing major historical events, portraits of an author or politician, street scenes depicted in paintings and watercolors may help make your points in a lecture.

■ as the basis for an assignment—for example, students can be asked to take photos to document activities outside the classroom, to create graphs or tables to demonstrate their work, or to find examples in the real world of the topics studied in class.

Finding Images

There has never been such a wealth of images available on the Web as exists today, especially photographs, now that digital cameras are ubiquitously embedded in our cell phones and photo-sharing sites like Flickr have encouraged everyone to post and make public their photos. You can save almost any image you find on the Web by clicking on it once, and then (if you're on a PC) right-clicking your mouse or (if you use a Mac) just holding the mouse button down. The dialog box will pop up and permit you to save the image to your hard disk. After that, you can easily upload it to a web page, into your CMS, or edit and change it for these and other uses. And of course, instructors can easily create their own photos for their courses using those same popular digital cameras.

Two issues are connected with finding and using images— terms of use (that is, are the photos freely usable or not within your own course or can you simply link to them?) and finding images that are relevant and appropriate for your class.

Using Google Image search allows you to insert a keyword to find a great variety of images related to your topic, but it is not always obvious which of these are royalty free. A sample search for the image of T. S. Eliot, even though further refined to look for only medium-size photos of the face, results in 4,300 images! When you click on each image, the standard Google language declares, "Image may be subject to copyright." To determine copyright, you must then go to the original site and see if there are any notations on the status of the photo. You can see that this might get very time-consuming so a better option might be to use the Google Advanced search tool that filters out those images that are royalty free from those that are not. By choosing the criteria "any size," "photo" in "JPEG" format and specifying that the usage rights should be those "labeled for reuse," the results are much more manageable—106 photos, of which only four or five actually include images of T. S. Eliot.

Flickr allows one to search for photos that are offered under the terms of the Creative Commons. If I would like to find a photo of a pine tree, I can use the Advanced Search to "Only search within Creative Commons-licensed content" and I can further refine it to those images that I can modify, adapt, or build upon in case I want to alter the images. Such a search results in over 11,000 different photos of pine trees.

Another site to try is PicFindr (www.picfindr.com) which allows you to search multiple sites for royalty-free or inexpensive stock photography, a search further organized by the type of usage or license you are looking for. A search for pine trees here produces a large number of photos, most of which are royalty free with a few others offered at a small price.

Google | Advanced Image Search

Find results	related to all of the words	TS Eliot	
	related to the exact phrase		Google Search
	related to any of the words		
	not related to the words		

Content types	Return images that contain	○ any content ○ news content ○ faces ● photo content ○ clip art
		○ line drawings
Size	Return images that are	Any size ❯ Use my desktop size
Exact size	Return images exactly the size	Width: Height:
Aspect ratio	Return images with an aspect ratio that is	Any aspect ratio ❯
Filetypes	Return only image files formatted as	any filetype ❯
Coloration	Return only images in	any colors ❯
Domain	Return images from the site or domain	
Usage Rights	Return images that are	labeled for reuse ❯ More info
SafeSearch	○ No filtering ● Use moderate filtering ○ Use strict filtering	

Figure 9.2 Advanced Google Image Search to find royalty-free images. Source: www.google.com.

Clipart   There are several collections of clipart illustrations. For example, Clipart ETC (http://etc.usf.edu/clipart) is a collection sponsored by Florida's Educational Technology Clearinghouse, containing tens of thousands of pieces of clipart suitable for students and teachers, offered free for educational use of up to fifty items without permission. (No T. S. Eliot here when we searched, but several illustrations of Emerson and other notable writers.)

Computer Screen Grabs   Sometimes all that's needed is a screen grab or screen shot of a portion of the computer screen. Perhaps you want to show a portion of a web page or the way that a form should be completed. Whatever the reason, if it resides on your desktop, you can snap a picture of it. Computer "print screen" keys can provide capture of an entire page, but when you only want the menu on the left hand side of the screen, you need to use screen grab software for that purpose. There are a number of free or inexpensive tools that can do this and screen capture is also included in image editors like Adobe Photoshop—check first to see if your institution has a license for such software. Also check to see if you already have this type of software on your computer. For example, Mac OS X owners can take screen shots of any portion of their screen using the existing keyboard shortcuts. Windows Vista may offer a Snipping Tool that can take similar screen shots. (Keep in mind that depending on what they are and how you intend to use them, you may need permission to use those screen shots. See Chapter 8.)

If you do not have suitable software, you can do a simple web search for free screen grab software. At the time of this writing, there is Faststone (www.faststone.org/index.htm) and Screen Grab (www.screengrab.org) offered free as a Firefox browser plug-in. Among commercial software, there is the popular and very easy to use Snagit (www.techsmith.com/screen-capture. asp), available for a free trial.

Scanning Images   Scanning means converting printed material (whether graphic or text) into a digital format that a computer can read. No matter how many images you can find searching on the Web, you can't find everything. If the images you want reside in a book or magazine, you will have to scan the image into a digital format that you can then further manipulate through editing. Your institution is likely to have scanners available through the library, your department office, or through a unit that handles instructional technology, but as is increasingly the case, many inexpensive home printers contain scanning capabilities. Such printer-scanners contain their own software which allows you to save the image in the format and to the folder on your hard drive that you select—the built-in menus and steps to make a simple scan are generally easy to follow.

Editing Images   Some found or scanned images need a little help. Some look dark and dreary, and others, such as those gleaned from magazines or newspapers, seem tinted, grayish, or full of dots. More common still, the image you scanned is upside down or tilted. Or the photos and images you saved from the Web may be too big or need cropping to cut out unwanted portions of the picture.

It's fun to fix up these images, but to do so you're going to need some sort of image-editing software. There are many programs available. The venerable monarch of all image-editing programs is Adobe Photoshop. This is the program you would want to use if your goal were to show a politician standing next to a beautiful young woman he had actually never met. In other words, it's pretty sophisticated and expensive. In our view, for most faculty members such a program amounts to software overkill. It has so many features and special effects that remembering them after two weeks or so is a considerable feat. GIMP (www.gimp.org) is a free program of similar complexity to Adobe Photoshop and is available for multiple languages on multiple platforms.

But the lesser-known and often free or low-cost image-editing programs are often a better choice for educators. They are also easier to use and to learn and will let you do almost all of the things you need to do to fix up your images.

For photos, Picnik (www.picnik.com) is a free editor, available online without a download, that allows you to do such things as resize or crop photos. It is cross-platform so it works for those on Windows, Macs, or Linux.

If you just need to quickly resize images to fit more appropriately into your blog or web page, there are free programs like Fast-Stone Photo Resizer (www.faststone.org/FSResizerDetail.htm).

Picasa is software that is offered free by Google to edit and manage collections of photos, but is for Windows only. If you have a Mac, you can use the iPhoto editing software that comes installed on your machine.

For free editors for images and photos, there is Paint.NET, www.getpaint.net—it is available in many languages and requires a download to a Windows computer. If you have Microsoft Office suite for either Windows or Mac, you may find it includes Picture Manager, an image editor.

If you want to explore some of the different options and features of editors, including platforms, prices, and other data on each, an excellent comparison page for image editors may be found on Wikipedia at http://en.wikipedia.org/wiki/Comparison_of_raster_graphics_editors.

Now that you've fixed up your image, the last thing you must do is to save it in a format you can use on the Web. Fortunately, there are only two common choices for this purpose.

If your image is an artist's illustration or a piece of line art, then the file format you should use is **GIF**. It was developed by CompuServe, an Internet service provider, many years ago as a way to send or display graphics on the Web. GIF remains an excellent choice for an image with relatively few colors.

If, however, the image you are saving is a photograph, GIF is not an appropriate format. You should save a photograph as a **JPEG file**, a format developed specifically for this purpose. The acronym stands for Joint Photographic Experts Group. JPEGs aren't so good, though, for simple line art with just a few colors; with that type of art, the JPFG format often smudges lines or makes them look ragged.

Note that some editors like Picasa that are designed solely or mainly for editing photos save only in JPEG format, although most can import images from different formats and convert them to JPEG.

The How and Why of Audio

How about sound?

Sound is a much-overlooked element in courses. But it can do a lot. You can search for sound files on the Web and perhaps discover a radio show or speech that is relevant to your class. Or you can record an interview with a colleague in your field, make the recording available on your web page, and then ask your students to comment on what your colleague said. Here are reasons and ways (apart from the use in language and speech classes previously discussed) to use audio:

- Introduce yourself to the class in a personalized manner. Even without a visual element, the voice conveys a sense of who you are and your attitude toward teaching the course. Encourage students to do the same but make it optional.

- Use audio for feedback on assignments—this can range from comments on papers to projects to insertion in online gradebooks. It is especially helpful for delivering sensitive criticism—your voice can easily soften what might seem like hard criticism in text.

- Record your lectures in a natural manner—the idea is to record lectures and commentary prepared specially for your online students rather than trying to capture something recorded from your delivery in a face-to-face class. For best effect, keep your lectures and commentary short. It is tedious to listen to long audio clips—we recommend you keep such clips to no more than fifteen minutes. If you have the equivalent of an hour-long lecture, it is best to split this up into fifteen-minute segments. That way, students can more easily play back just that topic or topics that they need to review. If you decide to do this on a regular basis, consider using a podcast format to which students can subscribe.

- Allow students to create presentations that include audio. Some students are best at expressing themselves through the spoken word while others may excel in writing or video. Role playing, debates, and interviews are all examples of assignments in which audio may play an appropriate part.

- As discussed in Chapter 7, use audio to bring interviews and guest speakers to your class.

It used to be that if you wanted to play a sound file (usually in the WAV or AIFF format) that you found on the Web, you had to download it first. That was often a tedious process. A sound file one minute in length might take ten minutes to download. If the file was particularly important (such as a clip from President Kennedy's inauguration speech), you might have accepted the inconvenience. But for anything else … well, you had to think about it.

Then, with the advent of streaming media technologies you no longer had to wait for the entire file to download in order to hear it. Instead it began playing, and continued to play, within fifteen seconds or so of your making the request. That's what the term "streaming media" means: information is fed in a continuous stream, rather than in one huge hunk, to your computer.

There are three major types of streaming media (and a number of lesser ones): QuickTime, RealNetworks, and Windows Media Technology. By "types" we mean formats, that is, the methods by which visual or audio information is assembled, compressed, and delivered. Each type has a "player" of its own—a piece of software residing on the user's computer that can play the multimedia file once it arrives from the server via the Internet.

Suddenly, however, all that has again changed. The second major development that has affected the availability and practicality of using audio for instructional purposes is the **MP3 audio format**. This is a compressed file—meaning that it produces a file many times smaller than the earlier formats and has thus enabled the explosion of downloadable music and music players such as the iPod and cell phones—that has been taken up as the leading format for listening to and sharing music. While it does not have the same audio quality as a WAV or AIFF format, it has proved good enough for most listeners, and in any case, if you are creating instructional material such as lectures or interviews and not a symphony, we don't think you or your students will find it lacking.

These days, you can capture digital audio through a microphone onto your computer, via your smart phone or other device. Again, it has become easier than ever for a rank amateur to do this. Let's look at a few programs and web site services that offer you some different approaches to recording audio for your classes. Which you choose will depend on the purpose of the audio as well as some other factors. Before discussing any of these, we recommend that you do purchase a headset microphone with a boom mike that automatically positions itself to the side of your mouth. This need not be an expensive one—$30–$60 is sufficient to obtain a decent quality headset with microphone. In addition, we recommend that you choose a headset microphone that connects via USB because these offer the most flexibility for different types of use, the best sound, and they detour around any limitations of your computer soundcard equipment. (Non-USB or "analog" microphones have a set of plugs—one for the microphone and one for the headset—that work through the soundcard of your computer.) Using handheld microphones or those that are built in to your computer do not work well for recording or real-time conversations as they are apt to create muffled sounds, lack of clarity, and background noise. You invariably move the mike about and it's difficult to place the microphone at just the right distance. Generally the microphones built into web cams that sit on top of your computers are not the highest quality and you will still have to deal with background noise.

Companies such as Logitech, Plantronics, or Altec sell decent inexpensive headset models that have USB connections, but they and others include higher-end versions that include more noise-canceling features or more comfortable padding on the headset. (For a more detailed explanation of this issue see https://admin.adobe.acrobat.com/_a295153/microphones.)

What Kind of Microphone Do You Need?

Purchasing a headset (or earpiece) with a microphone boom (one that you can situate at the side of your mouth) along with a USB connection is recommended for the best sound quality in recording audio and for communicating via real-time synchronous tools.

To use audio for quick feedback on student papers, try out Adobe Acrobat PDF—follow the help instructions to quickly insert and record short audio clips after converting student Word documents to PDF. All you need are the Adobe Acrobat program and a microphone. The virtue of this is that the audio clip is directly inserted at the relevant spot in the paper and the student needs only the Adobe PDF Reader to listen to the clip.

You can perform a similar task in MS Word, but the resulting file will balloon to an alarming size, whereas the PDF file produces a much more manageable size file.

A free recording and editing program called Audacity (http:// audacity.sourceforge.net) will also allow you to simply and quickly record an audio file and encode it in MP3 using a LAME encoder (software that is available for downloading at the Audacity site) so that you can upload to your course management software, web site, or blog. We have used Audacity with great numbers of faculty who were complete neophytes and yet able to produce good audio to suit their instructional objectives. It must be downloaded to your computer and is available for Windows, Mac, or Linux. It will allow you to create several types of audio files and to import and convert files as well.

Many people use Skype (www.skype.com) for making phone calls over the Internet, and this is a tool that can be used for providing feedback and consultations with students or to permit students who are collaborating on a project to communicate. When recorded using a plug-in, one can create

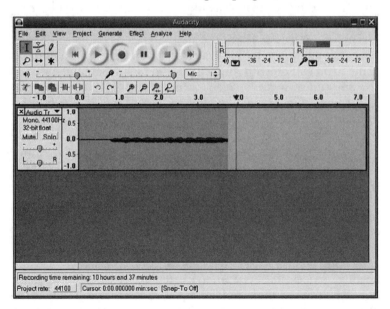

Figure 9.3 Recording on Audacity, from http://audacity.source-forge.net/about/images/recording.png.

recordings of interviews. Bethany Bovard teaches several courses in the Online Teaching and Learning Certificate Program in the College of Extended Learning at New Mexico State University. Bovard is a versatile and enthusiastic innovator and her TekTrek blog (http://tektrek.wordpress.com) is a good source for critiques of new Web 2.0 tools. She notes that Skype is a regular item in her toolbox for both instructor–student and student–student communications in her courses. Bovard mentions that Skype can become even more valuable through the use of such plug-ins as Pamela MP3 Call Recorder (www.pamcorder.com) or other tools that extend the use of Skype. (Such tools can be found in Skype under Tools>Extras or https://extras.skype.com).

Podcasting Services

Some of the online hosting services that are used for podcasting may also be used to create standalone audio files. But true podcasting is generally used to make a series of recordings, publish those recordings to a web site and to enable others to subscribe to those podcasts. Your own institution may facilitate your setting up podcasts. There are many types of podcasting software that allow you to not only record and edit your audio file (which you can do with Audacity or the Mac's GarageBand) but also to publish it to the Web, using wizards to create the RSS feed code and tags that will allow others to find and subscribe to your podcast. There are also podcasting services that will take your MP3 recordings and do all the coding and hosting for you.

Podomatic (http://podomatic.com) is a hosting service that allows you to create podcasts for free. It also features Web 2.0 types of sharing on the site. There are limits on monthly bandwidth data transfer for free users—in other words, the free service would not accommodate large files and large numbers of students accessing his or her podcasts.

Two other online browser-based services are Gcast (www.gcast.com) and Gabcast (www.gabcast.com). While these are free hosting services, if users want to use telephones for recording the podcasts (rather than uploading already-created MP3 audio files), each service charges for that mode of recording, the former by a yearly subscription and the latter with a per-minute charge.

A free tool that makes the entire process of podcasting nearly automatic is Posterous (www.posterous.com). Using Posterous, one can create an individual or group blog to which images, audio, or video can all be sent via email. Posterous accepts files in such formats as Word documents, PowerPoint, Avi, and MP3. Posterous places audio files into a player within your blog and allows you to set up an RSS feed. It automatically converts video files into Flash, and if you provide URL links, will even embed content (such as a YouTube video) when possible.

Bethany Bovard has used Posterous in her courses and points out that there are many instructors in higher education and K–12 teachers,

> *who just don't have the time or support to create and just want an easy way to post for themselves, and since pretty much everyone has email accessible to them, they are able to get content online without even having to use the term "blog."*

Bovard is particularly pleased by a feature in Posterous which allows her to create a group blog,

> *Place student email addresses into the system and simply tell students to just send an email here to contribute to the blog. While they need to register and put in a password to view the blog, they are able to contribute without having to learn blogging.*

Also, she notes that on Posterous,

> *you can set it up so that when you send an email to the Posterous account, you can arrange for it to simultaneously crosspost that new information to your other accounts on Facebook, Twitter, etc. So it can do double duty for those who have multiple sites to update.*

Narrated Slide Shows

So now you see that for minimal or no cost at all, you have the ability to make web pages, insert graphics (which you've scanned and fixed up), and create audio that you've made yourself. Though we don't want this to sound like a sales pitch for miracle kitchen devices, there is more, much more.

A narrated slide show can be a very useful tool for any instructor. With it, you can take a series of slides—say, for a biology instructor, pictures of a cell dividing—and create an illustrated lecture in which you talk to your students directly, explaining the significance of the images they are seeing.

There are a number of ways to create narrated slide shows. Probably the simplest way is to use PowerPoint's own "record narration" option—all you need is your slides and a microphone. Follow directions to set your voice volume level and to choose other options. Once you have saved the presentation, you have the option to re-record one or more slides to correct or revise as you like.

However, your resulting file may be quite large. For this reason, many educators like to use other programs that can reduce the size of the narrated PowerPoint slide so that it is more convenient to post online. Many of these conversion programs also provide a measure of protection from others changing or editing the presentation. Some of these conversion programs are free and others are low cost.

A popular choice is Impatica. It greatly compresses your PowerPoint and creates a new file that then plays on any site without a plug-in or download. Check with your institution to see if it has a license for this product. If not, a free trial version is available at their site, www.impatica.com.

iSpring is a product that converts your PowerPoint to a Flash (SWF) file. Flash file conversion can make a large PowerPoint file that may include animation, images, video clips, and hyperlinks from your PowerPoint into a more compact size and one easily accessed on a web site. A free version of this program is available at www.ispringsolutions.com/free_powerpoint_to_flash_converter.html. The software must be downloaded onto your computer.

Slideshare (www.slideshare.net) is a popular hosting site that allows users to upload and share PowerPoint slides (before narration has been added) and other types of files like PDF. The slides are converted to Flash format and enclosed within a player. It's free and one can create files as large as 100 MB. It adds Web 2.0 features like the ability to add "tags" that indicate what your presentation is about, to easily share with others—either the public at large or specific users on your contact list—embed it in your own web site, or create a special URL that you distribute only to a specific individual or group. You can set up your slide show with a Creative Commons license or mark it as "all rights reserved."

However, to add narration, music, or other audio files, you must synchronize separately recorded MP3 audio files that are available on your own web site in a streamable format. The process is a bit awkward in that the audio files are not actually uploaded to the Slideshare site but instead your audio file needs to be already uploaded on another web site.

The previously mentioned free version of VoiceThread (http://voicethread.com) also accommodates PowerPoint presentation but many find it less complicated to convert the slides to PDF documents. But it is possible to use this tool to go beyond the PowerPoint presentation format since image files, video, and text documents can all be uploaded directly to this tool. This allows you to build up your own slide show presentation out of many different sources. Adding your narration is easy and because the tool allows for the addition of student comments by webcam, microphone, telephone (for a fee), and uploaded video files, displaying student comments adjacent to the presentation portions upon which they comment is an ideal way to provide for interaction at the same time that you or your students are presenting. Also, the VoiceThread presentation can be embedded into your own web site so that students need not leave your online classroom to access it. See a sample of Michele Pacansky-Brock's use of VoiceThread for a lecture presentation for her Art Appreciation class at http://voicethread.com/library/4.

Scripted Versus Unscripted Narrations and Presentations

There are two ways to do a narration or audio/video presentation: scripted and unscripted. Scripting—that is, writing out exactly what you want to say in advance, word for word—is effective for those instructors who are dealing with complex or detailed material and don't want to make a mistake. Unscripted narrations and presentations, with the instructor speaking to the students from notes or even from memory or off the cuff, replicate more of the face-to-face classroom experience.

With the advent of YouTube and iTunes, students may be becoming more accustomed to hearing casual presentations and there seems to be a movement away from overly formal presentations. The ad-libbed quality of unscripted presentations, even with an occasional hesitation or error, creates a sense of intimacy between instructor and student. On the other hand, the ad-libbed presentation may ramble on too long.

If you have software that allows you to easily edit audio, video, or narrated slide shows, you may opt for the more unscripted production since you can still clean up any major gaffes or shorten long-winded passages and need not re-record.

The How and Why of Video

Larry Ragan is director of faculty development for Penn State World Campus. He notes that in the past, there was always a barrier to creating video—the cost, the learning curve, the staff resources necessary to help instructors. Now there are video cameras built in to computers, or small web cams that can be hooked onto the monitor or sit on top of the desk for those clips that don't require you to leave your desk. And if you want to capture something outside your office, many digital cameras and cell phones allow for the making of short video clips. Video clips can be transferred to your computer through a USB or Firewire cable or perhaps through a service offered by your cell phone service provider—you need to consult the documentation and cables that come with the device that you use to make video. Finally, beyond the great range of available dedicated video cameras which are getting more compact and convenient to use all the time, there are low-cost pocket-size mini video cameras like the Flip Video, Creative's Vado, or Kodak Zi6 that are specially designed to plug directly into the USB port of the computer. While these may not have the features and versatility of the more expensive video cameras, they do make it convenient to create on-the-fly videos, are unobtrusive because of their size, and easy to use. Sometimes easy to use translates into "more likely to use" as well.

Many video cameras come equipped with their own video editing software that allow you to manipulate, cut, or splice together segments. Computers are often preloaded with video editing software such as Windows Movie Maker (for PC) or iMovie (Mac). The Flip video comes with its own editing software but you can also export its video to work in a different editor.

Ragan talks about some of the creative opportunities this greater ease of use presents to instructors. He mentions a few examples of how video can be used in a course:

- Making a personal introduction video to form a personal connection with your students. Ragan advises instructors to do what is comfortable and true for them—that means you can just as easily film yourself sitting at ease at your desk or petting your dog or presenting a more formal pose.

- Creating transitional bridges between segments or at the end of a course. Ragan displays a video clip at the end of a lesson to reflect and summarize, "I've watched the dialogue around these discussions this week. Now let's talk about next week, when we will be moving into topic X ..."

- Enriching course content by adding the voices of other individuals in the community or profession, through interviews on the fly. Ragan notes that using a small video camera like the Flip (which is about the size of a pack of cigarettes) makes interviewing a more casual and seemingly less intrusive activity, "What you said is interesting," Ragan typically finds himself saying in approaching a potential interview subject, "may I just capture that?"

- Asking students to use video to do similar interviews in the community and in their workplace. For example, Ragan suggests, a student in health policy might do an interview with a public health administrator or even interview other students about what they think about a concept. Ragan notes that this in effect helps moderate the responsibility of the instructor for having to generate all course content and puts some responsibility for learning into the hands of the students themselves.

- Taking a virtual field trip. The instructor might go out in the real world and show a sample of something for the benefit of the students who can't be there in reality. For example, an agronomist can demonstrate local soil samples for the benefit of his online students who cannot be there with him. Or the students may be sent out on their own discovery quests. For example, Michele Pacansky-Brock, the Art Appreciation instructor, encourages her students to create their own video or find video on the Web that pertains to art in everyday life and to share it with their fellow students through easy uploading to their class Ning online social network.

Sites and Tools for Video

The YouTube and TeacherTube sites mentioned previously, or others like Vimeo (www.vimeo.com), have some features in common. They allow you to share videos publicly or with groups, to "tag"—categorize your video to make it searchable by topic—and often facilitate embedding by providing code you can insert into your own web site.

Another service that offers these and some notable additional features is Viddler (www.viddler.com). Viddler allows you to upload in a wide array of video formats and there is a choice of making your video private, shared, or public. "Shared" means you can specify who can see it. There is also a interactive commenting or annotating feature that permits users to not only add comments below the video, but to add comments via text or their own video clip at any point during the streaming of the video. Bethany Bovard explains why Viddler features can really enhance communications,

> *Rather than have to comment, "2 minutes into your video you said X and I wondered what you meant by that" you can just click on the video timeline and directly add your comment. I've found that my students are pretty comfortable making comments in this way, some commenting in text and others using their own webcams to make video clip comments.*

Bovard uses Viddler "to create discussions around lecture materials, for presentations and a host of other things—it just generally allows me to increase my presence in the classroom." She also appreciates the wide variety of files that can be uploaded—for example, even cell phone videos can be uploaded via computer.

Screen-Capture/Screen-Casting Video Software

These programs do not only capture the still shots or screen grabs of something on your computer screen but actually record a short video (say, 5–10 minutes) of your movements onscreen as you click and scroll or otherwise manipulate the software you have on the screen. For example, if you want to demonstrate to students how to use an online library electronic database in order to find a full text article, how to use an Excel spreadsheet, or how to use an online chemical experiment simulator, you can capture the entire process, along with your narration (if you have a microphone), by using screen-capture video software. Bethany Bovard says of this category of tool,

> *I use this type of tool for everything from course and lesson overviews to student tech support. My students use these tools to show me what they are seeing on their monitor so that I can better support them or to help out their classmates. These tools are easy to use by anyone with basic Internet skills, and since they don't require a download but work in a browser, you can use them from virtually any computer.*

Three easy-to-use and, at the time of this writing, free programs are Screencast-o-Matic (www.screencast-o-matic. com), Jing (www.jingproject.com), and ScreenToaster (http:// screentoaster.com). Screencast-o-Matic allows you to make and host your video right on their web site without even having to download anything. (Be aware that makes your video public.) You can provide a link for your students to their site to view the video or embed it in your own site. Or you may want to export it to your own computer as an AVI file (for Windows Movie Maker, for example), a QuickTime file (MOV) or Flash (SWF) file, then edit and finally upload it to your own site. Your CMS or one of the video hosting sites we have mentioned make uploading a matter of following a series of menu-driven directions. Like Screencast-o-Matic, ScreenToaster is accessed through a browser. Bovard uses both but notes that ScreenToaster has some handy features like the ability to add subtitles and to download a video. Content can be controlled as private or public content. Bovard likes the "picture within picture" feature, that is, she can include her webcam image in a corner of the screen: "It allows me to personalize—I use that when I am at the beginning of a course and want to introduce both myself and the course and help students navigate through the online classroom."

Jing allows you to take screen grabs as well as screen-casts and the latter are limited to five minutes. Jing does require a download but can be used with either Windows or Mac.

Step-by-step tutorials on the respective web sites provide helpful instructions on how to use their programs and you might want to search for additional video tutorials on YouTube.

For those who want more sophisticated or longer screen-casts, we recommend a program like Camtasia Studio. Your institution may already have a license for this program. One of the authors of this book, Steve Rossen, was an early adopter of Camtasia and taught his first multimedia classes a decade ago using Camtasia videos to demonstrate software while also instructing his students how to use Camtasia for their own work. Camtasia offers a free trial of their software for thirty days, which can be ideal for student use, and there is individual educator pricing for Camtasia and Camtasia/SnagIt.

Student-Generated Content

Let's take a moment to further consider how encouraging your students to create content as part of their course work is now a feasible and attractive approach to teaching and learning. The Web 2.0 tools we highlight in this chapter and that we have mentioned in previous chapters are often those that can be wielded by students. So why should you think about trying this approach to course work?

■ Students learn by doing.

Hands-on projects, when properly planned, compel students to research, experiment, and discover their strong points, as well as reveal the areas of difficulty they may encounter. The instructor can then give feedback and provide guidance to resolve these areas of difficulty and help the student move forward.

■ Students add diverse perspectives and approaches.

Students all have different learning preferences and see issues from diverse vantage points. By allowing students to make these differences more evident through creating content, the instructor can mediate, discuss, or help students learn to evaluate or critique ideas. By allowing students to express their ideas or solve problems through the means of diverse media, individual student learning may be better facilitated while new perspectives may also be brought to bear on an issue.

■ Students learn by sharing and collaborating.

By working together or sharing ideas, students are often led to reflect on their own ideas, to learn to work as a team, to negotiate different approaches, and to learn how to communicate their ideas in an effective manner.

■ Student interest is sparked by choice of format.

While some students will prefer to simply write a paper on a given topic, others will find their interest stimulated by a creative project that involves finding or creating multimedia resources or collaboration and sharing online. While the instructor must decide what the relevant options are for a particular assignment, giving students some measure of choice in how to accomplish the assignment may increase the student's involvement and interest in the task.

In encouraging student-generated content, there are just a few issues to keep in mind.

First, find out if your institution has any regulations about the use of sites external to the university. In regard to considerations of student privacy—before recommending a particular site or tool, investigate the privacy options. Some sites have special provisions for educational use and some do not. Some services maintain the right to use content created on their site in connection with publicizing their service. Second, if there are materials that will become publicly accessible online, suggest that students do not use their full names (you and their classmates can still know who they are), that they are familiar with any opt-in privacy options, and caution against divulging any private identifying information.

Bethany Bovard notes that while you can often make a blog private, if you do so, you can no longer set up an RSS feed for that blog. She also makes the point that, from both a philosophical and a pedagogical point of view, carefully and selectively providing opportunities to create and share information with the world outside the classroom has a value in itself.

> There are different levels of knowledge among the students in each course and by sharing information, they can be helpful to their classmates or even to students in other institutions. We feel it's very important that they are providing opportunities for others to learn and contributing to knowledge. And knowing that what they contribute is public often makes them work harder to perfect what they create. So we let our students know this and if they still don't want others to see their works in progress or they have privacy concerns, we show them how to create an email account with a pseudonym and then they can become a member of our blog or wiki using that pseudonym. We generate a list for the class and circulate it so that both instructor and students in the class are aware of the identity but it maintains that student's privacy on the public site.

Bovard also emphasizes the importance of not posting any grades or records of evaluation in the public site itself, reserving all such information for entry in the secure course management system.

● ● ● ● ●

Other Tools

Polls and Surveys

Polling or surveying your students on a frequent basis is a quick method to track how your students are faring in the class. It is an easy way to conduct formative assessment. For example, you can ask students whether or not they are finding a particular assignment difficult, or having a problem working through a solution, and depending on the response, you can provide some additional explanations. While you may have already invited students to post their questions or note any problems in the asynchronous discussion forum, many students hesitate to raise questions until they are really in a muddle—a poll can make the matter seem less weighty and students are more likely to indicate problems are afoot. Some course management systems have built in polling and surveying instruments. But if you do not have access to these, for polling, Polldaddy and Pollanywhere are two easy-to-use programs that offer free versions of their software to create polls or surveys for your courses. The free versions include a branding element from the company—a link that leads back to their web sites. Polldaddy's free version offers the ability to have an unlimited number of people responding to a single poll and unlimited number of polls per month with surveys limited to ten questions and 100 survey responses per monthly. Text, images, and even video can be used in the polls. Polleverywhere free version for educators allows no more than thirty-two people to respond to a single poll, but educators can use the polling software for an unlimited number of different classes. Students can respond to the polls using text messaging or from a web browser as they sit at a computer or via a smart phone. In both cases, you create the poll or survey on their site, using your browser, but you can also embed the code in your own online course management software or other course site so that students do not have to leave the precincts of your class.

Linda Smelser at University of Maryland University College has used Polldaddy with her undergraduate course in Principles

Create A New Poll

Account Home » List Polls » New Poll

Figure 9.4 Creating a poll using PollDaddy (http://polldaddy.com).
Reproduced by permission.

and Strategies of Successful Learning to insert polls into the
announcement section of the classroom software. This allowed
her to calibrate the progress of students on assignments. For
example, she created a simple, "Yes, No, Doesn't matter" choice
of responses to query students working on group projects to
determine whether or not the groups needed to extend their
preparation time for an additional week.

Other instructors might similarly ask students to rate the
class readings—"Which of this week's readings has proved most
helpful to you in understanding the X concept?"—or to get a
quick count of how many students want to sign up for virtual
office hours in a particular week.

Surveys   A popular online survey creation tool is Survey
Monkey (www.surveymonkey.com). The free version allows
one to survey up to 100 people with up to ten questions per
survey.

Quizzes

Please see the Chapter 6 discussion of quizmakers. We will simply note here that free versions of quizmakers like Quiz School and My Studiyo include some Web 2.0 features that allow for the inclusion of multimedia, embedding the quizzes into your own web site, and tagging and sharing.

Mind-Mapping

Either you, as instructor, or your students might want to create a **mind-map** to illustrate relationships between various categories of things, to present an outline of an upcoming project, to brainstorm, or for any other number of creative purposes. A free browser-based program that allows you and your students to do this is Mindomo, www.mindomo.com. You create the mind-map online and can either link to it on the Mindomo site or embed it on your web page. Users can delegate permission to edit to other users so a group of students could work on a mind-map together. The mind-map can also be exported to a text-based outline format.

There are other programs of this sort, both those that are hosted online and browser-based and those that require downloads of software—an excellent source to find continually updated reviews of mind-mapping software (or any of the other categories of tools for learning) may be found at Jane Hart's Top Learning Tools site, www.c4lpt.co.uk/learningtools.html, or the previously mentioned blog of Larry Ferlazzo. See the Guide to Resources for other sites that review and constantly update information on the latest Web 2.0 tools.

Avatars

The use of an avatar may be an option for students who are shy about introducing themselves through photos, or who might want to speak through an avatar presenter. Some instructors use them to inject a note of whimsy. To create an avatar it is not necessary for students to enter a virtual world. Programs like Voki (www.voki.com) make it very easy to create a 3-D avatar and then record a short (limited to sixty seconds) introduction

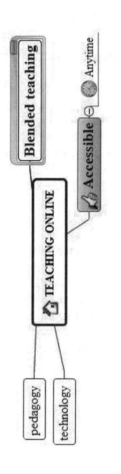

Figure 9.5 Creating a Mind-Map on Mindomo.com. Reproduced by permission from Mindomo.com.

or short presentation of opinions. The recordings can be made using telephone, microphone, or uploading a pre-recorded audio file. (If you don't want to use your own voice, it is even possible to type in text and have it rendered by Voki into audio.)

Animated Movies

There are a number of sites that will enable you (or your students) to make simple animated "movies" using site-supplied cartoon-like illustrations or, in some cases, your own artwork. These include DoInk (www.doink.com), Digitalfilms (www.digitalfilms.com), and Fuzzwich (www.fuzzwich.com). DoInk contains its own drawing tool so you can create original drawings. The main instructional use of these sites would be for story-telling (especially for those teaching K–12), art, or short explanatory pieces, but they also lend themselves creating short scenarios for teaching a foreign language.

Figure 9.6 Creating an Avatar on Voki.com. Source: Voki.com™. Reproduced by permission. Copyright 2007 Oddcast, Inc.

●　●　●　●　●

Using or Creating Multimedia: Why and When Is It Worth It?

Okay, now some of you may be asking, is it really worthwhile for me to create audio or video, search for appropriate existing multimedia, or even ask my students to create multimedia? Many of you will have neither the time nor the desire to make your own audio, video, or narrated slide shows even as you recognize how much easier this is to do than ever before. If you decide it is not worth your time, you should be aware that a lot of material is already available on the Web, as noted in Chapter 7. In addition to some of the sites mentioned in that chapter, there are some search directories like Intute (www.intute.ac.uk/arts) dedicated to accessing resources in the arts and humanities, engineering, mathematics, and technology that have been selected and evaluated by subject specialists. So while you may not want to create multimedia, you still have many other sources that you can incorporate into your course.

If you teach art history, then using graphics of an artist's work will seem a self-evident reason for employing multimedia. But if you teach mathematics or philosophy, the need to enhance your pages with graphics, sound, or video may not seem quite so obvious. Such subjects are traditionally taught with nothing more than plain old text or at most some graphs or tables thrown in. So why would an instructor choose to spend the extra time and effort to create or integrate existing multimedia?

To summarize and build upon what we have discussed in this chapter, here are some possible reasons:

1. *To illustrate the mechanics of how things work.* Often, instructors in seemingly abstract subject areas are called upon to describe the process of how things work. An economics instructor may need to illustrate how demand affects cost, or an electrical engineer may want to demonstrate how digital information flows through logic gates. These needs call for multimedia. Sometimes the process in question can be illustrated with a graph or a series of illustrations. At other times, an animation showing the process in motion is preferable.

2. *To clarify or emphasize abstract concepts.* Complex abstract concepts are often difficult for students to sort out or remember. Often, graphics can serve as memory jogs for students who are attempting to keep a host of such concepts straight. For example, a history professor teaching the Spanish Civil War might want her students to visit a web site in Spain exhibiting posters and paintings from the period as a way of keeping track of the seemingly bewildering array of acronyms for the anarchists, trade unionists, socialists, Falangists, and other political groups of the period.

3. *To provide another approach or perspective to learning.* Sometimes what is learned through more than one medium is more effectively retained by the student. Listening to a narration of slides may reinforce the content on the screen, and watching a video may be more enlightening than simply reading a text description of a place, culture, or event.

4. *To enliven or illustrate unfamiliar material.* Whether you're dealing with historical or geographical contexts (poverty in nineteenth-century London, the ecology of Central American rainforests), the identification of organisms or structures (spirochetes, postmodern architecture), or the way things function (human ambulation, a four-cycle engine), the use of graphics and animation can greatly enhance your students' comprehension. A major value of textbooks is the profusion of illustrations, graphs, and tables they provide. The Web provides a vehicle by which individual instructors, using comparatively inexpensive tools, can "publish" their own textbook-quality material and make it available to their students.

5. *As the basis for an assignment.* Illustrations can be powerful and fascinating stimuli for an assignment. Newspaper articles, advertisements, photographs, even articles found on the Web or scanned and displayed (following copyright prescriptions), can provide the basis for an assignment requiring students to critically evaluate the material and post their analyses. Students can also be asked to capture something in the real world on audio or video and present it online as part of an assignment. All of these options are becoming more feasible through the availability of digital devices and Web 2.0 software tools.

•••••

When to Avoid Multimedia and Web 2.0 Tools

Putting together a site enhanced by graphics, animation, or video poses an immediate problem: How much is too much when it comes to the time and effort involved in creating and assembling these multimedia elements?

For those fortunate enough to work at an institution that provides ample financial, administrative, and staff support, this question may be moot. However, for the majority of instructors, the burden of putting together such materials falls squarely on their shoulders. How can you gauge in advance whether creating a graphic or an animation is worth the time you will need to produce it? And when might you be simply overwhelming your students? Here are some factors to consider.

1. *Institutional support and your own priorities.* Some institutions encourage innovative teaching by rewarding faculty members with either merit promotions or release time. Other institutions provide support through labs, media centers, or paid student assistants. In such situations, taking time to enhance your course with multimedia makes sense.

   If, on the other hand, your university will regard your extra work with indifference, putting in the extra effort becomes strictly a question of how much experimentation with new forms of expression means to you personally. It *does* take time to learn even a simple menu-driven program or tool let alone devise the lesson plan underpinning its use. Even an advanced user needs a few hours to put together a presentation, for example, or to find or search for multimedia objects. If the effort cuts into your ability to do your own research and if your institution offers no compensation for your endeavors, then obviously you will want to use discretion before embarking on anything too ambitious. But many instructors have found that simple multimedia elements have the power to greatly enhance their teaching and their students' learning, sometimes resulting in less work for them and better outcomes for students after that initial investment of time to create or find resources. If that Web 2.0 tool or multimedia resource helps you to do your work more effectively and saves you time in creating lecture material, explaining processes, or grading students, this itself will likely be a compelling reason to pursue it.

2. *Relevance of the material.* It may seem that using an animation or video will encourage your students to dig into the material you are presenting. All too often, however, instructors sacrifice relevance to convenience, using a graphic that almost, but not quite, expresses the concept or the subject they are trying to illustrate. In these cases, students are often more confused by the material than aided by it. In such situations, it would be better not to produce the material at all.

3. *Availability of the material elsewhere.* Before you create a multimedia presentation, make sure that the material doesn't exist on another publicly accessible web site. Spend some time searching online. If you find what you're looking for, create a link from your web page to the site, thus saving yourself the considerable time and effort to create the material from scratch.

4. *Accessibility or ease of use of the material or tool.* Before embarking on the production of a complex multimedia element, consider whether your students will be able to view it or use it easily, as the case may be. Readers of this book range from those whose students will have no problem at all accessing content to those whose students have severely limited computer equipment and even more limited Internet access. Always test out your content under the real conditions in which it will be used. If you're linking to another site that has videos or animations, make sure you tell your students if there are particular types of software or plug-ins that they will need to access it. In the end, you must ask yourself:

   ■ Is the material you're planning to produce so complex that viewing it online may be more tedious than helpful?

   ■ Does it necessitate the downloading of software or accompanied by other conditions that would make it not worth the time expended to access it?

5. *What does it add to enhance the course experience and learning objectives?* Multimedia and Web 2.0 tools should add something to the learning experience that might otherwise be unavailable or less readily available. These considerations can be very practical in nature or more complex to discern. For example, screen grabs and text or a screen-capture video program may allow you to more easily demonstrate step-by-step instructions than would be possible with just directions in text. Less tangible but equally important is the increased interest students might register in the course content and activities having been stimulated by the multiple perspectives on the subject available through external and multimedia resources, or through their direct participation by creating and sharing content with their classmates. Finally, many instructors have found that multimedia elements and Web 2.0 tools provide a refreshing and stimulating element to their teaching. Enthusiasm on the part of the instructor is certainly communicated to students and may in itself be a valid reason to embark on this activity. And while you may decide that your presentations do not gain much with the addition of multimedia, allowing your students to fulfill an assignment using multimedia might be a true enhancement to the learning process.

Focusing on Web 2.0 tools, Bethany Bovard has produced a succinct and focused checklist for selecting appropriate tools for your needs, available at her TekTrek blog, http://tektrek. wordpress.com/2009/03/02/web-20-selection-criteria.   Her selection criteria are Access, Usability, Privacy and Intellectual Property, Workload and Time Management, and Fun Factor. She advocates using the checklist to quickly eliminate those tools that will obviously not do the job for you and then dedicating some time to further experimenting and trial and error to find the best tool to match your objectives. Bovard's blog entry for this checklist provides some helpful examples of how she used the criteria to conclude whether or not to use a particular tool. Her discussion may provide a useful model for you in formulating your own set of considerations.

● ● ● ● ●

Pulling It All Together

As the possible resources and tools dramatically increase in number, so does the responsibility for the instructor who must exercise his or her discretion in selecting what to use and how to use it. Some concerns have been voiced about the use of Web 2.0 sites that pull students out of the course management system environment and into other web sites where educational purpose is invariably mingled with non-educational and non-student content. To some extent, as we have noted at many points, instructors can avoid much of that by choosing services catering to educators or with special environments for educators, by embedding content from external sources within the classroom software. In other cases, instructors will simply need to scout out where they send their students in order to issue appropriate warnings or for the purpose of giving better directions to finding the sought-after objects.

But the greater responsibility is to devise a plan for your course that will integrate all the elements you have chosen, and to provide a rationale and purpose that will be clear to you and your students. If integration of tools and resources is lacking, the course will simply seem a bothersome or diverting but often irrelevant collection of content and activities to your students. We recommend that you always maintain a focal or gathering point for your students, a sort of virtual "homeroom"—whether that is a home page or blog, the course management system classroom, or, in the case of blended courses, an actual face-to-face meeting place.

Finally, a reminder about the changing and sometimes ephemeral nature of Web 2.0 tools:

Important! *Free sites in particular may not provide you with advance warning of their demise or major changes. Always keep a copy of your presentation documents and multimedia files and advise students to do the same for material they create. In regard to discussion, comments or chat, you will want to capture and save any content and transcripts that may be necessary for you to use in evaluating students.*

III

Teaching in the Online Classroom

10

• • • • •

Preparing Students for Online Learning

Learning online can be as exasperating for the student as for the instructor, particularly for those taking an online course for the first time. Suddenly thrust into a world in which independent or collaborative learning is heavily stressed, students accustomed to traditional classroom procedures—taking notes during a lecture, answering the occasional question, attending discussion sections—must make unexpected and often jolting adjustments to their study habits.

In addition to these pedagogical concerns, students must contend with varying web site formats requiring special equipment or software. Indeed, it isn't unusual for students at the same university to encounter two or sometimes three different course management software systems during a single semester. With unsophisticated equipment and busy schedules, perhaps unsure whether they should communicate by email or by posting queries on discussion boards, students often feel frustrated, abandoned, or confused.

Students' problems fast become those of the instructor as well. Instead of teaching their course, posting information, and responding to legitimate queries on the discussion board, instructors often find themselves trying to troubleshoot technical queries for which they have minimal expertise. Tussling with why a student using a particular browser can't see part of a given web page or why another is unable to install a program on her home computer, instructors expend too much time and energy providing support and maintenance while struggling to keep up with the normal duties of teaching a course. Ideally, every institution should have 24/7 tech support to which every student can turn for help. But we realize that some readers do not teach under those conditions.

This chapter will address these and related issues concerning preparation of students for the online learning environment. The key is to identify and be forewarned about potential problems and to learn some effective methods for handling them.

● ● ● ● ●

Problems That Students Typically Encounter

A student logging on to a course web site for the first time has a lot to contend with. To begin with, there's the terminology. Those neat rows of icons, either along the side or across the top or bottom of the screen, meant to guide students to the course material often bear names, captions, or titles the users have never seen before. For example, a button might say "Course Notes," "My Course," "Course Information," or "Main Page," all of which generally mean the same thing. The icons under which such captions appear may look like an open notepad, an owl reading a book, or a blackboard.

Similarly, an area set aside for students to post information about themselves, including a small digital photograph, might say "Course Information," "Student Home Pages," or "Biographies." Most variable of all is the button or caption leading to the conferencing system. In some course management systems it is called the "Threaded Discussion," while elsewhere it might be called "Conference Board," "Discussion Area," or "Electronic Message Board." Tests are sometimes called quizzes, sometimes assessments, and the areas where students collaborate on projects may bear names like "Group Pages" and "Student Presentations."

Often these mysteries of nomenclature and icons are just the beginning of the puzzles a student must solve. There are also technical problems and communication difficulties.

Technical Problems

When they begin a course, students may find themselves unable to view the web pages properly, either because the browser they're using is too old (for one reason or another they haven't updated it), or because they haven't installed the necessary plug-ins. Another common experience is not being able to share word-processed documents. Even if students are using the same program, those with earlier releases may not be able to read documents created by classmates or instructors with more current versions without the help of a plug-in.

Problems Related to Learning Style and Online Communication

Far more significant, perhaps, is the variance in learning styles required of those learning online. Students used to instructor-directed learning may feel somewhat lost in an environment that relies heavily on individual initiative and independent learning or even more dismayed to hear that collaboration with peers is an expected element of the class.

Even though the requirements of the course are clearly outlined in the syllabus and in the class announcements, the effect isn't the same as seeing an instructor glare severely at the class and announce that the essays are due the following week, without fail. Assignments are completed at home, often in solitude, and submitted through the click of a button, without that warm feeling students sometimes get when they pass in their exam papers or hand their essays over to their teacher in person. Indeed, without the discipline and structure imposed by the requirement of physically sitting in a classroom, students often feel cast adrift.

The complicated mechanisms of human expression—facial expressions, voice intonation, body language, eye contact—are also no longer available. In their place are the contextual and stylistic conventions of the written word, a mode of communication that favors verbal over visual or kinesthetic learners, thus leaving some students curiously unsatisfied. Learning how to modulate their own speech is also a concern for online students. Most of us rely on body language to deflect the impact of what we say; we convey our true intentions through gestures and vocal intonation. The absence of these conventions sometimes causes students real distress.

The asynchronous nature of much online communication adds a further dimension to this problem. We are all used to instant feedback: Susan says something, and Steve responds. Online, Susan may still say something to which Steve responds—but the reply may come a day later. This spasmodic flow of communication takes some adjustment.

None of these problems is beyond the reach of a dedicated instructor. Now that there are so many ways to easily incorporate audio into classes, we encourage instructors to think about selecting opportunities to add these personalizing elements to the classroom, both in the form of their own short recordings as well as permitting students to do the same in their projects. Dealing with these problems effectively can save both the student and the instructor valuable time, reducing some of the tensions inherent in learning something new. The key is to understand the need to prepare students adequately for what they are about to encounter and to provide them with the necessary tools to get through the course. These efforts will complement the work you put into designing your course and syllabus.

●●●●●

Preparing Your Students

To address the kinds of problems we've been describing, the most successful online programs offer student orientations as well as continuing technical support and resources. They may also offer study-skills courses that include a strong focus on the issues particularly relevant to online learning. But instructors who are left mostly to their own devices can also find effective ways to meet their students' needs. In the following pages, we suggest approaches for both the individual instructor and the institution as a whole.

Readiness Programs

Many institutions have short online quizzes or lists that allow students to judge their readiness for online classes. Some of the areas they seek to gauge are:

■ whether students are proactive, self-disciplined, and well-organized;

- whether students are comfortable communicating entirely online without face-to-face meetings (for fully online courses);
- whether students have access to adequate computer equipment and software, and if not, whether they are willing to update their equipment.

Two examples of different types of readiness quizzes online are:

- Sierra College: http://lrc.sierracollege.edu/dl/survey/OL-student-assess.html;
- Manchester Metropolitan University in the UK: www.celt.mmu.ac.uk/studying_online/readiness/index.php.

Orientation Programs

Ideally, your institution should devise a student-orientation program that will take care of major issues such as these:

- equipment and browser requirements;
- a general introduction to the software platform and its major features;
- instructions and links for downloading necessary software plug-ins;
- information about issues that arise in an online class—perhaps in the form of a checklist about what one can expect as an online student.

Lists of frequently asked questions (FAQs), referral email addresses, and toll-free numbers for reaching support staff are other useful features often included.

Many institutions or their hosting and delivery partners have created such orientation programs. Most are simply self-paced series of web pages, some interactive and some not. Many incorporate self-assessment surveys that seek to help students identify whether they are suited for online learning. Others test knowledge about computers, the institution's procedures, and so forth. At the University of Maryland University College students can actually try out the classroom environment and interact with others through enrollment in a demo course, UMUC 411 (see www.umuc.edu/spotlight/411.html).

Once students have enrolled, some orientation programs contain an element of human supervision and feedback, so that students must complete a few tasks in order to "pass" the orientation and be admitted to the classroom. These requirements are particularly effective in ensuring that students have the minimum skills, resources, and knowledge for an online course.

Having well-prepared students will mean that you as the instructor can concentrate on teaching rather than on resolving extraneous problems. There's enough for you to do once your online course has begun without having to divert attention to these preparation issues. Effective student orientation is also beneficial to the institution, because it makes a significant difference in the retention rates in online programs. Students who start off with a good orientation are most likely to have a positive experience and to return for further courses.

Preparing Your Own Orientation Program

What if your institution hasn't yet made arrangements for an adequate student orientation? What should you do?

Two methods will resolve your dilemma. First, you can devise a simple orientation of your own, one that will satisfy at least the minimum requirements. Second, as noted in Chapter 5, you can give clear directions in your syllabus for dealing with documents, as well as explicit explanations of how and where you will handle material and activities in the classroom. If you are teaching a blended class, we suggest using the first class meeting as a chance to take the students step by step through an orientation to the software used in your class and to answer any questions students may have.

Before you begin creating your own orientation, you may want to take a look at some of the information and orientation pages that other institutions and institutional partners have set up. The following offer useful examples:

- Portland Community College's "Online Learning Orientation" at www.pcc.edu/about/distance/orientation;

- UCF Learning Online: http://learn.ucf.edu/index.html.

Some orientation programs address the issue of basic computer skills and suggest how to find assistance. Others try to give students insight into the classroom environment. For example, Arkansas State University, Fort Smith (see www. uafortsmith.edu/Online/OrientationInfoForWebBasedClasses) provides a series of videos (with text transcripts) to orient their online and blended course students to their course management software, Blackboard. It includes study tips, manages expectations, and also addresses software-specific issues.

Elements of an Orientation

If you create your own student orientation, there are several elements you should consider, as outlined below.

1. General introduction, including our expectations for online students

A general introduction can be made available to students even before they enroll in your course. Michele Pacansky-Brock created such an introduction for her students at Sierra College, combining a short video, "Preparing for Your Online Class," with a text introduction, all linked from the distance learning web page at her institution so that students could view this as early as when they were shopping for classes. She also provided a transcription and subtitles for her video, using a program called dotSUB (http://dotsub.com). She tells students in the video,

> *I created this website in an effort to increase the success of your learning by providing you with some very important information about my classes before the semester begins.... This page is important for all my online students but especially for those of you who are about to embark upon your very first online learning experience ... You're going to find, as you embark upon your journey with me that I really love teaching online and I work very, very hard to make your experience exciting and relevant.*

Pacansky-Brock discussed the attributes of successful online students and referred students to her institutions's online student-readiness quiz and a video of a Student Success workshop she had created, "Are You Ready for an Online Class?"

In the video, she explained how communications worked in her class,

> *This may sound a bit odd to hear from your instructor but communication is the foundation for any successful relationship ... yep, that's right. I expect you to fully communicate with me throughout your semester learning experience. You'll have plenty of opportunities to interact with me in our discussions and activities but if you, at any point, need further help to successfully meet a specific learning objective in our class, it is your responsibility to reach out to me and let me know.*

She comments on this, "I try to explain what my class consists of ahead of time so I can be more assuring of having prepared students enrolled on day one. I know there are students who do NOT want such a technologically enriched learning environment, and they have the right to be informed about the components of my class before they enroll so that they can find another class that suits their preferences."

2. Requirements for computer equipment and software (other than the platform being used)

State these as simply as possible. Realize that many people don't actually know the "numbers" for their computers, such as how large the hard drive is. However, they can easily identify their modem speed and the version of their software and browser, so be specific about these—for instance, "Must have Internet Explorer 8 or Firefox 10 or higher" or "Should have a high-speed Internet connection." You can also devise your own "tests" of certain requirements. For example, if students need to be able to access audio in your course, give them a sample to test—either on your own site or elsewhere on the Web.

Many institutions can make a common word-processing program available to your students, or they have site licenses for other software. But if your students don't have access to a common program supplied by your institution—and this is often the case for continuing-education students—you will need to stipulate how documents will be shared. You might ask students to save all documents in a particular format or to use software freely accessed through a browser like Google Docs. Or you might want students to paste their documents into text boxes provided in your course management software.

Gather information about the software possibilities ahead of time, and let students know whom they can contact for technical support or to obtain software. Include links on the Web where students can download any free programs, such as Adobe Acrobat Reader, that you intend to use in the classroom. In regard to technical resources, don't overload new online students with many different references; instead, choose a few carefully evaluated resource links that will meet the students' needs.

Pacansky-Brock addressed the issue of technical requirements humorously in a section of her introductory materials called, "Your Transportation to Class":

"What?! Why do I need transportation for an online class?!" Well, you wouldn't enroll in an on-campus class if you didn't have a reliable way to get there, right? So, you shouldn't enroll in an online class unless you have regular and reliable access to the internet. This class requires high speed internet access (DSL, cable or satellite) due to the large, multimedia files you'll regularly be accessing.... Reliable "transportation" is paramount to your success in this online class.

3. Computer skills needed

Depending on your student audience, you may want to suggest a computer skill set necessary for taking your course. In most cases, this is fairly simple: "Students should know how to cut and paste, how to email and send attachments, how to use a browser, and how to download from the Web." Refer students to web sites for Internet neophytes which can help those who are unsure about their basic skills. Urge them to check their skills *before* entering your classroom. In some cases, you may be able to refer students to on-campus workshops as well. In an online language or speech class, you will need to discuss any software that you will be using to facilitate audio communication.

4. Introduction to the course management software or other programs you will use to teach the class

Some course management software companies have already put together a general introduction, student manual, or classroom demo for their software. Whenever possible, refer students to such pre-made resources. You may also be able to find examples of software introductions at the sites of other institutions that use the same software your institution does.

Michelle Pacansky-Brock added information about the technology and programs students could expect to use in the class and how she planned to use that technology in a section entitled, "How Much Technology Does This Class Require?"

> *As you may have heard from other students, my online classes employ many forms of emerging technologies as learning tools. This is a topic I'm passionate about, folks, and I assure you I have carefully evaluated each technological tool before integrating it into my class and requiring you to use it.*

She continues,

> ***Podcasts*** *(Art 10 and Art 1E)—Both of my online classes offer options to my students. Lectures are offered in printed PDF form and in podcast form so you can select between reading or listening, based upon your own reading preferences. Interestingly, nearly 40% of my students have shared that they read and listen to my lectures because it enforces their learning. The other wonderful option that podcasts provide is mobile learning! If you have an iPod, you are welcome to export the podcasts onto your mobile device and learn on the go! Podcast lectures are accessed through Sierra College's iTunes site and requires students to have iTunes software installed on their computer. You will be required to download this software in the first week of class.*

VoiceThread (Art 10 and Art 1E) If you enroll in either of my online classes, you will also be engaging in weekly discussions and activities using an online tool called VoiceThread. Voice-Thread allows you to leave your comments in text or voice, it enhances our class community and enforces visual learning through image-based, interactive discussions ... If you're interested in using the voice commenting feature of VoiceThread, you are encouraged to consider purchasing a USB microphone for your computer or you have the option to purchase one hour of phone commenting through VoiceThread for $10. The phone commenting option allows you to leave comments through your telephone, just like leaving a voicemail (pretty cool!). Voice comments are encouraged but not required ...

5. A first assignment that requires students to demonstrate some familiarity with the software being used

This might be combined with one of the icebreaking activities described in Chapter 7. Typical of such assignments (depending on the software features available) would be these:

■ Write a short self-introduction and post it in the discussion forum.
■ Take an orientation quiz using online testing.
■ Fill in the template of a basic web page or blog with some biographical data and an optional photo of yourself. Add a video clip or audio recording if you like.

A Final Note

We recommend that you avoid beginning any orientation with material that consists only of a streaming video or animation that requires the downloading of a plug-in. Although it may look snazzy, it could intimidate students who are already nervous about their ability to take an online course. If possible, provide students with a text transcript of the video, or permit them to return to the orientation pages so that they can refer back to this information as needed once the course has begun. End the orientation on an upbeat note. This might include an assignment or a self-assessment quiz that provides feedback and encouragement and reinforces students' sense of readiness to begin their online course.

• • • • •
Providing FAQs

Take a good, hard look at your syllabus and ask yourself if anything you're requiring your students to do will require special additional skills or equipment. For example, if you've devised an exercise that entails uploading or downloading software, using a plug-in or accessing a useful but difficult to navigate site, go through the steps yourself and jot down any parts of the exercise that may not be obvious. You may think that all of the operations involved are commonly known, but you'll be surprised to discover how many students don't understand them. If you don't provide some way for students to readily find out, you may spend an inordinate amount of class time filling in the blanks.

One approach is to gather all these possible sticking points into one FAQ file. You can compose it using a word-processing program, or create it as a web page. In this FAQ you should list each procedure your students may encounter and provide a short explanation of what they need to know to complete it. The web convention for composing such FAQ pages is to list all the possible questions at the top of the page and then create a link to each one with a bookmark (in Word) or an anchor (in HTML), thus permitting your students to find the question they want answered without having to search the entire document.

• • • • •
Introductory Techniques

Your initial postings in the discussion forum, your first messages sent to all by email, or the greeting you post on your course home page will do much to set the tone and expectations for your course. These "first words" can also provide models of appropriate online communication for your students.

Your introductory remarks should reinforce what is contained in your syllabus, your orientation, and other documents students will encounter as they commence their online class. Note some of the examples we have already given of instructor remarks that set a tone and reinforce expectations.

The last thing we would like you to remember is that you must establish a presence and rapport in your classroom that are evident to students as soon as they walk through the online classroom door. Even though this would seem to be a matter of instructor preparation, it is also an important part of what you can do to foster your students' readiness to begin the learning process.

Here are a few tips for establishing your presence:

■ Convey a sense of enthusiasm about teaching the class.

For example, you might say:

Welcome to our course! I look at teaching Intro to Biology as a chance to share my enthusiasm about this subject with all of you, whether you are taking this class to fulfill a general requirement, have a personal interest in biology, or because you are exploring whether or not to major in this area. If you are one of those who feel some trepidation about science classes in general, I hope that you will soon realize that biology is all about the life around us and I look forward to helping you discover the underlying principles of this subject.

■ Personalize and provide some touchstones about yourself and encourage students to do the same.

A biology instructor might share the following information about himself:

I first became interested in biology as an undergraduate, changing my major from business. My particular interest is in the biology of marine animals and I have spent many summers at a research center in California. Here's a photo of me chatting up the sea lions ...

or,

I have been teaching biology for 20 years here at State College. In my private life, I am a member of the chamber music group here in Smithtown and play the violin.

Or an instructor might share her enthusiasm about online education,

I began teaching online two years ago and found that it has opened up a new world for me, broadening the range of students with whom I come in contact to include those from many different places in the world and diverse backgrounds. Please tell me and your classmates a bit about yourself and what you hope to learn in this class.

■ Indicate your availability for questions and communications, the protocol to follow, and that students are not stranded on their own when it comes to online learning.

For example, you might say:

If at any time you have a question, please post it in the Q&A discussion area after checking the class FAQ. If it is something relevant only to yourself, please send me an email. I log in each day and should respond to you within 24 hours. Sometimes your classmates will come to your assistance, but please don't wait to contact me if you are encountering a serious issue. If you have a technical problem, contact the 24/7 help desk as soon as you can rather than endure frustration and delay trying to figure out the problem on your own.

A well-organized course, with signs that you have anticipated the students' problems, plus a welcoming attitude apparent in your first communication, conveys your appreciation of student concerns. Your initial efforts set the tone, and when these are followed by a responsiveness to students throughout the course, they will go a long way toward instilling student confidence in the online learning process.

11

•••••

Classroom Management and Facilitation

Classroom management, as we use the term, includes all the organizational and procedural measures that keep a class moving along. Like any class on the ground, an online class can get out of hand if you don't manage it properly. *Facilitation* is defined as the way in which an instructor interacts within the online classroom to set things in motion and to respond to students, focusing here on discussion and student presentations in the classroom. In this chapter, we'll look at record keeping, class communications and participation, facilitation of both asynchronous and synchronous discussion, different approaches to facilitating discussion, providing feedback, and arrangements for team teaching. Chapter 12 will deal with special issues, such as student behavior problems.

Your classroom software, whether a full-scale course management program or simply a set of web pages, Web 2.0 tools, and discussion boards, will have an impact on your classroom management and facilitation alternatives. We urge you again, therefore, to become familiar with your software in advance, so that you can exploit its capabilities and compensate for its shortcomings.

•••••

Record Keeping and File Management

Teaching online can be a nightmare for record keeping. By the end of a course, there may be thousands of postings and emails from students. Where and how will you save this information? How will you organize it?

Begin by finding out what the rules are for the server on which your course is housed. Will material be left on the server after the course is over or archived in a way accessible to you? Even if you're lucky enough to have such an arrangement, it's a good idea to prepare a system for saving material on your own computer. Moreover, if you intend to save any discussion materials, it's important to do so at intervals during the course rather than trying to sort through them all at the end.

If you are using Web 2.0 applications outside your institution's control, you will want to be even more assiduous about developing a system to capture the content you create and you should encourage your students to do the same for their own content.

Tips for Record Keeping

Here are some suggestions for setting up your record-keeping system:

1. When you compose major pieces of information, do so first in your word-processing program or your HTML composer software rather than directly in your online classroom. If you are writing online and your connection is interrupted, you may lose all or part of your material. Also, if you start out in your word-processing program—and save your work there— you will already have created an instant "archive" of your material.

2. On your computer's hard drive or on a flash drive, create a series of folders that parallel the divisions of your course. For example, if your course is organized by week, create a folder on your computer for each week and then subfolders for "Discussion," "Lecture," "Exercises," and whatever other components you may have.

3. Create folders for student work on your computer and make sure that you've set up folders for student assignments in your email program. If possible, don't leave students' assignments in your email program only, but download and store them along with the other classroom folders. Some instructors like

to house all Assignment #1 papers from students in the same folder, while others keep all assignments from an individual student in a sort of portfolio set aside for him or her alone.

You may also find it useful to take notes on the contributions of individual students while you read postings in the discussion forum, particularly in a large or active class. This can be done with simple paper and pen, in your word-processing program, or even by copying and pasting representative snippets of a student's postings into a folder for that student. Some course management systems make it easy to assemble and store or print discussion threads. Any measures that help you build up a profile of individual students will assist you in following their progress and evaluating their work.

4. Make sure that all student email is sorted automatically or manually as it arrives at your email address. One of the greatest organizational perils is email from students that becomes commingled with email from other sources. This results in misplaced assignments and late responses to communications.

If you're working from a business account or a personal email account, you may want to consider establishing a separate email address for your class communications. There are many free email services available on the Web but be certain to ask about the limitations for size of individual attachments and total storage capability. If your students send you multimedia files, those may exceed the service limits.

In regard to IM or text messaging, you will need to sort out the ephemeral from the potentially worth saving communications from students. You may simply want to keep a log of questions asked and answered via these means.

5. As noted earlier, make sure you specify how students should use the subject line in email communications with you. For example, you may want to specify that the subject line consist of *student's first name + last initial + number of assignment*. Gently remind class members if there are lapses (and there will be) during the progress of the course.

Extend this system to students' attachments as well, whether text or multimedia: make sure that students put their name and assignment number in the body of the attached text itself.

Often, attachments are downloaded and saved separately from the emails that delivered them or the course management assignment folders where they were submitted. In this case, if students remember to affix their names and assignment numbers, you will be able to print out assignments, if you wish, without having to guess who authored each paper!

Relabel assignments and emails if necessary before saving them to folders. Keeping the nomenclature uniform will enable you to sort quickly through your students' contributions. This is a valuable time saver.

For multimedia files uploaded to a third-party site—put the onus on students to maintain their own copies in the event of a third-party host incurring disruptions or even going out of business. With the ephemeral nature of many of the new Web 2.0 sites, such a loss of service is not an idle notion. Or, if you prefer to view such files offline and want your own copies, clearly express that wish to your students as part of the rules for creating these types of assignments.

6. If you are using external web sites outside your institution's control—for example, a blog or other Web 2.0 tool—be sure to create a system for handling student communications and student-generated content housed there. These sites can change or even disappear with little or no opportunity for you to recapture content. Even as you caution students to keep a copy of their work, few students would think of pre-serving their discussion postings. Your review and record keeping (or downloading as the case may be) of student activity at these sites is essential as an *ongoing* procedure. You would be wise to keep tabs on communications on at least a weekly basis. Depending on the nature of the content, this might mean anything from copying and pasting every-thing into a word-processed document or simply taking notes on student contributions and copying and pasting only graded assignments.

Electronic Files versus Hard Copy

In contemplating the multitude of online activities and student assignments, you may be wondering how much you need to read online and how much you should download and print out.

This is really a personal choice. However, don't feel somehow less "cyber-expert" if you want to print out and read most assignments or even some discussion offline. It can be very hard on the eyes to read a great deal online. Some instructors print out and read all assignments offline, preferring to make their notes in the paper margins while on the train, at the coffee shop, or lying in bed. Others read the papers offline but make their notes in word-processed documents, which they then copy and paste into their emailed correspondence with their students. Still others may create PDF versions of documents to read on their mobile devices and take screen shots of assignments posted on third-party sites.

The same issues apply to record keeping. If you want to keep paper records as well as electronic ones, that's fine. In any case, always keep a backup copy—either on a flash drive, computer hard drive, or on paper—of your gradebook and any other important class records. You may want to have a paper chart that you use while online, to tick off credits for student participation as you read. This may save you the time and bother of having to toggle back and forth between the classroom and your word-processing program. You may also want to keep a paper journal of events in your class. Perhaps your course management system gradebook can be saved to a spreadsheet—if so, plan to download it on a regular basis so that you have your own record of the class as it proceeds.

You may have to experiment to find out which system works best for you. The factors to balance here are flexibility, economy of time, security of records, and how much time you want to spend online. But do devise a system of your own and follow through with that system.

● ● ● ● ●

Managing Communications

Not surprisingly, many online classroom management issues involve communication—between you and your students and among the students themselves. Designing an effective communication system and monitoring it are key steps in teaching online.

Creating a Uniform Announcement Area

You need some area within your course where students know they can receive the latest updates and corrections. If you cannot easily update a web page area linked to the course's home page, consider using a mailing list to email students your updates. If you have a discussion board, you can also choose that as your venue: let students know from the first day of class that each time they log in, they should check a particular area for the latest announcements. Depending on your preferences and those of your students you can also send SMS text messages to students that repeat online announcements or simply remind students to log in to view those announcements. Some faculty have experimented with using Twitter for this purpose. Twitter has an advantage in that its communications can be followed on mobile devices as well as via the Web. If you send a weekly message via email or some other format, make sure these are identical to any announcements in your online classroom—one way to do this is by starting an email with words to that effect— "This message is a duplicate of one posted in the classroom." Since Twitter messages are very limited in length (140 characters) you may need to remind students to visit the classroom to see the remainder of the announcement. For example, you might send out a "tweet" that says "Reminder essay assignment due Fri, see classroom for details or to ask questions."

It's a good habit to make regular announcements on a weekly or biweekly basis—to keep students on task, and get them in the habit of checking in, even if there are no special changes or updates to announce. Simply give an overview of the week ahead or of upcoming due dates for assignments and exams. Here are a few examples of the types of information that might appear in announcements:

1. Reminding students about upcoming due dates and stages of the course:

   As we start week 5, all of you should now have chosen your topics for the final essay. It's a good idea to start outlining your ideas now for the rough draft that will be due at the end of week 6.

2. Offering a preview or overview of the week's activities to reinforce the students' attention to tasks:

   This week we will be focusing on the romantic poets. Be sure to visit at least one or two of the recommended web sites for additional background information before taking part in the discussion about the readings.

3. Taking stock of progress and encouraging students:

   We are now entering the seventh week of the course. I am pleased that so many of you are participating in the weekly discussion forums and that the quality of those conversations is so evident. Nearly all of you have turned in your journal entries for week 6. You can expect to receive your grades and comments from me during the next week. Feel tree to email me it you have any questions about how I determined your grade.

4. Noting problems in computer access:

   Our server experienced a shutdown this morning from 8:00A.M. to 9:00A.M. EST. If you tried to access the classroom at that time, you would have received an error message.

5. Updating, clarifying, or changing the syllabus or schedule:

   Please note the following change in the reading for this week: pages 10–25 in White (not 110–125 as recorded on the syllabus). Quiz #2 will be postponed until after the holidays— therefore, it has not yet been posted. Also, there will be no on-campus meeting this week, due to the holidays. However, I will be holding live online chats throughout this week, by prior email appointment only. Student groups who hoped to meet on campus are encouraged to use the live chat as well.

6. Reminding students about special events or introducing speakers:

   This week we are fortunate to have as our guest Dr. Basstone. I have posted Dr. Basstone's lecture in Unit Three. He will be available on Tuesday and Thursday of this week only to answer your questions in Discussion Forum Three.

7. Maintaining your presence: Bring in the outside world when relevant to demonstrate your own active interest in the class topics and to involve your students:

> *Don't know if any of you have seen the news today about the economic stimulus plan, but it highlights the importance of our current discussion concerning that issue. I was very struck by the fact that the New York Times editorial challenges the findings that have hitherto been accepted by nearly everyone, including me, on this issue. Take a look for yourself at the following URL and post a response to my message on the discussion board....*

Setting Rules and Establishing a Protocol for All Communications

One key to handling the email problem—the potential deluge of email you may receive—is to divert individual email, as much as possible, into the common classroom space. This prevents your having to make the same response over and over again, and it also has the positive effect of promoting students' consciousness of the online classroom as a shared space, not simply an assemblage of web pages. If you make your presence felt primarily in the online classroom and only secondarily in the private email realm, your students will look for you in that public space. When you receive an emailed question or comment that isn't really private in nature, praise the student and encourage her or him by requesting that the student post the item in the classroom—or offer to do so yourself. A common protocol is to ask students to first post a question in the appropriate discussion forum or a separate Q&A area and wait twenty-four hours for a reply before attempting to email the instructor.

The more tools and avenues of communication that are available to students, the more important it becomes to establish a protocol for communications. For example, if you are using blogging or other Web 2.0 communication tools you will need to add those to your mix in thinking about where and when and what students should communicate in each type of forum. For example, a logical rule might be that blog comments are only for postings directly related to the blog content, while all general questions are to be asked in the course management system discussion area.

Among younger students, you may find that the email influx is diminished by the tendency of these students to favor text messaging and instant messaging for their communications. With synchronous communication tools—whether text messaging, chat, instant messaging, audio messages, and the other options in Web 2.0 tools that we have discussed in this book—you will need to set rules for your own response times (or perhaps you don't want to be available via text message or instant message at all) and for your students in regard to using these tools for course-related work and assignments. For example, if you allow students to do their group work using synchronous tools, do you want them to save a transcript for you to see? If you do communicate with your students via instant message or text message, how will you keep a record of your communications so that misunderstandings are avoided?

These modes of behavior and protocols will not evolve among students on their own—you must set the rules and procedures early in your course and carefully consider how to structure the channels of communication.

Important! **With the increasingly diverse channels of communications that might be available to you and your students, it is necessary to establish rules, procedures and expectations for all chosen forms of communication.**

● ● ● ● ●

Encouraging Participation and Managing Your Workload

Most instructors would like to promote as much interaction as possible in an online class—not only between instructor and students, but student to student as well. Instructors who run large, lecture hall, on-campus courses with an online component would perhaps like to use the online environment not only to replace some of the lecture time, but also to give students additional opportunities for discussion, presentation of projects to their classmates, and other forms of participation that are difficult to manage in a large classroom meeting. In previous chapters, we discussed the variety of activities you can set in motion to engage students. Here we want to take a look at how you can promote participation in these activities. At the same time, we will examine how the choice and design of activities may affect your workload.

Two factors determine the level and quality of participation and interaction in a class—your course design and student dynamics. The second part of this formula, student dynamics, is really not wildly different online than it is in the on-campus classroom or discussion seminar. Students will bring their own expectations and work habits to your online classroom. To some degree, you will be able to shape and influence their behavior, but in other respects it's the luck of the draw. Experienced instructors can fairly quickly identify the core group of students who are active participants (perhaps including obnoxious students as well as the most delightful), and these can be enlisted to get the classroom dynamics moving. Here, though, the factor of course design comes into play as well: instructors need to design the course so that other students are drawn into the orbit of the core group and begin to participate, even if in different ways and to a lesser degree. The trick is to get enough of the reluctant or shy students to be active in the classroom, at least occasionally, to make the class more diverse and interesting for all.

The Effect of Class Size

The way you use classroom design and organization to promote student participation will probably depend on the class size. As in the handling of email, your own workload can become an important factor in your decisions. Let's look at the issues involved in an online classroom or online component for classes of various sizes.

Classes of Ten to Thirty Students   If you have a class of only ten students, your major problem will be how to encourage participation and student-to-student interaction. Given that, in a class of ten, perhaps only three to five students will have a tendency to be very active, while the others will be nearly inactive or only moderately active, that group of three to five may become discouraged, fatigued, or bored if it spends most of the course carrying the load for the entire class. While you can give each of your students more individual attention than in a larger class, you presumably would like to avoid having the course become a de facto independent study class. So you have a real incentive to encourage student-to-student participation.

With a class of twenty, you may have several active coteries of students, and if even half of the students are active in discussions, they can potentially generate hundreds of messages for you to read—not to mention homework or exercises. You need to achieve a balance of energy between relating to students as individuals and relating to groups of students. This means not only getting students to talk to one another, but also apportioning your assignments and activities so that at least a few are group efforts or involve peer contributions.

In a class of thirty, your potential problems are your workload and the risk that students will disappear into the corners of cyberspace. In a class of thirty on the ground, you can see the rows of students and generally keep track of them visually. Online, you really do have to remember the names and check your records and notes to keep track of all of them. At this level, group work and presentations become a necessary part of your course design. You'll want to create smaller groups for the purposes of at least some discussion topics and projects. This arrangement will give shy students a more comfortable environment for airing their views and asking questions. It will also allow students to form social connections with other students and build up a sense of camaraderie. In any class of more than twenty students, you will probably also want to use some type of self-assessment or an automatic assessment vehicle such as online testing.

Classes of 40–100 Students (or More)   Beyond thirty or so students, you will find it difficult to operate without the assistance of a teaching assistant (TA) unless you dramatically redesign the class. There are two approaches you can take if you do not have a TA—first, the implementation of group strategies, and second, replacement of some instructor–student interaction with built-in *interactivity* of content. The latter can be accomplished by an individual instructor investing a good deal of time in creating modules, but it is more commonly done by a course development team.

Group Strategies and Interactivity of Content

In a class of forty or more students, even with a TA, and the addition of rich content and exercise modules, you must interact more with groups of students than with individuals. In such classes, if possible, you should use online testing with automatic grading for at least one-third to one-half of your assessments, and you should have students working in groups and making presentations to the entire class.

In such a large class, discussion forums can be established for groups of 10–15 students. You (and your TA or team teacher if you have one) can then observe the groups, noting the interaction and responding when necessary. You can think of this as the party-host model. You and your colleague circulate among the various groups of guests, joining in on conversations at times and making sure there are no wallflowers sitting by themselves.

In order for students to benefit from ideas and questions that arise in groups other than their own, you should set up dual levels of the classroom—one for the entire class and the other for the group level of organization. Establish a forum where students can ask general questions about the course; this will prevent your having to answer these questions in each group. But also establish discussion areas where student representatives from each group can address the topics of discussion with the entire class.

For example, in Week 3, if students are discussing the chapter reading assigned on the French Revolution, you might have students meet first in their groups to discuss and summarize the main ideas of the chapter on Robespierre or to reach some conclusions about the dominant causes of the Revolution. You would set a time limit for these group discussions to conclude. Then you would post the same discussion question or assignment in the discussion forum for the entire class, asking the student spokesperson for each of the various groups to exchange and discuss their groups' ideas.

When there are individual assignments for a large class, you can choose examples that typify the responses and the problems encountered, then post these anonymously (without the student's name attached) for all students to view. In this way you can create a lesson by means of your comments. This method works best for courses with much factual or objective material—computer science, math, and so forth. For courses that involve more subjective responses, you can spotlight those you think are full or good responses. Some instructors do this by creating presentation pages, while others use the discussion forum areas for this purpose. To comment on problems the students may be encountering, you can derive principles and illustrations from the poorer student work without actually posting individual examples.

Christine Appel of Universitat Oberta de Catalunya (Open University of Catalonia) in Spain and Jonathan Matthews from Pennsylvania State University were previously highlighted in Chapter 7 as those who teach large online classes and rely on group strategies and interactive content to manage their teaching load. Both of these instructors are able to avail themselves of strong instructional design or course development and technology units on campus to provide interactive content.

Christine Appel notes that the Modern English 1 course she teaches to fifty students consists of five major types of assessment tasks. "Some are self-correcting, like reading exercises for which students can check their answers after a certain date," she notes. There are three tasks involving writing and/or speaking for which students receive individual feedback from the instructor, while another two projects are based on group work, with the instructor offering feedback to the group midway through the project, "intervening in the process, highlighting changes that need to be made." The final versions of the group projects in this highly standardized course are set up so that the instructors give feedback to the groups but can use their own discretion to decide whether or not to give additional individual feedback as well. Matthews and his TAs similarly use computerized quizzes, interactive modules for content, rubrics, and group projects to deliver feedback and assess their students. Such a strategy of providing a mix of different assignments in which feedback may be given to individual students, to small groups of students, and through automatic computer programmed or pre-written feedback, allows for effective assessment of students in a large online class.

If you find yourself in a situation where you alone teach and provide nearly all course content for a class of forty or more students, a good solution is to find appropriate Web 2.0 tools that enhance the small-group capabilities that might exist in your CMS and to seek out relevant enriched content available on the Web. At the same time, seriously rethink the objectives of your assignments and assessments so as to target a smaller number of assignments for individualized feedback. If you formerly gave individualized feedback on five separate assignments, you might replace a few of these with rubric-guided grading, designate one as a group assignment, or consolidate closely related assignments into one larger project.

Rich, interactive content can also serve to help instructors who may not have expertise in a critical aspect of a subject. In the area of nursing education, there has long been a shortage of nursing educators. Pam Taylor notes that this shortage is even more pronounced in the subject area of nursing informatics. Taylor creates nursing informatics content (see her company site at http://nivateonline.com) required by nursing credentialling organizations so that nursing programs can incorporate this approved content. Her modular, self-paced materials were developed for entry-level informatics courses and are currently incorporated in a host of nursing courses within the U.S.. Taylor comments on the potency of truly interactive content:

> *Online learning is not just reading a screen of text. Presentation of content needs to be paired whenever possible with an application that provides the student with an opportunity to evaluate if they understand the content presented. Too often educators rely on 4 or 5 screens of text plus a short quiz to meet the 'interactive' definition. In my online modules, we discuss how databases work as the foundation of the electronic medical record. Once the content has been presented,*

the student is then presented with a series of mock medical record screens where they actually enter data using the techniques that were presented. This tends to promote better retention of the content since it has been applied to a real-world situation rather than just having students answer a question.

Changing Class Sizes

Perhaps the hardest thing for instructors to adapt to is a sudden change in their class size—one gets used to teaching within a particular design and context and to suddenly be confronted with an increase of even 25 percent—say, from twenty-five students to thirty—can be a challenge. If you are faced with this situation, what you need to do is think about is redesigning, not merely adapting, your syllabus and manner of interacting with students.

There is really no one ideal class size for an online class—the quality of teaching and learning hangs on understanding the model, purposeful design, and the instructor's skill in managing the class. A poorly organized and haphazardly designed course for twenty is not going to promote better learning than a richly enhanced and carefully designed course for forty students. As an instructor, you may prefer teaching under one model rather than another just as those who teach face-to-face may prefer small seminars to large lecture hall classes. But if you do find yourself facing a change in the model to which you are accustomed, (especially if it is not in the nature of a radical change), you may find it comforting to realize that by implementing a few changes in design of activities and content, you can attain the same level of effectiveness in your teaching and perhaps find equal enjoyment in the teaching experience as well.

Here are a few tips for adjusting class design to a larger class:

■ Trim the number of topics in the main discussion forum to a manageable number of items or create a new forum to handle additional topics. When the discussion area is overcrowded with large numbers of topic threads and postings, it becomes difficult for students (and you) to follow the discussion.

- Consider reducing the minimum number of postings you require of students each week and weigh the participation grade more heavily on the quality of the responses.

- If appropriate, replace at least one individual assignment with a small group project. Have groups present their projects in a common discussion area. Consider having students use a peer-review rubric to evaluate themselves and other group members.

- Use detailed rubrics to give guidelines and to supply general feedback on assignments. Save your more detailed individual feedback for key assignments—at least one of these should be on an assignment given early in the course so that the student receives the necessary feedback that will enable him or her to improve.

- Revisit the class schedule, consolidating assignments if possible, and revising due dates or expected feedback times for assignments if necessary—don't set up unreasonable deadlines for yourself in regard to returning long assignments.

- Maintain a pattern of frequent visits to the classroom to avoid feeling overwhelmed by a backlog of postings you must read. Frequent visits will also help promote a sense of your presence in the classroom.

- Prepare a list of resources to which you can easily refer students who may need assistance in writing, the use of the library, or computer skills. You may also want to prepare a FAQ of questions and answers about assignments based on your past experience teaching the class. While both these ideas constitute a helpful approach for any class, they are even more effective for a larger class in which your feedback time is at a premium.

Finally, find comfort in meeting the challenge of a larger class with the knowledge that the diverse backgrounds and potential for greater interaction among students may actually make the course more stimulating than one of a smaller size. Keeping yourself organized is the key to maintaining your enthusiasm and energy for teaching, and transmitting that enthusiasm and energy to your students.

The Debate about Class Size

Class size of totally online courses has been an issue since the inception of online education. Often overlooked in this controversy are the underlying assumptions about the online instructor's role in the classroom, the nature of the course, and the design considerations that are appropriate for the course.

We can state one point quite emphatically here: You can't have a high level of instructor-facilitated interaction with individual students in an online class of forty or more students. Having said that, a course design based on small-group strategies, highly interactive content, and targeting of key assignments for individual feedback may adequately compensate for this overall lower level of individual instructor–student interaction.

Some institutions have applied the same rules to their online courses as to their on-site versions—for example, assigning one TA for every 20–25 students if a class exceeds thirty or forty students. Applying such equations is a good start. However, the cut-off point for the "average" class served by one instructor should be lower for the completely online class than for an on-campus version, assuming that the same level of instructor–student interaction is desired. From the experience of those who have taught in both formats, it appears that one instructor in an on-campus class can comfortably handle a class of 30–50 by herself, whereas the equivalent online is closer to 15–30 students, with the latter number dependent on the level of instructor–student interaction desired in the class.

Some instructors who have taught online would put the number even lower—say, 15–20 students for one instructor. Although this estimate may come from a heartfelt reaction based on their experience, it cannot necessarily be applied to all cases. Our observation is that many who teach online automatically fall into a pattern of very intense instructor-generated activity and a great deal of one-on-one interaction. In fact, the workload issue is usually the number one complaint of first-time online instructors, whether they have fifteen students or twenty-five.

The very seductiveness of the online environment, with its seemingly endless avenues of communication, can cause an instructor to become far more interactive online than he or she would be in a traditional on-campus class. Student expectations also play a role here: online students tend to be more demanding and to need more affirmation and attention than their on-campus counterparts. Further, the fact that one can see and review one's interactions with students may make an instructor more acutely self-conscious and eager to respond more often and more elaborately than in an on-campus class.

While this high level of instructor responsiveness may be a desirable thing in itself, it may not be practical for some programs to have classes small enough to make it feasible. More importantly, it is not necessarily true that actual student learning outcomes are higher in small-scale models. Programs should ideally base their decisions as to class size on the type of course, design of course, resources available, and workload that may be expected of instructors. And institutions need to prepare instructors to teach under the resulting new model rather than assume that instructors will simply continue to teach the same way for forty as for fifteen students!

●●●●●

Finding a Balance between Student-Centered and Instructor-Centered Activities

No matter what the class size, most students appreciate a balance between student-centered activities and those that focus on the instructor. In other words, they want the instructor to contribute something unique, something they can't "get from the book," but they also respond well to an environment that asks them to be active participants in their own learning. While there is strong consensus that the online instructor needs to emphasize facilitation of student learning, we believe that it is a mistake to think that students have ceased to seek inspiration and the imparting of experience or the sharing of expertise from their online instructors.

In a class of fifteen, you might wish to do away with the formal lecture mode and simply provide a segmented lecture as described in Chapter 3: a running commentary of short paragraphs that offers the initial material—the thread topics—on which students can base their discussion. But in a larger class, you will want to provide a more structured presentation of instructor-generated materials. Students would quickly lose their way if they had to find the tidbits of lecture material hidden among hundreds of discussion topics or anecdotal comments.

Your ideal mix of instructor-generated and student-based activity depends on the number of students, the length of the course (for instance, whether there is enough time for several projects and how long students will have to get organized for group efforts), the number of TAs you have (if any), and any matters related to the level or type of course you teach. We recommend that you include some calculations for your ideal mix in the planning stage for your course.

We also encourage you to take advantage of the increasing ease of use of Web 2.0 tools to allow students more opportunities to generate content whenever this choice seems appropriate and relevant as a learning activity.

● ● ● ● ●

Some General Guidelines for Student Participation

One of the most effective ways to promote student participation in an online class is to make it required and graded. As explained in Chapter 5, this should be clearly stated in your syllabus, and the criteria must be defined.

Participation online ranges from "attendance"—defined as logging on and (presumably) reading in the online classroom—to actually posting messages in discussion forums and taking part in small-group activities. It is not possible to gauge pure attendance unless you have tracking features in your software that monitor the opening of files or time spent in a particular portion of the classroom. These tracking capabilities can help give you a clearer picture of a student's activities, but they are generally not sufficient for assessment purposes. For example, they may tell you that a student opened up a particular document and kept it open for a period of time, but not whether the student actually read the document. So it's best to think of the information you gain from these features, if you're lucky enough to have them, as merely a small piece in the puzzle. They are chiefly valuable for alerting you to a negative—i.e., telling you that a student has never accessed a portion of the class

To be an effective goad to activity, participation grades for a completely online class or true blended class should constitute somewhere between 10 and 40 percent of the student's overall grade. If you include a separate category for contribution to small-group activities, you might end up with 50 percent of the grade in the "participation" category. For an online component in a mainly face-to-face course, we recommend that at least 10 percent of the total grade for the course be reserved for online participation.

You may want to establish criteria for both quantity and quality of participation. For instance, one-third of the participation grade might be based on the student's meeting a minimum quantity level (say, posting a comment or question in the discussion forum once a week), with the remaining two-thirds based on the quality of participation. Or, if your course involves lots of teamwork, you might divide the participation grade between individual accomplishments and contributions to the group.

Depending on your course objectives, presentations—either group or individual—may be an essential part of student participation. You might define participation to mean completing all weekly classroom exercises, taking part in discussions, *and* presenting a project to the class. The use of presentations, whether group or individual, fosters interaction among students, but it is most effective if you emphasize that student comments and questions about their classmates' presentations are counted in participation grades or are separately graded.

Important! *However you choose to define "participation," make sure that a significant part of the grade depends on what the student does in the shared classroom, not simply on the completion of assignments submitted to you alone.*

So think about how you can structure opportunities for student-to-student interaction—it's not something that will necessarily happen without your deliberate effort.

Asynchronous or Synchronous Discussion?

Some instructors are firm believers in synchronous communication for fostering a sense of online community while others find it difficult and exhausting to facilitate synchronous sessions with a large group. Both asynchronous and synchronous communication have their advantages as well as disadvantages. Asynchronous discussion allows time for reflection and encourages more careful consideration but often lacks spontaneity and it may take longer to arrive at a conclusion or for a group to reach a decision. Synchronous communication provides a sense of immediacy and cultivates a feeling of responsiveness among participants while allowing for quicker problem solving, but at the same time the greater speed and short-hand expression can lead to misunderstandings, superficial interaction, and poorly considered decisions. Many of the shortcomings of synchronous discussion can be alleviated by software that provides a means for archiving or replaying as well as by careful preparation leading up to a synchronous session. The disadvantages of asynchronous discussion are downplayed when the discussion prompts and questions are well-constructed and stimulating, the facilitating instructor has some skill in tending discussion, and there is a clear beginning and ending schedule for the asynchronous discussion, with students willing to post throughout the week rather than all jumping in during the last two days of a week.

Tips for Fostering Asynchronous Discussion

In Chapter 6, we discussed the impact that a particular discussion software structure may have on the way you organize your discussions. However, no matter how your software may be organized, there are techniques you can use to foster greater participation and clarity among your students.

1. *Start the major topic threads yourself.* It's a good idea for the instructor to start all major topic threads unless you have designated a forum for student presentation or have designated students to act as the moderator. If you wish to (and your software permits), you can allow students to contribute additional threads as they feel the need. This arrangement should be considered with great care, however, because students often tend to create new topics without real necessity, and your discussion area may soon be overwhelmed with too many threads on duplicate topics.

2. *Narrow down topics.* A good discussion needs pruning and shaping. An overly broad topic thread—say, "The French Revolution: What Do You Think of It?"—will often result in very fragmented discussion. This is especially true in an introductory class, in which most students know little about the subject. If you divide up broad topics into logical subtopics—say, "Economic Conditions on the Eve of the Revolution" or "The Execution of the Royal Family"—you can prevent the discussion from going off in too many directions. In an introductory class, you may want to provide even more guidance. For example, a discussion based on specific readings in the textbook, on a focused web site visit, or on assigned exercises, coupled with your guideline questions, will likely be more productive than simply pointing students to the forum and expecting them to find their own direction.

A short series of closely related questions can allow students to jump in on any one of the points and still find themselves "on topic." In our example of the French Revolution, a topic thread might contain several questions about the economic conditions and invite students to choose one to which to respond:

> *Please address one of the following, "What were the land-holding patterns? How important was foreign trade? Had the average well-being of the citizens improved or worsened in the years leading up to the Revolution? Give a rationale and provide support for your response."*

The shaping of discussions takes some genuine forethought. You might think of this task as similar to creating chapters in a book or long article you are writing. Threads will stay of manageable length if you keep topics specific and allow a place such as a lounge or question-and-answer forum for off-topic conversations.

Sometimes, of course, a thread goes off on a digression that is so valuable and interesting in itself that you don't want to curb it. The pruning and organization of threads is for the purpose of sustaining discussion, not stifling it. Allow students to digress, but if you think that the new direction in the conversation calls for an entirely new thread, you might create one or suggest that a student begin a new topic message to explore the subject further.

3. *Organize forums and threads to reflect the class chronology or topical sequence and suggest a pattern for posting.* The organization of discussion forums should complement the class structure but also provide some reminders of the course chronology and sequence. For example, creating one forum for each week or unit of the course helps students know at a glance where they should be looking for that week's activity. Even if you don't have a forum structure, you can designate all the threads for a particular week under the rubric "Week 1" or "Unit 1."

   Suggest a schedule for posting that is appropriate to the topic, assignment, and your student audience—for example, if you want students to comment on other students' postings, you might suggest that everyone post their first responses to your question by midweek and to classmates during the remainder of the week. You may even set up your system of credit for the discussion participation rubric to reflect that. (If you have many working students who must do the greater portion of their schoolwork on the weekends, and you are able to do so, you may want the class week to run from Tuesday through Monday rather than Monday through Sunday.)

   If you have a general forum area for ongoing questions about the course, you might want to divide this up by week so that students can more easily find questions that pertain to a particular week's activities.

4. *Address students by name and encourage students to signal topics and clarify responses.* Mention the student's name in responding to their message: "Joan, your point certainly reflects on the issue of the previous chapter." Change the subject line to reflect the topic of your response ("Response to Joan," or "Joan and the previous chapter's issue," etc.) and encourage students to do the same. Clarify the portion of the message to which you are responding through copying of the statement before your own reply, quotation marks or whatever means your discussion software features most readily allow and remind your students to do the same. (While some

discussion software automatically repeats the entire message to which one replies, you may need to pinpoint the relevant portion.)

5. *Key the thread topics to appropriate and relevant activities.* Keying thread topics to the assignments, readings, projects, and exercises for a particular week will help keep students on topic in their discussions and also provide an obvious place to discuss anything that occurs in the course during that week. While you may have some key topics in mind, do allow students to ask related questions that you may not have anticipated. Adding a prompt at the end of the discussion question such as "If you have another question based on this week's reading, feel free to post it in reply/post it in a new thread." Or you may create a thread each week that is a placeholder for "other questions about this week's readings and activities."

6. *Establish a pattern of frequent response.* Students tend to follow instructor expectations for online participation, and these expectations are communicated not only by the declarations of the syllabus but also by the instructor's behavior. During the first week or so, if your class size allows (this would be in a class of no more than thirty students), greet all students individually in the classroom as they arrive and engage as many as possible in discussion. Thereafter make an effort to respond to a diverse group of students each week—not just to the same one or two individuals. If you have a large class, you will find yourself rotating your time among all the small groups, as well as tending to any all-class forums. For a class of fifty, Christine Appel notes that instructors in the Open University of Catalonia's (UOC) Modern English 1 are expected to monitor the group discussion areas, and are expected to post in either the announcement area or the group discussion areas at least once every forty-eight hours. A rhythm is established so that students visit the common forum at the beginning of each major project, and return again at the end of each project to the common forum to share what their groups have accomplished.

In such large classes, rather than engaging in long, concentrated visits to your classroom, it is best to establish a pattern of short but frequent activity. When students see you "poke your head into" the classroom (that is, see your postings), it makes them feel that you are truly present and actively responding to the class. In contrast, when students see that an instructor rarely engages with them, they are discouraged from posing questions and comments aimed even indirectly at the instructor, and they may also conclude that the instructor will be unaware of what is going on in the classroom.

Think in terms of three to five short periods of logging on each week, rather than the one or two sessions you may be used to in your on-campus courses. If you have only four hours to devote to the classroom in one week, spend an hour for each of four days in the classroom, rather than two hours twice a week. This will allow you to keep up with the flow of student discussions and will also reinforce the impression that you are responsive and on the scene.

If you are teaching a primarily on-campus course that meets once a week and also has an online component, you will have to decide how important student discussion online will be in your class. If you really want students to make use of this venue, then you too must actively attend to it. The discussion forum is a great place for you to continue conversations you started in class or for the TA to extend the weekly discussion section. Initiate topics on a weekly basis and require some weekly participation from students in the online forum. This is also the best place to update the class on changes and errors, to pose and answer questions, and to help students review material. Again, unless you are actively "showing the flag" in this area, students will quickly learn that they can ignore it with impunity.

7. *Facilitate and build on participation.* While the instructor needs to be seen as engaged, don't try to respond to every posting in the classroom. Even in a class of twenty, this will quickly overwhelm you and can actually put a damper on student discussion. The quality of your postings is as important as frequency. And you want to encourage students to interact with each other, not only with you. So make comments that address a whole train of thought—responding, for

example, to five or six related messages in the thread rather than to each of the five individually. In this way you will do your part to encourage participation as well as interaction among students. Think about jumping in or tending to the conversational fires at critical junctures, working as a facilitator to help move the discussion forward and keep the fire going.

Don't merely post friendly expressions of affirmation. You should also contribute comments that summarize what students have posted, as well as follow-up questions that stimulate further discussion. In some cases, it might be appropriate to invite students' responses to their classmates' ideas: "Anyone else want to comment on Tom's observation?" "Did anyone reach a different conclusion about this issue?"

If a class is fairly quiet, it may seem that it's a good idea to jump in and reply as soon as someone finally posts something. The truth is, instructors feel uncomfortable when nobody's talking. Resist the temptation to jump in too quickly and risk squelching student voices with an excess of chatter or by answering the question you have posed to them. There are also times when there will be a lull in conversations because students are working on a major assignment. Some instructors may even schedule a "quiet time," such as a few days during which students are encouraged to devote most of their time to a project.

8. *Provide feedback that stimulates higher-level thinking.* Look for student postings that imply unspoken assumptions or suggest a line of other questioning. Provide follow-up responses that ask for more information or deeper consideration, from the student posting and/or the other students in the class. For example, ask students questions like, "What are the implications of your statement?" "What evidence is there to support your point of view?" "Does anyone want to add to/dispute/verify that?"

Equally important is to confirm when students are on the right path but then help guide them to the next step: "What Joe has said about X theory is sound, but when we look at it operating in the area of Y rules, how would we go about testing that theory? Anyone want to tackle this?" It may also be appropriate to ask students to apply issues to real-world situations—"Several of you have posted comments on the economic price of environmental protection. Can anyone think of a current example in which economic development has been negatively impacted by environmental degradation and explain how?"

9. *Be aware of cultural patterns as well as differences in personal styles in discussion.* If you have a classroom that includes students from another country, be alert and request information from informants (rather than making assumptions) about the best way to ask questions. For example, a group of students from a particular culture may not respond very well to questions and topics that call for volunteered responses. In this case, a question like "Anyone want to comment on this?" is better altered to "I would like to hear what you think about this. Please post your response to this question by Wednesday afternoon."

   Be aware, too, that not all students respond well to the same approaches to discussion. For example, some students respond poorly to a question that asks them to share personal experiences, while others are not at all shy about divulging information about their background and preferences. We think it's important to respect these differences and not make students feel boxed in by the way you frame a question. A way around this problem can be to split the question in such a way as to offer an alternative: "Can you relate this to your own experience or one you have heard or read about?"

10. *Prepare a strategy for potentially controversial discussions.* It is even more important to have a strategy for approaching potentially controversial subjects online than in a face-to-face class since it is more likely you will see a wider range of students posting online than might have been willing to venture an opinion on-campus. If you have a code of conduct or netiquette stated up front, that will help matters as you gently remind the class as a whole when people tend to stray from the rules. When strong opinions are expressed that seem irrelevant to the subject matter, you may redirect as needed. When relevant but unsupported opinions arise, don't hesitate to ask for facts to back up assertions or to ask for clarification. Avoid irony or heavy-handed phrasing—remember that as

the instructor, what you say automatically carries a lot of weight and without vocal cues, students may easily misinterpret irony. If you know that the subject matter is inherently controversial, you may want to ask students to debate an issue and either assign them randomly to a particular viewpoint or ask them to take the side most opposed to their own personal view. Having to research and defend a position with logic often helps students discuss highly charged subjects.

A Study in Workload Management

A community college instructor, Fred is assigned to teach an online course in American history. He finds that he has been asked to teach a class of fifty students, the same number as in his on-campus course. He has always prided himself on promoting active discussion in his courses and wants to continue to do so in his online course, so he requires that all students contribute to the discussion on a weekly basis in order to receive participation credit.

Two weeks into the course, Fred is overwhelmed by the time it takes him to read through and respond to the student discussion postings. Instead of the dozen students who usually dominate the class discussion, a much larger percentage of his class freely express themselves on the discussion board, to his surprise and delight. However, most students seem to respond directly to his postings and seldom to other students. This means a substantial amount of his time is needed to read and respond to students.

Also, the sheer number of postings on the discussion board each week makes it hard for him to follow the conversations. Students often arbitrarily start new threads instead of replying to a thread, making it hard to follow the continuity of a discussion.

Following the advice of a colleague, an experienced online instructor, Fred divides the class into five smaller groups of ten students each for the purposes of discussion. He refines his participation credit so that students must respond to at least one other classmate each week rather than only to the instructor's initial discussion threads. He asks students to remember to reply to a message rather than start new threads for a response and to save new threads for new topics or clearly divergent subtopics.

Fred finds that he is able to circulate among the five discussion groups, addressing his remarks to each group as a whole as much as to individuals. Discussions are easier to follow, and as an added benefit, students begin to provide more follow-up questions and comments to their classmates, raising the overall quality of the discussion.

• • • • •

Tips for Establishing Effective Instructor-Facilitated Synchronous Communication

The most common form of synchronous communication available to instructors is text-based chat. However, voice-enhanced and video-enhanced chat and presentations have become more widely available.

You should carefully consider any requirement that students participate in chat as a graded assignment. When students live on campus, chat arrangements are not a difficult problem, but if your group includes working adults or students from a mix of time zones, chat can be a real impediment to their full participation in the class. In such cases, you will have to be very flexible about scheduling times for chat. It is best to offer some variety in the choice of times. If possible, too, you should copy the chat to post asynchronously (if archiving is not automatically generated by the chat) for the benefit of those who cannot attend. If you are supervising group work, request that groups post their chat transcripts in a group asynchronous area or email it to all the group's members and to you.

Gila Kurtz, who teaches a course in Synchronous Technology in Distance Education for the Master of Distance Education program at University of Maryland University College, differentiates between instructor preparation for a text or audio- and video-enhanced chat. "With audio/video synchronous presentations, I prepare content in advance, allowing time for questions and discussions after finishing a topic. This type of synchronous audio/video presentation is an instructor-led mode and can accommodate a larger group than for a text based chat session. For the latter, I don't recommend preparing a story-board or script in advance. Live chat is a learning event and not a show that needs to be perfect."

Here are some further tips for organizing an instructor-led chat or other synchronous session with more than one student:

1. Try to limit group chats in which students are expected to fully participate to four or five participants.

2. If you must have a group of more than five students, establish a system for granting turns to speak. If your chat software includes a crowd-control function (the equivalent of raising hands to be recognized), then you should definitely make use of it. If your software doesn't have such a built-in system, you can design one: for instance, a question mark, asterisk, or some other sign that, when typed, will appear next to the student's name, allowing you to recognize him or her to speak.

3. Allow some time at either the beginning or the end of the chat for students to ask off-topic questions and to socialize. Announce this before the chat or at the opening of the session. Budget an extra two minutes as well for greetings and goodbyes.

4. For synchronous presentation formats like Adobe Connect, Elluminate, Wimba LiveClassroom and other such software, make sure participants test out their equipment ahead of time to ensure that browsers, microphones, etc., are all available. As presenter, have a backup plan in place for those who encounter problems speaking or hearing the presentation. When presenting, it can be helpful to have an assistant to help handle technical issues. If this is not possible, make sure you practice before the presentation under realistic conditions.

5. Chat may be used to bring in a guest speaker. This is best done in conjunction with an assigned paper or lecture by the guest, and it may follow the guest's participation in an asynchronous discussion for a period of a few days. This technique is most effective when you adequately prepare students for the guest chat. You should time the chat to coordinate with associated activities and give students an interval to formulate questions they can pose to the guest. If the guest is not available for a particular time, consider a one-on-one interview which can be replayed for students—you can even gather the questions ahead of time from students and ask the guest on their behalf. Gila Kurtz emphasizes that it's important to also verify that the guest is familiar with the technology if if he or she is expected to directly interact with students.

6. Limit each session to approximately one hour or less and announce the time limit before the chat. An hour period

allows for the social niceties that smooth the way, as well as some spontaneity, but also provides a substantial period of time during which all can focus on the pre-announced topics.

7. Prepare students for the chat by posting the topics or agenda, assigning readings or activities, or giving them questions to consider before the chat. Ask them to keep these questions or notes at their side while chatting. Have ready your own notes or outline so that you can keep track of all the items on the agenda. In some chat software, students entering late can't read anything that was said before their entrance. In such cases, strongly emphasize in advance that students should appear on time. You won't have time to keep recapitulating the "plot."

8. Whenever possible, preface your response with the name of the student to whom you are replying, or include bits of the question or comment to which you are responding. Using student names is particularly effective when you answer two students in one reply:

   Joe, I think reading the book before seeing the film would be best. No, Elsa, Exercise 1 is not due until the day after tomorrow.

   Including bits of the question also helps pinpoint the object of your response. This is often necessary when several comments have been made in rapid succession.

   Joe, book before film is best, but, as Linda reminds us, there are some films that are merely loose adaptations of books.

9. If the software you use does not indicate when someone is typing your students will not know (without a video cam of your actions) when you are thinking or entering a response. Students are often impatient in chat, trying to keep alert and anticipating your answers. So, in a fast-paced chat with a group of students, break up any long responses into two or three parts each ending in a word that indicates the thought is incomplete. This will let students know you're actually formulating a reply, not ignoring what they've said:

FIRST RESPONSE: Joe, book before film is best, but,

SECOND RESPONSE: as Linda reminds us, there are some films that are merely loose adaptations of books, while

THIRD RESPONSE: at the same time it is true that some books are created after the fact, to capitalize on interest in a movie.

This technique can also help you set the pace of the chat. Students automatically slow down, knowing that you're still sending your response. A similar slowdown tactic is to type just the student's name with a comma and send that, and then send the rest of the message in your next segment. As students see "Joe," they will await the remaining phrase, "book before film is best."

10. Have a backup plan in place, in the event that you or some of the students encounter a computer crash, lose the Internet connection (in countries where connections are unstable) or experience a dropping out of the audio. For example, note all participants as they come in, so that you can email everyone in the event of a break. Remind students that they can use the text chat if unable to use their microphones. If you have twenty-four-hour technical support, make sure the phone number is available ahead of the session.

Chat and other Synchronous Communications: Benefits versus Drawbacks

Let's be honest about the shortcomings of chat and other synchronous communication. Real-time communication is often productive of disjointed or widely digressing conversations, sloppy or impressionistic responses, bad spelling, poor grammar, and flippant attitudes.

The lines of communication are often out of sync. While you're creating your response, the other participants may already have moved on to other questions. An instructor-led chat with more than five people can quickly become difficult to follow. In fact, real-time chat is probably the most exhausting intensive activity an online instructor will ever encounter. Your attention must be attuned to rapid-fire comments and questions from several students; you must respond quickly, and, if your typing on the keyboard (or thumb-typing on your mobile device) isn't the most skillful, you may struggle to keep up with more nimble-fingered students. Worst of all, while your students may allow themselves less than complete sentences and partially formed ideas, they are still likely to take everything you write as official pronouncement.

Given all these shortcomings, why use chat or other synchronous communications at all?

And when is it most appropriate or effective? Here are some answers:

1. One use of chat is to provide reinforcement and immediate feedback for students. When there are no face-to-face meetings in the course, chat can provide a forum for such communication.

2. Virtual office hours and personal consultation can be provided by chat (or Instant Messaging). Such real-time communication can serve in lieu of an email or phone conversation, or provide clarification for communications by those methods. For example, you may have a student who writes cryptic emails with key information missing. You may be able to clarify his questions via a real-time chat. If a Whiteboard feature is available as well, you might be able to assist a student with a problem that requires more hands-on demonstration. You might also want to schedule individual chats with students for the purpose of asking follow-up questions about their work.

3. The social aspect of chat and IM may be one of the most important uses. Students may appreciate the opportunity to use chat and IM among themselves without its being an official class activity. It can help students form bonds with others in the classroom. Casual group chats (or even text messaging) may add to the sense of cohesion among group members collaborating on a project. Some students miss the spontaneous interaction common to on-campus classes, and chat may provide a suitable outlet for humorous exchanges, social chatter, and team-building conversations.

4. Chat may be used in conjunction with asynchronous group areas for group project meetings and discussions. Typical reasons for holding a chat are brainstorming and finalizing unresolved issues.

5. Chat may be used to bring in a guest speaker. This is best done in conjunction with an assigned paper, lecture, or even asynchronous discussion with the guest. To be most effective, you should carefully prepare students for the guest chat. You should time the chat to coordinate with associated activities and give students an interval to formulate questions they can later pose to the guest during the chat.

● ● ● ● ●

Team Teaching Online

Team teaching, whether online or on the ground, presents some unique challenges as well as opportunities. Students can derive the benefit of the multiple perspectives and teaching styles brought by two instructors, while instructors may appreciate the intellectual stimulation of the collaboration as well as the prospect of sharing some of their duties and workload. However, instructors who have experience of team teaching know that being half of a two-member team doesn't necessarily mean doing only half the work. Moreover, the difficulties involved in coordination can be legion.

Important! *Team teaching online requires even more advance planning than its on-the-ground counterpart.*

Even though you and your colleague aren't together in a physical classroom setting, you are very much occupying the same online classroom space, and you can easily trip over each other there as well! Once teaching begins, differences in teaching style and approaches will invariably appear, so it's best to discuss your pedagogical approach as well as practical procedures before the course begins.

Avoid team teaching a course with fewer than fifteen students. Such a small group of students will tend to feel overwhelmed by two instructors seemingly vying for their attention.

There are three basic models you can adopt in team teaching: shared responsibility, division of labor, and primary–secondary. Let's look at each of them in turn.

The Shared Responsibility Model

In the shared responsibility model, both instructors do everything; that is, each of you shares the responsibility for all activities in the class. Online, this means that both of you read and respond to all discussions and assignments. Students will know which instructor is which in the discussion forum, because your name will appear next to your comments.

Assignments can be graded by consensus (very time-consuming if you're communicating with each other only online) or by averaging. However, unless you have an online gradebook in which to enter grades, one of you will have to take charge of notifying students of grades and passing along the corresponding comments by email. If you wish, you can sign both names to the grade and add comments.

One risk in this form of team teaching is that students may not know whom to address a particular question. Students may also become confused by the two instructors' different teaching styles and approaches. No matter how much we instructors like to imagine that we have a student-centered classroom and an anti-authoritarian style, students do tend to adjust themselves to the prevailing classroom mode that we set.

This model of team teaching also presents some of the same problems encountered by two parents. You want to be two individuals, offering different opinions, but you don't want to contradict or undermine each other. You must also avoid being played off, one against the other, by students.

A further risk of this model is that neither of the instructors may have the course firmly in focus. Areas of the course can become relatively neglected if no one takes responsibility for them. Finally, this model can be exhausting for instructors because not only are they responsible for teaching the entire class, but they also must spend additional time coordinating with the other member of the team.

Nevertheless, in some situations you may decide that the shared responsibility model is the best approach for you. If so, here are some tips on making this "everything" model work:

1. Ask students to send any emailed queries to both instructors.

2. Each instructor must assiduously read all discussion threads in the class. If one instructor has more comments than the other on a particular topic, that's fine, but the other should make at least a few responses to the same topic.

3. In your syllabus or introductory messages, clearly state the procedures for students to contact you and to submit assignments.

4. For grading and evaluating student work and participation, work out a procedure that you can easily follow. If you're meeting with your co-teacher online, you'll need a way to smoothly exchange any emailed assignments and to maintain record keeping as well.

The Division of Labor Model

The division of labor model involves just what the name suggests: the two instructors divide their responsibilities according to a pre-arranged plan. Like the shared responsibility model, division of labor also requires a great deal of planning and coordination, but it is generally easier to implement.

The division of labor may be arranged by weeks (Joe for week 1, Mary for week 2); by topics (which may overlap with weeks); by types of class activities (Mary handles the research project, and Joe supervises all group reports); or by a combination of these factors (Joe takes on the research project and weeks 2, 4, and 6 of the discussion, while Mary handles all individual presentations and weeks 1, 3, and 5 of the discussion). You may also want to have some activities handled separately by each of the two instructors, while other activities are a joint effort.

The biggest risk in this model is that one instructor may lose track of the classroom while the other instructor is taking his or her turn. Here are some tips for making the division of labor model most effective and least frustrating:

1. Make sure each instructor contributes something to the overall effort. This contribution should start with the selection of texts and planning of class activities.
2. Decide how you wish to divide up the classroom responsibilities, and state the arrangement in your syllabus so that students know who has the primary responsibility for any particular activity.
3. Make sure that your introductions during the first week of class, or your comments during the first topic of discussion, are carried out jointly with your co-teacher.
4. Ask students to copy (cc) the other instructor on any queries sent to one instructor. This will ensure that each instructor is kept "in the loop."

5. Even if you divide up the discussion responsibilities by week, make sure that the instructor not assigned to that duty in a particular week reads through the discussion. The "off-duty" instructor might want to make a comment as well, and he or she can best do so after the other instructor and the students have had their say.

6. Divide up grading of assignments as evenly as possible but in alternating cycles so that neither instructor loses track of students. In other words, Joe grades assignments 1 and 3, while Mary does 2 and 4. Each instructor should cc the other on any emailed evaluation comments to a student. Each instructor should have copies of all grades and comments. If there is no central gradebook online, the two instructors need to keep identical records. This may mean that after each grading turn is taken, the instructor who did the grading emails a list of grades to the other.

The Primary–Secondary Model

In the primary–secondary model, one instructor assumes the primary or dominant role in managing the class. This approach is necessary when one instructor cannot participate in the class to the same extent as the other, yet is still making an active contribution. For example, one instructor may have less Internet access or more workload issues than the other, or one instructor may feel less expert in certain areas of course content.

Tips for making the primary–secondary model work include the following:

1. Make sure that each person is fully aware of the responsibilities he or she has agreed to take on. Work this out by going over the week-by-week activities of the course.

2. Try to balance the workload to each person's satisfaction. If one instructor cannot participate online as much as the other, for instance, let him or her take on more of the record-keeping duties or slightly more of the grading of assignments.

3. Clearly indicate to students the respective responsibilities for each instructor, but ask students to cc each instructor on any email correspondence sent to the other.

4. If one instructor does not have as much uninterrupted Internet access as the other (this would be particularly true for partners who have no home access), set up a system so that the partner with good access does the posting. For example, if you need to post a message but lack ready access to the web page or discussion forum, you can email or IM to send the material to your partner, who can then post it for you. In this case, your name, as the instructor who wrote the actual message, should be typed at the top of the message itself (because the posting will automatically bear the name of the person who puts it online). Students need to be reminded about this practice to avoid confusion about the two instructors' contributions.

Classroom Management: Special Issues

In addition to the issues discussed in Chapter 11, several other problems may arise in conjunction with managing your online classroom. Some, such as student behavior problems, aren't unlike those that may occur in an on-the-ground classroom, except that the online environment may introduce further complications. Other issues, such as privacy concerns and the difficulty of confirming student identity, are unique to the online environment.

Privacy Issues

It's hard to argue that anything on the Web is truly private: computers automatically make records, students may share their passwords, and so on. Password access to classrooms and discussion forums brings us some measure of privacy, but short of encryption and identification by eyeball, voice, or fingerprint, it is hard to ensure complete privacy or security. Perhaps, however, we can speak of "more or less private."

In previous chapters, we have mentioned the new privacy issues raised by the use of Web 2.0 communications taking place on sites and servers external to your institution. It is worth reading the "terms of use" for each such site and giving your students fair warning or the option to use an alias on public sites if you are not able to or do not choose to create a private group area.

Beyond the security measures afforded by our software and hardware, there are other things we can do to protect privacy. For example, we must be careful about distributing student work, discussion transcripts, and email outside the classroom without permission. It's surprising how many otherwise discreet and caring instructors will think nothing of posting student materials, complete with names, on an open web site for the entire world to access without permission or even notification.

Important! *What is said in the classroom is originally said in a defined context. Those later reading these words outside the classroom may not understand that context.*

Similar privacy concerns affect your own contributions. You can expect that students will copy and download your words for the purpose of learning. Do give some thought to what you wish to disclose about your private life and opinions in the classroom discussion. If you're concerned about students distributing your material, then make sure you state up front that words and materials are for class use only, not for distribution. With social networking sites like Facebook, many instructors would do well to separate their private profiles from an academic one. And it doesn't hurt to remind students who are networking with their classmates about the many privacy options available in Facebook that can help them control what information they want to release to classmates as well as the instructor.

We recommend that instructors teaching completely online classes never give out their personal phone numbers to students unless absolutely forced to by the program. If your institution requires some phone "office" hours each week, use either your campus phone or your work phone. It is also sometimes possible to work out an arrangement by which students who want to contact you by phone call your department, which relays the request to you via phone or email. You can then return the student's call. The prevalence of Skype as a communication medium provides another option—you may create a Skype account just for the purpose of communicating with your students.

Most issues can be resolved in the online classroom or by private email. This has the advantage of giving you a record of the communication with the student. It also means that the student has to think a bit about his or her question and perhaps has a greater opportunity to reflect on your answer as well.

●●●●●

Identity Issues

How do you know the real identity of the person you encounter online? The truth is, sometimes you don't. If students are registered with the university, we can assume with some degree of certainty that they are indeed the people they say they are. Presumably, they had to show an ID at some point. Yet in the continuing-education classroom—and especially for students who live far away from campus—this authentication may not occur. Generally, institutions are more concerned about identity confirmation when a student is enrolled in a state certification or degree program. In those cases, students may be required to take at least one live, proctored exam or to prove their identity when applying for and exiting the program.

In terms of our daily interactions with students online, we cannot always detect gender, ethnicity, age, and other characteristics that are often more easily detectable in a live classroom. This type of identity might be thought of as social identity as opposed to the authentication of those enrolled. Some institutions may give you a roster with no more than name and ID number and address, while at others you will have access to computer databases holding extensive information, but most instructors are unlikely to have ready access to more than the most limited details about students.

Although there may be clues—for example, a name that sounds Italian or references to foods and customs belonging to a particular culture—these are all merely guesses unless the student confirms our conjectures. Approximate age is sometimes easier to detect but also prone to error. Are those references to television shows of the 1950s or music of the 1960s the product of firsthand experience or a love of retro fashions?

We are particularly prone to mistakes about female students, because their surnames are often not those they grew up with, but instead represent new identities taken on through marriage.

Immigrants may also take on new names that they think are appropriate to their new country. Students with names such as Pat, Dale, Sasha, Kim, and Ming may be male or female. Or your student's name may be in a language so unfamiliar to you that you have no way of knowing whether the syllables signify a particular gender.

You may ask for voluntary submission of photos, but even photos, short of the student's official ID photo, can be less than revealing of the truth. Is that your student in a photo taken ten years ago, or is that your student's handsome friend?

There's no point in trying to stop ourselves from imagining our students (and them from imagining us); our minds can't help trying to categorize. But be alert to the possibility that you may be dead wrong about the identity of your students. Avoid making statements and assumptions that aren't based on information actually provided by the student. The best policy is to allow students to self-identify. Unless you think fraud may be involved (for example, one person masquerading as another to take a test or complete an assignment), we would advise you not to worry too much about such identity issues. Just keep an open mind and watch for clues.

The use of virtual worlds such as Second Life and the creation of avatar identities can present unique identity problems. When creating the name of their avatar in Second Life, students are unable to use their own surnames but must instead choose one from a list of names. Instructors using Second Life for course activities will want to immediately create and publish a "cast of characters" so that all participating students know who's who in the virtual world. Some instructors request that students incorporate their real first names when choosing a first name for the avatar to aid in this process of class identification.

● ● ● ● ●

Managing Student Behavior Online

When it comes to the topic of handling "difficult students," we think that most problems can be averted by the skillful management of student expectations such as we have outlined in earlier chapters—the comprehensive syllabus, clearly written assignment instructions, protocols for communications, codes of conduct, and clearly stated policies and criteria for grading, as well as instructor responsiveness, are all ways to ensure that students understand how to do their best in your online course. Some students are being "difficult" because they are having problems handling the conventions and habits of learning online (or the complexities combining online and face-to-face classes). Such students can benefit from a quick explanation, some patience, and possible referrals to appropriate resources.

But there is another important point to keep in mind: sometimes the "difficulty" actually resides with the instructor, not the student! So, before jumping to the conclusion that you have a "difficult" or intractable student, do a quick self-review to make sure that you have not been ambiguous or lacking in clarity about your expectations and instructions for students.

In the online asynchronous discussion forum, the blog, the wiki, or chat room, the range of student types remains pretty much the same as in the on-the-ground classroom. There are the quiet ones, the nurturers, the take-charge types, the class clowns, the disruptive ones, and the imaginative procrastinators. There are a few aspects of the online environment, however, that create new opportunities for the "usual suspects" to manifest their trademark styles.

Noisy Students

A noisy student in an online classroom, much like his or her traditional counterpart, spends much energy raising issues that are only tangentially related to the topics under discussion. One way this occurs online is that the student will begin new topic threads even when the comments he or she has to contribute actually fit in with pre-existing threads. Such students often avoid replying to anything but the instructor's comments. And when they do join in the discussion, they generally ignore the direction of the conversation and simply pepper the thread with inane comments.

This type of student is actually easier to handle online, in asynchronous discussion, than in the regular classroom. There are more space and time in an online classroom for such students to perform without seriously affecting others. When they start a new thread on what is already an ongoing topic, most other students will simply ignore this detour in favor of continuing the more active and peopled conversation. In the interest of housekeeping and to prevent the area from over-blooming with threads, you may want to drop this individual an email note. Ask him or her to please reply to an existing thread if the aim is to participate in a conversation rather than to break out a true new topic. Or, treat the problem as a technical one. Remind the student of the difference between replying to a subject and starting a new one. Many students are actually confused by the differences in software response methods.

When the student peppers the existing conversation with inane comments, this isn't really as disruptive an influence as it would be in an on-the-ground setting. Classmates will read this student's inane comments but simply not respond to them and move on to the next message in the thread. Other than the moment required to read the inane comment, nothing is really lost. The noisy student hasn't forestalled the comments of others because the clock isn't ticking away in the asynchronous classroom, and no "air time" has been consumed.

A good way to deal with the noisy student is to give him or her some personal attention in the form of a personal email. Sometimes a noisy student is just feeling a bit lost and anonymous, and wants some individual attention. Suggest that the student share some of his or her ideas with others in a lounge forum. In the public discussion area, acknowledge the student, but then steer him or her back on track: "What you say about X is interesting, Joe, but how would you respond to Ian's comment about Y?" or "This is an interesting point. We may be able to take this up later, in week 5."

In the synchronous chat room, a noisy student can take up precious "real time," so setting rules and procedures for chat will make a major difference. Some forms of chat software will actually allow you to eject a student who isn't following the rules. While that is an extreme measure, it may be necessary if the noisy student crosses the line to become disruptive. Other software permits you to call on students, supplying the equivalent of the raised hand. However, even if you don't have such software, simply requiring students to type an asterisk, exclamation mark, or question mark to be recognized before speaking will have the same regulating effect. The noisy student will have to wait his or her turn along with everyone else.

There are ways to deal effectively with the noisy student. Be gentle and remember that the noisy student may prove to be your salvation when the classroom discussion hits the doldrums and you desperately need someone to respond to your prodding!

Quiet Students

Quiet students can present even more of a problem online than in the traditional classroom situation, because you can't see them nodding their heads in assent or shaking their heads in disagreement. If the quiet student doesn't post anything, whether by text or audio comment, you can't readily tell if he or she is even in the room, occupying a virtual seat.

Two strategies can come into play here:

1. If tracking is available through your software, you can follow the quiet students to see if they are present, how often, and what they are reading.
2. By requiring a minimum level of participation by posting, you can probably coax a few contributions out of them.

You can also use private email to gently urge quiet students back into the classroom discussion space. Send a message saying that you've noticed that the student has been accessing the classroom but not actually posting and that you wonder if he or she is having any technical problems. Or say that you wonder how the course is going for the student—does he or she have any special questions about procedures?

Often you can find a way to bring the student into the classroom discussion by virtue of his or her special talents or background—information you've gleaned from the biographical introduction. Sharon Packer, a psychiatrist who has taught online courses in psychology and religion for the New School, suggests that asking questions in the introduction phase, such as "What do you want to get out of this class?" (rather than the usual "Why are you taking this class?"), often elicits information that the instructor can later use to motivate students to participate. For example, in a comparative religion class, if Joe has mentioned that he lived half his life in Japan, you might address a question to him directly during the discussion of popular religious practices: "Joe, is there anything you can recall from your experience in Japan that relates to this type of folk practice?"

Some students may actually be "learning while lurking," but if participation constitutes a major portion of the grade, they must be reminded that a lack of active participation will have consequences. Look to their written assignments to gauge whether learning is indeed occurring. Also, once the student has completed an individual assignment, see if there is something worthy of note in it that you might ask him or her to share with the class. If the quiet student happens to send you an email or reply to an inquiry of yours, grasp that opportunity to say that his or her presence is missed in the classroom. Emphasize that a good question is as valuable for discussion purposes as a brilliant comment, and that he or she should feel free to contribute in a casual tone to the conversation. Some quiet students are really just overly self-conscious about writing and posting their thoughts, imagining that anything seemingly "published" to the world in this manner ought to be perfectly expressed and articulated.

In audio- and video-assisted communication modes, quiet students may shy away from using voice and appearing on a web cam—if the class is not one that requires audio (for example, a language or speech class), consider allowing such students to choose the text option that is usually available.

Disruptive Students

The disruptive student will attempt to take over your class by commandeering the discussion and questioning the major thrust of your course or some essential aspect of it in the public forum. He or she may answer questions addressed to you, contradict you, and in some cases become abusive. This is one of the worst situations an instructor has to face online. Few students will stage such behavior face to face, but more feel emboldened to do so online. The situation is considerably worsened by the fact that the comments will sit there for days, to be read by all.

At the extreme, when a student uses foul language or is abusive or threatening, you should immediately notify your administrator. Copy and save all posted or emailed communications with that individual. Although you may be moved to delete (or ask your administrator to delete) outright four-letter words and the like, knowing how to handle comments that don't sink to that level may be more difficult.

Some instructors post their own classroom codes of conduct at the beginning of the class to help set boundaries for students. Sharon Packer, whose online classes concerned the psychology of religion, history of psychiatry, and approaches to dreams, was particularly sensitive to discussions that might elicit personal or controversial topics. She recommends that instructors keep objective criteria in mind when formulating a code of conduct. These criteria often must be keyed directly to the type of course being taught. For example, in her courses she often included such guidelines as "There will be no discussion of personal use of illegal drugs" and "This isn't the place to discuss personal psychiatric history." She also urged that students maintain a cordial atmosphere and use tact in expressing differences of opinion.

Many instructors provide a link to, or an excerpt from, the text of their institution's honor code and emphasize that the code applies in the online classroom as well. Often, such codes are not specifically related to online education situations and may not be sufficient to provide all necessary guidance for your students. Nonetheless, in terms of issues such as plagiarism, cheating, and so forth, these may provide useful material. Other institutions have been more forthright in addressing these issues. For example, Kansas State University has published guidelines concerning student behavior online (see www.k-state.edu/provost/policies/studentconduct.htm) to augment their regular student conduct rules, drawing a distinction between dealing with nonthreatening disruptions as well as those of a threatening nature.

Dealing with disruptive students

In dealing with disruptive students in particular, it's important to achieve a balance between asserting your authority in the classroom and overreacting to a student provocation. However, you must act quickly to prevent disruptive students from escalating tensions in the classroom, and you must take the lead in informing your department if students cross the line.

Following are some examples of different types of disruptive behavior and instructor responses, based on real situations we've observed or heard described. Please note that these are composite examples, not actual case histories.

Example 1: The Know-It-All   Midway through a course, one of the students, Janet, who had some real-world experience in the subject, began to answer questions that were addressed to the instructor in the asynchronous forum. At first this seemed fine, because Janet was contributing some good tips to the student questioners. The instructor simply acknowledged Janet's comments and then added her own remarks.

At some point, however, Janet began contradicting the instructor's information. Janet even offered her own web site information and suggested that students use it as their guide. The instructor checked her facts. She wasn't wrong, so she simply reaffirmed the information to the other students (and, by implication, to Janet as well) without responding directly to Janet's contradictory message. Her message was polite and generous, beginning with:

> *Although there may be some disagreement by scholars in the field on the details, the general principle I enunciated remains sound and is the one I would like you to use in this course.*

Janet wasn't directly mentioned, and she was able to save face; yet the instructor reasserted the primacy of her authority and refocused students on the objectives of the course.

Example 2: The Mutineer   Professor X's approach to the subject matter wasn't interesting to one of her students, Jerry. Jerry was a bright student and knew quite a bit about the subject. Therefore, he had already formed his own ideas about the way to approach it.

Jerry began to sound somewhat critical and condescending toward the instructor in the class discussions. But his first direct attack came in response to the instructor's comments on Jerry's public presentation. The instructor's comments were dry and very brief. Jerry commented in the classroom forum to the effect that the instructor had "not given me any constructive comments at all." Note that, at this point, the instructor had not responded in turn.

A few days later, in a private email to the instructor, Jerry blasted the instructor's teaching methods and complained about the poor quality of the class. The instructor got angry, but instead of answering Jerry's more abusive private email, she posted a public reply to his less strident public note:

> *I believe I have given you constructive comments, and I don't appreciate your tone here or the way you expressed yourself in your recent email.*

This set Jerry off, and he began to post angry messages in the classroom, trying to enlist students to his way of thinking:

> *I'm sure a lot of you feel the same way I do—this course is a gigantic waste of my time and money. I think we should ask the department for our money back.*

A few students actually posted affirmative replies, such as these:

> *I agree—am not satisfied with Professor X's responses.*

> *I feel that I was misled by the way this course was advertised.*

Professor X was well on her way to losing control of this classroom. Jerry's original public posting about not getting constructive comments was sharp and somewhat rude but hadn't yet overstepped the bounds of decency. In responding publicly, the instructor would have been better advised to hold her criticism in check, merely noting the sharpness of Jerry's public message by implication.

> *Jerry, I have been rather brief due to the constraints of time, and perhaps you did not get the full import of my comments.*

Any time students feel they need more feedback, I hope they will let me know via private email. I will send you a private email within a day or so that I hope will provide you with the additional details you have requested.

This response by Professor X would have had the effect of noting Jerry's complaint while ignoring the hostility behind it and addressing what she as a teacher could do to respond to the student's needs. She would also have succeeded in moving the conversation to the private sphere.

As for Jerry's private email, she should have responded to it privately and firmly.

Jerry, I'm glad that you have expressed these thoughts with me via private email. I'm sorry that you don't find my approach one that is helpful to your study of the subject. Because it is too late to withdraw from the class, I suggest that you do the best you can with the material and activities. You have many good ideas, and I welcome your airing of alternative approaches in the classroom, as long as this is done in an objective manner and in the appropriate forums.

The subtext here is this:

I did not appreciate the personal comment you made in the classroom; you should have withdrawn from the course when you could, but I will not penalize you for your opinions even though I do expect you to follow my syllabus. I appreciate that you are bright, and I will give you some opportunity to display your knowledge, but don't make any more personal comments in the classroom.

Note that even if an instructor doesn't normally express herself in a formal manner in the classroom, this is a situation that calls for a certain degree of formality. Formality in online forums signifies seriousness, clarity, and firmness to students. It is particularly effective when it contrasts with an otherwise casual instructor tone.

Example 3: The Belligerent Student Who Hasn't Kept Up   Andy barely participated during the first part of Professor B's course, but he seemed suddenly to reappear, apparently angry that he was finding it hard to catch up with the class. He posted angry messages in the public classroom that reflected his very real frustration arising from his lack of understanding of what was going on in the class.

> *What's this supposed to be about? I don't get it. What's the point of this assignment?*

In a case like this, Professor B should ignore the emotion in Andy's comments in the classroom forum. The professor should post objective, concrete suggestions in reply:

> *This concerns Lesson 5. You might find pages 10–25 the most useful.*
>
> *Andy, as I mentioned in my previous lecture, this assignment asks you to focus your attention on Problem 2. See the guidelines for Assignment #1 in the syllabus. All students: If you have any specific questions on this assignment, please feel free to post your questions here.*

Professor B needs to back this up by emailing this student and being supportive, while still calling him to account.

> *Andy, I have noted your expressions of frustration in the classroom and have responded. Since you were somewhat late getting started in the class, you may need to go back and review Lessons 1 and 2 and the guidelines. If you need further help, just email me and I will try to assist you.*

The subtext of this is:

> *I can see that you're frustrated, and that may be due to the fact that you didn't keep up with the work. I think you can do it—go back and try again. Read the relevant material, read the guidelines. You aren't the only one who may have questions. If you really don't understand after making a decent effort, I'm here to help.*

Example 4: The Belligerent Student on the Attack   Professor Y teaches an online course in contemporary American politics, in which students are encouraged to explore their assumptions about American political parties and hot topics of the day. Professor Y does have a code for students to follow in expressing their opinions; however, she likes to keep the classroom as open and free as possible.

During a particularly heated argument about school vouchers, Tom attacks another student, Linda, saying, "You're a right-wing bigot!" Professor Y cannot track the readership of individual messages, but she assumes that many students have read this one, because it has been posted for two days and the record shows that many students have logged on during that time.

She carefully copies and saves a record of the online exchange. She then posts a response, without naming Tom:

> *I would like to remind everyone to base your arguments on the issues. Please observe the code of conduct posted for this class, which asks students to refrain from personal attacks and labeling of other students.*

At the same time, she writes a private email to Tom:

> *Tom, perhaps this was not your intent, but your remark to Linda seemed inappropriate and insulting. I hope you will apologize by private email to her and then delete your comment.*

But then Tom attacks Professor Y in the classroom forum:

> *Who are you, the pope?! We should be able to say whatever we want to say.*

At this point, Professor Y telephones an urgent request that her department head deal with this student and, if necessary, officially remove him from the class. She follows up with an email that makes the same request but also includes a copy of all the online and email communications. She sends a brief private email to Tom, letting him know that she has referred his case to the department and warning him to refrain from any more personal comments; she forwards this to the department as well. She continues to monitor the situation and all classroom communications carefully until the matter is resolved.

There are a few particular things to note about this situation:

■ Professor Y felt that she had to post a public response, but she wanted to avoid targeting Tom in public, so she posted a general reminder to all in the class about the code of behavior expected. She emailed Tom privately to give him an opportunity to make things right. If Professor Y had simply responded to Tom in the classroom forum with an equally personal remark, the situation would have rapidly degenerated.

■ Even though Professor Y had the ability within the software functions to delete Tom's note, she felt that it was better to ask Tom to delete it himself and apologize to his classmates. Had Tom's note been even more blatantly derogatory, or had he used profanity, Professor Y may have chosen to delete the note immediately upon discovering it, after carefully copying and preserving a record. She then should have followed up this deletion by notifying the department and Tom that she had felt compelled to take this action.

■ When Tom escalated the situation by posting a direct attack on her, Professor Y decided to let the department handle the matter. As a last resort, she was prepared to delete any more comments by Tom.

■ Professor Y needed to back up her story and protect herself by forwarding a copy of the communications to the department. Otherwise, the department head might not have reacted quickly enough.

At this time, more and more institutions have guidelines in place for student conduct online, but where online education is new, guidelines may be lacking and there may be few administrators who have firsthand familiarity with online classroom management. Although you should keep your department or other relevant institutional authorities in the loop whenever special issues arise—and protect yourself by keeping scrupulous records—you may find that you, as an online instructor, are often out there on your own. You must be proactive and quick-witted when dicey situations arise.

Other Behavior Problems

In addition to students who are unusually noisy, quiet, or disruptive, there are other behavior problems that may create problems in the online classroom. We'll comment on a few of them here.

The Controller   Sharon Packer notes that a student who emails you before the class begins, to request all assignments in advance, may not be the conscientious eager beaver you assume, but one who actually wants to control the class. By getting a head start on everyone else, this student can be the first to post responses to the discussion questions. Perhaps this student will post in such extensive detail that the entire discussion is squashed. Or perhaps this student wants to seem in control of the material because he or she actually lacks sufficient background for the class.

Naturally, there are students who request assignments in advance for valid reasons. Maybe they will be traveling during the first week of class, or they may have a disability that could slow their assimilation of the reading material. Some students just want to see the reading list to find out what they're getting into before committing to the class. These valid concerns can be discovered by simply asking the student his or her reasons for requesting all assignments in advance.

The Staller   Packer also suggests that students who delay logging on to the class (barring actual technical problems) may be unmotivated or stalling. These students may not want to become part of the group process and may fail to create bonds with others in the class. Some students of this sort simply like to work alone, and they may eventually access the class, absorb the material, and do all the necessary work; many more, however, are likely never to finish the course.

Another possibility is that such students are deeply insecure about their abilities or intimidated by the unfamiliar online environment, even when they've gone through an orientation. The strangeness of the online environment can make those who are normally competent and professional in their chosen fields fearful that they will look foolish or somehow lose control. An email reminder to such students, to encourage their participation, can sometimes be the personal touch needed to bring them into the classroom. Technical problems are a wonderful face-saver: even if they aren't the real issue, asking a student whether he or she has delayed logging on because of technical problems may elicit the actual reasons or at least cause the student to realize that he or she shouldn't delay any longer.

If you can use your tracking features and observation to keep track of student progress in the classroom, you may be able to intervene to encourage students who delay or stall. It's also important to keep a record of student "attendance"—how often and when the student was in the classroom—because being able to document a student's participation may be necessary in the event that a student challenges you about a grade. If attendance reports aren't available from your software, you should keep a manual record. Unfortunately, a small percentage of students imagine that they can more easily get away with a lack of participation in an online course than in a traditional classroom.

The "Must-Have-an-A" Student   Although the student who tells you early in the course that she or he "has to get an A in this course" is a familiar phenomenon, these students may be particularly drawn to distance learning and online courses. Some find it easier to assume a pose of invincibility and grandeur when they know they won't meet you in person; this type of adult student may even claim honors and credentials he or she doesn't really possess. Some students may simply find it easier to harass you about their grades by email than they would by coming to your office.

In any case, those words, "have to get an A in this course," should definitely raise your antennae. Meet such declarations with firm, objective statements about your grading criteria and standards, combined with a mild rebuff:

> *Thank you for your note. It is good to see that students are motivated, but there can be no guarantees that any particular*

student will receive an A in this class. This online course is a challenging one, no less rigorous than its on-campus version. See my grading criteria listed below. Students will receive further instructions about the requirements for assignments as the course proceeds. To do your best in my class, follow the guidelines and schedule in the syllabus and pay attention to the rubrics for all assignments.

Keep every scrap of correspondence with this student and be cautious in your email to him or her. Be aware that this student will likely keep a record of everything you say.

●●●●●

A Final Word

The foregoing examples are offered to help you recognize and deal with potential problems. Naturally, each student presents a unique profile and must be responded to as an individual. Avoid jumping to conclusions, and don't hesitate to rely on those gut feelings derived from long experience in the traditional classroom to help you sort out one situation from another. Sometimes a phone call or Skype conversation will allow you to better evaluate the student through the aid of voice and tone (and perhaps the web cam video as well), but keep in mind the need to keep a record of such communications and follow up with an email that summarizes the conversation.

When in doubt, err on the side of softening your language in emails and postings. A "might" or "perhaps" in your advisory or disciplinary message can often provide the face-saving gesture needed to defuse a tense situation. Finally, don't allow yourself to become overly reactive or distracted by difficult students. Remember that there are other students who also deserve your attention, and don't get too caught up in one student's drama.

Teaching Web-Enhanced and Blended Classes

Although we've discussed issues as they pertain to "blended" classes throughout the book—classes that combine online and face-to-face activities—this chapter focuses specifically on them as well as those in which online elements play a merely supplemental role to the face-to-face class. You may find that material that was discussed in the context of the chapters in which it occurred is here summarized or treated in greater depth.

Today, the use of the Web by instructors is broad and varied. Some universities maintain their own "channels" on YouTube to stream video versions of their best instructors' on-campus lectures to the Web while others schedule just a few online discussions throughout the semester and post their lecture notes, while still others teach classes that regularly meet online one week and on campus the next. How can you best integrate the online and face-to-face elements of a class? What factors should you think about? Are there any pitfalls to avoid? To answer such questions, we'll try to offer helpful tips for blended classes as well as for integrating online tools for a primarily face-to-face class.

Let's look for a moment at those instructors who make minimal use of the Web. Perhaps they teach a traditional on-campus course but maintain a web site for the course. Typically, such web sites contain a course syllabus, a schedule of required readings and assignments, a listing of the course office hours, and some hyperlinks to relevant web sites in the instructor's particular subject area. They may also include a link to a discussion board which may be entirely an optional area, with students deciding whether to use or not use the site. In these cases in which students seldom look at the web site, the situation suggests that the instructor isn't using the web site to maximum advantage. If asked to provide a reason why their web sites are so lightly utilized, instructors might cite their students' lack of reliable access to the Web from off campus (a typical complaint for developing countries), or even a lack of interest on the part of students who are having their instructional and social needs met on campus. Instructors may also say that because of their own workloads, they don't want to spend more time creating material for the web site. They may even express the fear that if they use the Web more extensively, their students will no longer have a reason to come to class. In other words, instructors are asking why they should work more for the same pay, doing something that perhaps threatens their livelihood. The ultimate answers to this question are beyond the purview of this book. Academic senates and other faculty organizations, institutional administrators, and union representatives must work them out. But we don't believe that using the Web effectively requires you to labor twice as long for the same pay. We do think that it can improve the way you teach your traditional course. To that end, this chapter will also provide some practical suggestions for this skeptical audience.

As previously noted in this book, the Sloan Consortium definitions of Web Facilitated (what we call "enhanced" here), Blended/Hybrid, and Online are based on the amount of content delivered online. They term "Web Facilitated" as those courses with 1–29 percent of content delivered online; "Blended" courses as those in which 30–79 percent of the content is delivered online but still require some face-to-face meetings; and true "Online" as containing 80 percent or more online content with few or no face-to-face meetings. But another way to approach this is to look at the types of instructional *activities* carried out online and whether or not they are required or the degree to which they replace face-to-face time. (Still persistently termed "seat time" by many.) For the purposes of this chapter, we will use the following definitions:

■ *Web-enhanced:* A broad category of courses with associated web sites or course management system classrooms that contain materials relevant to the course (perhaps a syllabus, a list of web-based resources, a course calendar, a reading list, lecture notes or video lectures, discussion board, and/or real-time online meeting functions and chat). Actual online activities may be required or optional.

■ *Blended:* Courses in which both online and face-to-face instructional elements are required and complementary. A sizeable percentage of content is delivered online, there are required online student activities, and a significant portion of the student's grade is based on online activity.

● ● ● ● ●

Tips for Teaching Web-Enhanced Courses

While we want to focus first on those teaching web-enhanced courses, readers who are mainly interested in true blended courses may find that many of the following tips are also relevant to their needs.

Posting Lectures Online

The matter of online lectures is probably the biggest bugaboo teachers face when considering whether to use the Web. Why should students bother to come to class if they can simply read (or view video versions of) the lectures online?

Most lectures consist of a body of core material, factual or introductory in nature, followed by a discussion of more complex issues, proofs, or processes. The core material constitutes the main dish of the lecture. It's usually this material that students are expected to know. The other material serves as side dishes, which help differentiate the A students from the B and C students. If the core material were posted online, enriched by graphics and charts (perhaps with a few links to other relevant material available online), students would be relieved of the chore of reproducing this material word for word in their notes. That would allow them to concentrate on the finer points of the lecture. In other words, posting the lectures online frees the students to concentrate on what is being said.

Yet that argument still raises the question: Why should most students bother to come to class?

The answer may have something to do with learning styles. Some students learn better by listening and taking notes. Others do better by reading rather than by listening to lectures, and a third group seems to benefit by doing specific assignments based on the material covered. In that sense, posting lecture notes online helps some, but not all, students.

But the answer goes deeper still. It involves the basic approach to lecturing. Perhaps you need to rethink how you use your face-to-face time with students.

A Revised Approach to Lecturing

Admittedly, an instructor who posts lecture notes *and* reads them aloud in class may be in danger of putting students to sleep. But if the lecturer alters what he or she does in class, relying on the fact that the material is freely available online, then the experience of attending class may have a different meaning.

Say that the assignment for the week is to read the core notes posted online, along with whatever textual material supports it. In that case, instead of spending the first twenty minutes or so reviewing the core or introductory material, the instructor can concentrate on a particularly knotty issue or complex concept, examining it, elucidating it, debating it in class. Those students who have read the material beforehand will gain a deeper insight into the concept. (Of course, those who have *not* read the material will have considerable difficulty following what's going on. One hopes they will get the message and come to the next session better prepared.)

Online lectures offer other advantages as well. For the instructor, posting lectures can be an aid in re-evaluating older and possibly out-of-date course materials, improving organization, coherence, and comprehension. For the students, having the core portion of the lecture online provides an opportunity to review the material in its original form (rather than using their scribbled notes) or to catch up on material they may have missed because of illness or absence.

Important! **The point here is that using the Web to post lectures is neither a panacea nor a threat. It depends entirely on how effectively the web-based material is integrated into the class.**

How to Post Your Lectures Online

Posting your lecture notes online does add to your initial workload, particularly if you've never prepared them this way before. But once you've done it, you'll find it comparatively easy to update your notes the next time you teach the course. There are more and more choices available to accomplish this, which were discussed in Chapters 6 and 9 in some detail. You may post your lectures by uploading PowerPoint, by creating a PDF version of your word-processed documents, write directly into your course management system content area, or use one of the free sites mentioned in earlier chapters to create course web pages. You may also use one of the many Web 2.0 programs already mentioned in this book to create narrated slides or an audio or video lecture. You may want to experiment with these diverse ways of offering lectures before deciding on one that is easiest for you to create and for your students to access.

Using a Discussion Board

Most classes, particularly smaller, seminar-style classes, involve discussions of some sort. Ordinarily, students prepare for the discussions through readings. In some graduate classes, students prepare "position" papers, which are then circulated to other students for their consideration before coming to class. Using the Web in conjunction with the work done in class can enhance any of these techniques. Take the case of the seminar. In order to present the topic properly, the instructor will generally introduce it with either a short lecture or an impromptu talk. The students will then offer initial reactions to the discussion topic, setting the stage for the eventual discussion. A half-hour or so may have elapsed before the discussion is really joined.

An alternative approach is to have the students post their initial reactions to a discussion topic online and read the postings on each topic before coming to class. Although this would require more work from the students, it would not increase the instructor's workload except insofar as he or she had to read the work posted to the web site. What it would require of the students is perhaps a more carefully considered appreciation of the discussion topic and a greater awareness of where they stand in relation to other students in the seminar. Presumably this would make for a livelier and more informed discussion, and it would elicit remarks from all the members of the class rather than merely the most vocal.

A discussion board can be of use in large, lecture-style classes as well. For most students, "attending" such a class means finding a seat somewhere in an auditorium, staring at the back of someone's head, and listening to the instructor intone the lecture from a stage. Discussion in such a setting is usually fairly haphazard. The instructor pauses to solicit input from the assembled students. The more intrepid dare to raise their hands, while the rest sit quietly.

The Web can humanize such a class and permit students far more interaction with their colleagues and instructors than might otherwise be possible. An instructor can divide up the class into groups of twenty or so, depending on the number of TAs or assistants available. The instructor with a large class and no assistance might even devise a system of rotating student moderators who take turns facilitating their groups. Students using the discussion board will thus have a work group composed of class members whom they might not ordinarily get to know, a considerable advantage in schools where a majority of students don't live on campus, or in large universities where most students know only their dorm-mates.

Instructors and students can use these virtual study groups for a number of purposes. Students can post and discuss questions related to the material covered in class. Or, having delivered a lecture in class, an instructor might post a follow-up question, requiring the students to formulate an appropriate response as part of their grade. These responses might then become the basis of a future class discussion or lecture. They might also serve as an archived resource for students reviewing the material.

An instructor can monitor the comments posted in the discussion groups and use them as the basis of a frequently asked questions (FAQ) page containing general answers to the students' more noteworthy queries and concerns. This will save the instructor the extra time of having to respond to the same question over and over again, either by email or in one-to-one advising sessions. Finally, if the instructor creates some relevant and focused initial discussion prompts, the discussion group postings can provide the instructor with valuable insight into how effectively the material in lectures has been conveyed.

Enlisting Technology in Your Favor

Much has been made of the ubiquity of laptops, **netbooks** (small, scaled-down laptops), and smart phones and the distraction these pose to students in the on-campus classroom, taking attention away from the lecture or other activity that the instructor has so carefully prepared. Rather than fight it, try to enlist technology in your favor. This goes beyond the "clicker" personal response systems many universities have introduced on campuses whereby instructors can poll students or ask them to contribute questions. Why not make something on the Web the object of your attention (for example, a photograph representing a current event or a video) and ask students to log in and take five minutes to post their quick responses in a chat. Then display the chat and its results and discuss the issues. (For those students who may not bring an electronic device to class, you might provide the option of logging on after class to an asynchronous forum you have established to add their responses to those of their classmates.)

Similarly, there are ways to take advantage of the popularity of social networking sites like Facebook. However, be careful to allow students to preserve the boundaries between social interaction and "official" class participation. You can create a special Facebook group to communicate with students, or ask students to create a limited class profile with appropriate privacy settings for participating in your class. There are an increasing number of applications designed for Facebook that might enhance your face-to-face class, including the application previously mentioned, Blackboard Sync, for institutional customers that provides some integration with a Blackboard classroom. However, start by deliberating what you would like to accomplish and then try out these applications of interest to you within Facebook to judge for yourself whether it would be easier to use a course management system or one of the many collaborative sites like Ning rather than Facebook for your purposes. It may be that you decide to use Facebook primarily for community-building activities for the class or as a way to update students on the class activities.

Using Online Quizmaking Tools

If your course is enhanced or blended, you presumably can conduct your high-stakes testing in a proctored on-campus environment. But online quizmaking tools can provide valuable

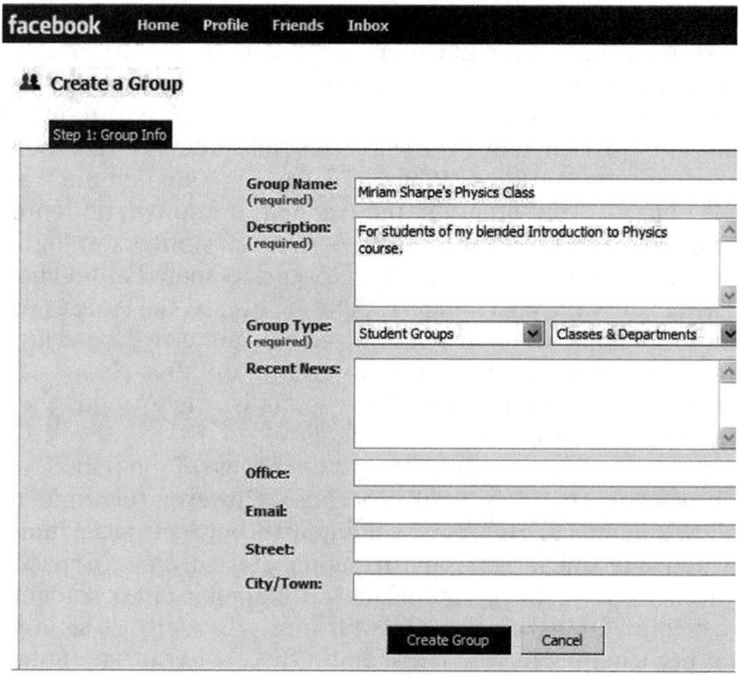

Figure 13.1 Miriam Sharpe prepares to create a group page on Facebook (www.facebook.com) in order to build community in her blended physics class. Reproduced by permission from Facebook.

assistance by permitting you to construct self-grading quizzes online. Most course management systems contain this feature. They permit you to construct a quiz consisting of true/false statements, multiple-choice questions, one-word answers, multiple answers, matching answers, ordered answers, or short or long essay questions. Even if your institution offers no access to course management systems, you can make use of the numerous free quizmaker tools available online. (See Chapter 6 for more detailed discussion of this.)

Students taking these tests can receive immediate feedback. This feedback can consist of a simple "correct" or "incorrect" message, or a statement explaining in detail why the student got the answer right or wrong. Questions can include embedded graphics. Depending on the software, they can even include sound or video files you've made, or links to such files that you found elsewhere on the Web. Another use of such online quizzes is to provide sample practice exams for student to use to prepare for midterm or final exams. Using one of the quiz generators, the instructor can provide answers as well as focused feedback, so that those taking the practice exams can learn from their mistakes. As with the preparation of lecture notes, creating quizzes can be time-consuming at first and then save you a great deal of trouble the second time around. One caveat, however: be sure to save the questions and answers in a word-processing file of your own. Sometimes institutions change their course management systems, and it isn't always possible to import a set of questions in one software system into another.

Providing Advice and Support

Providing counseling, advice, mentoring, and support is part of the job of teaching. Instructors list their office hours in their syllabi and, once or twice a week, sit dutifully behind their desks waiting for someone to knock on their door. All too often, nobody comes, leaving the instructor to wonder about the utility of sitting in an office for two hours a week. For some, the meager trickle of students is an opportunity to catch up on paperwork. Some may see it as a testament to their pedagogical skills—a sign that students aren't having any difficulties. To others, however, the lack of office visitors is a warning signal that something may be wrong—either the allotted time isn't convenient or the students don't feel they are getting what they want from the course. Using two of the online tools readily available to most instructors—email and chat—can improve the flow of communication markedly.

Counseling Students Online

With email, text messaging, instant messaging and chat, instructors can respond to student inquiries at a time and place of their choosing, leaving them freer to structure their activities during the day. Students can submit their inquiries as the need arises—for example, in their dorm room late at night when they're studying.

But shifting the counseling load to the Web has its obvious downside as well: it can significantly increase the instructor's workload if it isn't kept in check. To control your workload, we suggest the following guidelines, some of which we've recommended in earlier chapters as part of establishing a protocol for communications.

- Set strict parameters for responding to emails and other online messages and make these clear to your students in both your syllabus and your class. For instance, make sure your students understand that although you will accept emails from them, you will *not* necessarily respond to each one immediately and that you may provide responses to a question in the classroom if you see it is one that has been repeatedly posed.

- Specify which kinds of problems you will respond to: for example, personal problems, requests, or issues; or difficulties comprehending the subject matter. Steer clear altogether of administrative issues, such as dates for upcoming tests or questions about homework. Such information is either available in the syllabus or more properly discussed in an online or on-the-ground discussion session.

- Insist that you will not respond to any emails whose chief issue isn't clearly identified in the subject line of the communication.

This will save you the trouble of having to read through the entire email to discover the problem at hand. It will also allow you to forward a student email to a TA or assistant when appropriate.

■ Respond to a problem you perceive as being potentially a question for all by sending *one* email to your entire class, or by posting an announcement in the online classroom or by compiling a FAQ page with your answers and post it on your web site.

Establishing Virtual Office Hours

Online chat software can be used to conduct virtual office hours. It can, for instance, lighten your advisory load, or at least make it less onerous, if you use it in a focused way. Say, for example, that you tell your students that you will be available for consultations for an hour or two on certain days. If you're in your office, or even your home, you can open a chat session, leaving the chat window visible on your screen. As you wait for students to check in, you can do other work, glancing at the screen now and then to see if anyone has arrived.

Once a student has arrived, your conversation (depending on the chat software you're using) can usually be logged; that is, a record of your conversation is automatically saved to a text file. This permits you to edit the text file at some later date, extracting material for your FAQ page.

Some chat software tools now include a whiteboard function. The whiteboard, as you may recall, is a communal area where an instructor can draw or type. The students in the chat session can then discuss the instructor's display or present material of their own as part of the online give and take. Such software tools permit you to display in the whiteboard area any document on your hard disk (such as a PowerPoint presentation or an Excel spreadsheet) or any web page you have bookmarked; you can do this simultaneously while chatting with your students. More impressive still, the students can do the same thing. Thus you and your students can see the same documents, web pages, or applications at the same time that you are discussing them.

Many of the foregoing capabilities are now augmented by browser-based videoconferencing tools that permit one-to-one or even group video and audio communication without the need to even download software. (Some of these tools were described in earlier portions of this book, especially Chapter 9.) But as the pipelines carrying the information have improved, this form of communication has become more accessible and common. Today's instructor now has a broad array of communication tools with which to conduct advisory or small-seminar sessions with a class whether or not their institution provides such tools.

Assigning Group Projects

One feature commonly available in most course management software is the ability to divide large classes into small student groups, affording them a private area online in which to collaborate on the production and publication of group projects.

In these private areas the students have access to the full panoply of online tools—message boards, chat rooms, and whiteboards. They can create information, format it, and share these newly created items with each other, unseen by the rest of the class. This gives them a virtual workspace, permitting them to work together on a schedule convenient to them—a particular advantage to students with busy schedules or difficult commutes. It also permits you as the instructor to assign group collaborative projects with the assurance that they won't overwhelm the students' time or capabilities. Many institutions and course management systems also provide wiki software for such group collaboration purposes.

In a small private school, using a discussion board or other tools to promote online group work may seem superfluous. But in a large urban school, where students commute long distances, have jobs, or are raising families, the opportunity to work online overcomes a number of logistical obstacles while at the same time affording a level of intercommunication that wouldn't otherwise be possible. It also helps students learn how to collaborate with one another, a communication skill highly valued in the workplace.

Access to online group collaboration tools may permit you to assign more complex research projects than you might have before. By dividing the workload, students can tackle problems of much greater complexity than might have been possible if the assignment were for one student alone. With adequate preparation and planning, students from different institutions, cities, and even countries can connect via the Internet and may be able to work together collaboratively using the same set of group tools. Finally, the group projects can be released for viewing to the whole class and form the basis of a vigorous face-to-face or online discussion. To explore this subject further, see Chapters 6 and 7 for discussion of some of the specific options available for group activities.

Using the Web as a Student Presentation Medium

The Web is a powerful presentation medium, and it can be used in both web-enhanced and blended classes to display work created by students as course projects, either individually or in groups. Some instructors understandably prefer the more traditional means of expression, such as the research paper or the PowerPoint slide show delivered in front of the class. Frequently, however, an inordinate amount of classroom time is required to present such projects to the class. How much more efficient it can be to have students present their work online instead.

Using the Web to present such reports permits students to use a wider range of media to make their points. Students can create videos, narrated slides, blogs, and web pages replete with graphics, sounds, animations, and links. Even without such multimedia embellishments, web-based reports can be read and evaluated by all the students before or after they come to class, leaving more face-to-face class time for discussion, analyses, and critiques.

Assembling such projects should no longer be considered a hardship for students. In most cases, it is a skill they can master easily, and one they ought to learn. Using simple, menu-based Web 2.0 type tools described in earlier chapters, they should be able to assemble relatively sophisticated presentations with ease.

Web-Based Exercises

The Web is so rich in potential learning materials that traditional instructors would be depriving their students of valuable educational resources if they ignored it altogether. No matter what subject you teach, be it molecular biology or cultural anthropology, a multitude of sites can provide you and your students with information, simulations, or resources to consider, critique, analyze, or discuss. A list of some very useful sites on the Web to search for such resources is provided in the Guide to Resources at the end of this book.

Aside from visiting informational web sites, students can participate in global science experiments, perform experiments in online labs, collaborate and communicate with students from another school, state, or nation, analyze and critique articles published online and post reactions to them in a discussion board, and meet and discuss relevant issues with a "guest host" in a discussion board or chat room.

Here are some pointers for incorporating Web resources into your face-to-face on-site class:

- Identify each site you want your students to visit by its URL, both on your web site and in the syllabus. Revisit the site just before you begin teaching the class to make sure it's still alive (sometimes sites are moved to different URLs or simply no longer work).

- Be very clear when defining what you want your students to see or do when visiting a site. Be respectful of the time they must spend online to accomplish the assigned task. Generally, you'll want to avoid the treasure-hunt approach—that is, having your students hunt for information before they can critique it.

- Avoid wasting time displaying web sites in the on-site class unless it is for the purpose of discussing a specific assignment focused around that web page or it otherwise requires some explanation that can't be duplicated online. If your Internet connection in the classroom is not stable, you may want to prepare screen shots of a web site being used for this purpose.

Team Teaching

Just as students can collaborate easily online, so can teachers. Team teaching a large, lecture-style course requires a great deal of advance planning and preparation. Traditionally, this is done in face-to-face meetings, but using the collaborative tools available on the Web can ameliorate the process, speeding up the production of course materials and easing the task of approving them once they are done.

Once a course is under way, using the Web has its advantages as well. Instructors can spell each other at certain tasks, with one instructor handling lectures in the classroom while the other publishes backup materials on the Web and replies to student inquiries on discussion boards.

In less common cases, instructors may be situated too far apart to commute easily to the physical class. Using the Web is an obvious alternative, permitting the use of "experts" to prepare online lectures, but leaving the discussions to the instructor in the on-site class.

A Final Thought on Web Enhancement

In this discussion of ways the Internet can be integrated in an on-the-ground class, one key thought underlies our comments.

Important! *Making the use of the Internet optional rather than incorporating it into the curriculum dooms it to failure.*

When you make the Web an integral part of the course work, you automatically make it more relevant and valuable to your students and yourself alike. Treating the web site merely as a repository for chance comments or random postings reduces it to the level of a technological appendage and squanders its considerable potential to enrich what you are doing on the ground.

●●●●●

Tips for Teaching Blended Courses

While many institutions new to online education have surmised that the road to online teaching is made easier by first exposing instructors to blended teaching, there is little or no research that bears this out. In fact, many people who are experienced online teachers might tell you that blended courses can actually be more difficult to teach than fully online ones. Why is this? It is chiefly due to the challenge of integrating the two modalities of teaching in a way that makes both equally meaningful and effective.

Two of the biggest errors made by those attempting blended courses are:

- overloading students with a great deal more work than they would have in either a completely face-to-face or fully online course;
- not giving clear directions about what will be accomplished in each mode and how to coordinate the two.

The first issue has been termed the "course and one-half syndrome." The second is best handled along the same lines as fully online courses—with a comprehensive syllabus and schedule that clarifies how the class will operate.

The tips offered here in some cases reiterate principles already stated in this book and previously illustrated by examples, while in other cases, tips supply some additional information specially tailored for the blended format.

Preparing for the Blended Course

- Take advantage of any training or training resource materials offered on campus (or off- or online) if you are new to online teaching and blended learning. Look for training that not only focuses on how to use online software from the technical point of view, but also offers some insights into approaches to teaching and learning and design for a blended course. See Chapter 14 for some suggested training opportunities for blended teaching.
- Review the face-to-face version of the course if that's what you have been teaching. Consider what is best reserved for face-to-face delivery and be able to explain your rationale. Find the weakest points in the teaching experience as you see them and consider how these may be changed with the addition of online activities and resources.

- Review the schedule for your blended class. Are the face-to-face meeting dates already determined or can you determine the pattern yourself? The first class should ideally meet face-to-face so that students can be fully prepared for the blended format. On many campuses, students are accustomed to thinking about the first class day as provisional, a waste of time, or not a "real" class meeting. For this reason, it is a good idea to email your students ahead of time to stress the importance of not missing this first class date. If this would seem to be a losing battle on your campus, strongly consider making both the first *and* second class meetings face-to-face.

- Generally speaking, in putting together your syllabus schedule, it's a good idea to plan discussions of the most complex materials for a face-to-face meeting. This doesn't mean that complex issues cannot be handled just as well in a fully online class, only that you may find that it will be relatively quicker for you to clear up misunderstandings if you have the opportunity for a face-to-face session. Many instructors have found that scheduling the first small-group meeting for a face-to-face meeting week greatly facilitates the rate at which groups form and establish cooperation. Some instructors also recommend that groups be scheduled to meet face to face at other critical moments in a group project. Again, this doesn't mean that the same objective cannot be reached purely online, but if you have the opportunity to convene groups face to face, you may find that it simply accelerates the process of forming groups or reaching consensus on key aspects of the project.

- Be prepared to offer an orientation to students on your course management system or other software if this is not supplied to students elsewhere.

- Define how your blended class operates in the introductory area of your syllabus and what expectations are for students in regard to participation in online and face-to-face activities. Explain how the weeks will work in tandem as a fully integrated course. Make sure your syllabus schedule clearly delineates in a graphic manner (through use of bold font or other means) those weeks in which the class meets face-to-face and what online activities, if any, are expected for those same weeks.

Design Issues for the Blended Course

■ Pay careful attention to the transition between face-to-face and online activities. Ideally these two modes are not completely separate—therefore, always have some online activity, no matter how minor or brief, within the week in which the class meets face to face. For example, you might ask students to go online to the discussion board within forty-eight hours after a face-to-face meeting to continue to reflect on the topics broached at that meeting. This gives students who may be reticent about speaking in the on-campus class a chance to weigh in and it also provides an interval for all students to reflect on the preceding face-to-face discussion. It also signals to the students that what happens in these two modalities is not disconnected, but interrelated. The online work following directly upon the face-to-face meeting helps bridge the topics and activities of the two successive weeks, and can serve as preparation for the entirely online week. The opposite is also true—a carefully planned activity in the online-only week may be designed to provide essential background for the upcoming face-to-face meeting.

■ Consider the pacing and time needed to complete each week's activities, both online and face to face—calculate the total time expected for students to be on task—whether that means reading, researching, discussing, or completing other "homework." The total time should be comparable to that expected for a purely face-to-face class. This avoids the problem of "a class and one-half."

■ In devising a participation grade, be sure to define what participation means in the context of a face-to-face class meeting and an online discussion. Keep in mind that there generally isn't time for every student to participate in a 1–3-hour face-to-face classroom meeting. You may want to give students an opportunity within a face-to-face meeting week for participating in either format. In other words, if you give ten points for participation, you can stipulate that the ten points can be distributed over both the face-to-face and online meetings or confined to just the online. Or you can set up separate criteria or a rubric for each modality. Perhaps there are a certain number of points for participating in three of the fifteen face-to-face discussions with another total number of points for online participation in a face-to-face meeting week and yet another collection of points for those weeks in which the class is only online.

■ Carefully incorporate Web resources into your course content and instructional activities to provide more diverse pathways to learning and supply guidelines to help students devise a more critical approach to reviewing information.

■ Avoid scheduling all your face-to-face meeting time for lecturing! The on-campus meeting affords valuable time to explore ideas and gauge understanding by engaging students in active discussion and debate, case studies, or other active learning strategies.

Teaching the Blended Course

■ Post your syllabus online but depending on your student audience and expectations for the on-campus meeting, you may want to bring hard-copy printouts to the first class meeting (if that is indeed face-to-face) as well. At some campuses, students can be emailed in advance and instructed to read and bring the syllabus to the first class (on their laptops or in hard copy).

■ At the first and perhaps second class meeting, you will want to review the syllabus for the course. Additionally, here is when you may need to lead that orientation to the course management software for students. At the very least, you will want to clarify how and when and where to carry out online activities, as well as to point to your syllabus schedule to emphasize the face-to-face meeting dates and the required online activities.

■ Provide weekly announcements in the online classroom every week to highlight the week's activities ahead and guide the "handoff" from the face-to-face meeting week to the purely online ones and vice versa.

■ Send weekly emails to students to remind students of continuing online activities during weeks in which the class does not meet face-to-face. Sometimes students in a blended class tend to think of the weeks in which they do not meet on campus as "weeks off."

■ Send a personal email to provide a friendly reminder to students who at any time are not participating in the online portion of the class or the opposite—to encourage students to come to face-to-face meetings.

■ Use an online gradebook to allow students to follow their progress in the class. By grading students on their online activities on a weekly or biweekly basis, it is easier for you to keep track of student learning and for the students themselves to be reminded of an ongoing class in which they may seldom meet face-to-face.

■ Strive to interact with students online every week in some manner. This may range from active facilitation of online discussion to announcements or posted commentary that help illuminate the readings and assignments underway. Let students know that you will be monitoring their online activity.

■ In addition to any student course evaluations your institution may administer at the end of a course, consider asking students some of your own questions tailored to the blended course design you devised. For example, you may ask students questions such as, "Which assignments provided the best learning experience for you this term and why?" "Was it clear to you what needed to be done in weeks in which the class did not meet face-to-face?" or "Rate the following Web-based activities from our class ..."

Finally, after teaching your first blended class, carefully review it and don't be shy about enlisting the extra pair of eyes that a trusted colleague can provide. It's difficult to get the blended course "recipe" exactly right the very first time, but your effectiveness will improve with feedback from students and colleagues along with reflection and practice.

14

Taking Advantage of New Opportunities

Because online education is a relatively new enterprise, you have an opportunity to make a positive contribution to this growing field. To take full advantage of this new opportunity, you would do well to keep yourself informed of the latest trends and issues and to continually improve your skills and knowledge. Each time you teach online, you have the chance to acquire insights and experience that can be used as the basis for further exploration. In this chapter, we hope to point out some of the possibilities for your development as an online educator.

New Career Directions

The field of online education has become the preoccupation not only of most institutions of higher education but also of software producers, media conglomerates and publishing houses, and education-delivery companies. All of these players are beginning to appreciate the need to employ people with solid academic credentials, experience in the classroom, and, of course, an understanding of how teaching and learning can be effectively handled and enhanced in an online environment.

Because online education ranges from self-paced independent study modules to fully instructor-led courses, career prospects cover a similarly wide range. For instance, you can find new opportunities in areas like these:

■ creation of courseware for your own courses;

- design and creation of courseware to be used by other instructors;
- curriculum development for both nonprofit and profit-making entities;
- course development or instructional design and technology services;
- training and providing support for other faculty;
- administrative positions directing online education programs and training.

Academic and staff jobs related to online education are growing in number and even a cursory look at some of the online job-listing sites demonstrates the range of non-academia-based jobs for which educators with online expertise might qualify. As technology races ahead of content, those with the intellectual capital to create courseware and shape curriculum will be increasingly in demand.

The example of Pam Taylor, the nursing informatics expert, illustrates some of the possibilities. Taylor taught her first web-enhanced course in 1995, but within a couple of years she had transitioned to a fully online course. She became a leader among her peers, helping other instructors make the same transition to online teaching. Teaching online, she says, "has opened my classroom walls up to the world beyond." She has learned to work with tools like Dreamweaver for HTML pages, Fireworks for image editing, and Articulate for Flash-based movies to create interactive courseware. Building upon her experience in teaching and content development, she created her own business, the NIVATE online program (http://nivateonline.com) in early 2009, focusing on creating online content in the area of nursing informatics, content that could be incorporated into the nursing informatics curriculum of diverse institutions. As a result, she has made a positive contribution to alleviating the shortage of nursing informatics instructors nationwide. Taylor notes,

> *I have taught nursing for over thirty years, and have always felt it was wonderful to contribute in this way to patient care. But teaching online, and creating nursing informatics*

content, has allowed me to indirectly touch thousands and thousands of patients through these nursing students, rather than the more limited number of nurses and ultimately their patients that I would have reached through direct contact in the face-to-face classroom. This is a wonderful thing for an educator!

Already, online teaching has revitalized the careers of many longtime instructors, allowing them to experiment with new approaches to teaching and to create courses for an expanded audience of learners. Many have assumed new positions of leadership within their own institutions. For others, online experience has provided an opportunity to start a new career outside academia, to bring their needed expertise and perspectives to associations and companies engaged in education-related businesses.

Moreover, instructors who are ready to retire may consider extending their teaching lives with online courses. As part of regular online programs as well as continuing education, online teaching offers new opportunities to retired professionals who have much to offer students in the way of expertise and experience.

● ● ● ● ●

What to Do after You've Read This Book

Although this book strives to provide you with a comprehensive guide to online teaching, we hope that it will also inspire you to explore some additional pathways for your continued development as an online educator. Here we'll suggest a few of them.

Further Training

This book was developed as a practical guide for instructors who wish to teach online, but it wasn't meant to replace a formal training program completely. In fact, although a good training program would include at least some of the *information* provided by this book, a training program should also include the *experience* of teaching and learning online.

Important! *Whenever possible, opt for a program that emphasizes online training, not just on-site training.*

Most of us are used to learning in a workshop or lab arrangement, with an instructor hovering over us or directing from the front of the room as we struggle with a software program. Such personalized attention can be very helpful; the face-to-face interchange and the ability to ask questions "on the fly," gaining immediate feedback and support, can be quite valuable.

But trying to learn to use a specific course management system in a workshop environment can have its disadvantages as well. For one thing, some course management software programs are too complicated to master within a manageable amount of real time (three hours, for instance, which is about as much time as the average instructor has to spare in a single afternoon). This isn't because the software itself is especially difficult to use, but because it contains too many individual parts and functions to cover adequately in the space of a few hours. Learning how to operate the basic functions in software is one thing, but knowing what to do with them is quite another. In a workshop devoted to a course management system, most instructors, especially novices, find the information too plentiful to digest in one sitting. Without repetition over time, much of the experience is lost. Or—and this is probably just as harmful—instructors may leave the workshop thinking they know pretty much all they need to know.

Coupling an on-site workshop with further work online is often the best solution for those eager to learn enough to proceed confidently on their own. Until you've become a student, there's no way you can properly appreciate, or even identify, the problems and pitfalls of learning online. Sitting in a classroom with other instructors is a totally different experience from sitting at home and communicating with your instructor and fellow students online. Using the actual online tools to complete an exercise or post a comment on a discussion board is entirely different from experimenting with the tools in an on-site workshop.

An added advantage to learning online, rather than in a workshop, is that students can progress at a speed that suits them. Thus the novice can afford to proceed at a slow pace without worrying that he or she may be holding back the rest of the class, while more advanced users can proceed quickly to get to the material they need to learn.

You can learn some fairly complex and technical material online. For example, in a course we taught about how to make effective use of multimedia, instructors learned how to make animations, short videos, and narrated slide shows on their own, submitting their completed work to a web site. Most of these instructors had never used the various software tools before taking the class, yet none of them complained that they could not learn without a live instructor standing by. These instructors were not "techies"; they ranged from English professors to instructors of machine-shop technology in a trade high school. The instructional material supplied—narrated slide shows and video-capture demonstrations—guided them through the various exercises, and the online discussion board provided a forum in which they could voice their problems and concerns.

Training outside Your Own Institution   If you have a good training program at your institution, we strongly recommend that you sign up for one of its offerings. Your institution's center for teaching and learning, instructional technology or academic technology units, may all provide one or more types of training. What should you do, however, if your institution isn't offering faculty development training in online teaching?

First of all, you can enroll as a student in an online course of your own choosing. There are many online courses being offered now by institutions all over the world. You might base your choice on any number of criteria:

- a subject you've always wanted to study;
- a course that is in your field or similar to your own course;
- a course that uses the same software platform your own institution is considering;
- a course that simply suits your schedule and budget.

Even though such courses won't show you specifically how to teach online, they will give you vital experience as a learner in the online classroom.

In terms of specific training for teaching online, there are now a number of national and vendor-operated programs, including the following types:

- short online courses and tutorials in particular software platforms, offered by the providers of those platforms or their partners;
- short, site-based training courses and workshops for particular software platforms and tools, often available at conferences focused on the use technology in education;
- full-scale, comprehensive programs covering teaching methods, curriculum development, and tools that aren't specific to any software platform.

Many of these programs are available completely online, thus eliminating the constraints of geography. Online training is particularly advantageous in that it doesn't involve removing an instructor from the classroom in order to be trained, and it is particularly economical in that it doesn't require the travel and lodging expenses necessary for an off-site workshop.

You may be able to work on an interdepartmental, districtwide, or consortium basis to arrange discounted tuition for yourself and other faculty members. You can also investigate whether any regional or statewide opportunities are available. For example, the Illinois Online Network has developed a program of instruction in online teaching for all of its interested instructors and external partnering institutions.

Opportunities for Further Training outside Your Own Institution

For those interested in programs offering a certificate or graduate-level degree that are open to the public, there are such programs as the Sloan Consortium's Online Teaching Certificate Program and its separate Blended Teaching Certificate. The California State University, East Bay similarly offers a Certificate in Online Teaching, while the University of Wisconsin provides a certificate program in Distance Education.

For those interested in a deeper commitment represented by a graduate program, there are such programs as California State

University, East Bay's Master of Science in Education, with an Option in Online Teaching and Learning (MS-OTL). The University of Maryland University College offers a Master of Distance Education, now in its tenth year, as does Athabasca University in Canada while the University of Hull offers a Master of Education in eLearning. The Open University of Catalonia (UOC) in Spain offers a diploma or certificate in E-Learning Course Design and Teaching, delivered online and in the English language. The University of Colorado, Denver, offers both a Masters in eLearning Design and Implementation and a Designing eLearning Environments certificate. All these programs differ in regard to time involved, focus, qualifications, and cost but they are mentioned here because all are delivered online and all have reputations for quality.

It can also be advantageous to have several instructors from your single institution take an online teacher-training course together. You can point out to the administration that training several people at once will provide a seed crop of informed faculty who will go on to share their new insights with other faculty members. Faculty collaboration and sharing will often stimulate others to continue learning. But whether or not your institution is willing to offer financial support for you and your colleagues, taking a course together will provide a mutual support network for all of you.

General Characteristics to Seek in a Training Program   What characteristics should you look for in a training program? First, as we suggested earlier, it is essential that the core of the development program be conducted online.

The ideal training program should also have a flexible schedule, emphasizing asynchronous (not real-time) communication, although there should be a start and stop date to prevent participants from losing focus and motivation. Lessons and activities should be arranged so that students can work on them on a weekly basis, rather than on a specific day. Faculty should participate three to five times a week, for short intervals, in the discussion forums, rather than once a week for longer periods of time. This replicates the ideal online teaching experience.

Ideally, the program should be a minimum of about six weeks in length if it is to include some time for actual course development. This sort of time frame will allow a week for general introduction to concepts and time to get accustomed to the software. This would be the minimum to ensure that you and your fellow students have adequate time to get up to speed with the software, interact in the online environment, and begin to build your own courses. However, a program may also consist of a shorter series of focused modules, each only a week or two in length. In investigating the different training options, you will need to determine whether the course is comprehensive or organized into shorter courses on discrete areas like course design, facilitation, etc.

It is advantageous if the person leading or designing the training is someone who has experience in both teaching and learning online, has taught in a face-to-face or blended class as well as online, and has a working knowledge of course design. Perhaps you will find that the training is done by a pair or team in which one of the members is an instructional technologist or instructional designer. That's fine, as long as at least one of the trainers can share the perspective of teaching in a live classroom. Such a person is better able to comprehend the sensitive nature of transferring years of experience in the face-to-face classroom to an online setting.

Content to Seek in a Training Program   What content and topics should you look for in a training program? We think there are five important categories of training content: software training, facilitative or methods training, course design, personal consultation, and supervised start-up.

1. *Software training.* Naturally, software training is important. In an online teaching program that isn't platform specific, you will learn the software being used for the program and perhaps be introduced to several different platforms. As in the process of learning a foreign language, you will find that learning one platform and analyzing others will improve your facility in learning further platforms. Sometimes these programs will ask you to produce a demo in your own chosen platform. If your program has been specifically designed for your institution,

then the software training may include having each participant build a basic shell for a model classroom.

Training in HTML code used to be automatically included in training programs. However, with the rise of built-in HTML editing through WYSIWYG tools, this is often an unnecessary expenditure of time. Other software training may include specialized topics on multimedia production, whiteboard, and synchronous conferencing systems or mobile learning. Good programs combine observation and analysis of how tools are used with opportunities for hands-on experience.

Overall, how much do you need to learn about the software you'll be using? Naturally this will depend on how much help you can expect to receive from support staff. But even if you have technical support, including instructional designers or instructional technologists to assist you and do a good deal of the work for you, we suggest that you learn as much as you can so that you can provide direction and make informed decisions. In the end, because decisions about design and organization affect curriculum, a wise online instructor will seek to be fully involved.

2. *Facilitative or methods training.* The next layer of training is what may be called "facilitative" or "methods, approaches, and techniques." A good training program will give you the chance to explore the differences and similarities between live and online classrooms. For example, it will help you confront the sometimes-troubling issue of the instructor's "voice" and style in the classroom. In large part, a sense of your own online voice will develop as you engage in online communication with others. The trainer as well as other colleagues can help you achieve this vision of yourself through interaction and positive reinforcement. It's difficult to achieve this sense of ease about oneself in a one- or two-week training program; that's one reason why we recommend a longer course or a succession of shorter ones.

Any comprehensive training program should also include classroom management, course preparation, methods of handling student participation and interaction, the use of web resources, and other areas explored in this book. Moreover, we believe that a substantial portion of the training should involve analysis of case studies in online teaching and learning. You'll want a chance to observe real online courses, at your own institution or even elsewhere if the latter is possible. The program should offer guided discussions of the diverse teaching methods and styles present in online courses. Especially in a short-term program, we believe you will find analysis of teaching models as they are actually used in a real course to be more valuable than instructional design theory in the abstract.

3. *Course design.* This need not involve extensive exposure to traditional instructional design training, but it should involve real, hands-on practice under authentic conditions and it should cover the basics of planning a course, writing instructions for assignments, and other issues related to design and development. The training course itself should provide a model for good course design, and there should be opportunities to observe and analyze examples of actual online classrooms. Many training programs are now using the Quality Matters™ rubric (see Chapter 3) or other such formulations as their framework for exposing instructors to online course design.

4. *Personal consultation.* In either the final portion of your training or as a follow-up to the training, some personal consultation is desirable. Ideally, training instructors or other staff should be available to work with you on a one-to-one basis or to provide individualized feedback in the context of the training course to arrive at a model that will satisfy your particular goals and objectives. Finding a good fit for your own preferred teaching methods and style is paramount here.

5. *Supervised start-up.* Finally, in an ideal training program, the last stage should involve a supervised start-up of your actual course. If this isn't available to you, we recommend that you ask another instructor with experience teaching online to critique your online classroom setup. At the University of Maryland University College, new online instructors are provided with a peer mentor who is an experienced online instructor. For the period of one semester the peer mentor helps the novice online teacher to bridge the gap between completion of training and confronting that new online classroom on one's own.

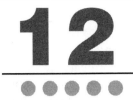

12

•••••